LLEWELLYN'S

2014

Magical Almanac

Featuring

Barbara Ardinger, Elizabeth Barrette,
Penny Billington, Blake Octavian Blair, Deborah Blake,
Calantirniel, Emily Carding, Dallas Jennifer Cobb,
Autumn Damiana, Raven Digitalis, Ellen Dugan,
Denise Dumars, Eli Effinger-Weintraub, Emyme,
Sybil Fogg, Karen Glasgow-Follett,
Ember Grant, James Kambos, Sandra Kynes,
Mary Pat Lynch, Lisa Mc Sherry, Mickie Mueller,
Susan Pesznecker, Diana Rajchel, Marion Sipe,
Cassius Sparrow, Kelly Surtees, Ellen Coutts Waff,
Charlynn Walls, and Charlie Rainbow Wolf

Llewellyn's 2014
Magical Almanac

ISBN 978-0-7387-2153-8. Copyright © 2013 by Llewellyn. All rights reserved. Printed in the United States. Llewellyn is a registered trademark of Llewellyn Worldwide Ltd.

Editor/Designer: Ed Day

Cover Illustration: © Tammy Shane

Calendar Pages Design: Michael Fallon

Calendar Pages Illustrations: © Fiona King

Interior Illustrations © Meraylah Allwood: pages pages 48, 50, 104, 145, 146, 149, 255, 257, 259, 260, 303, 304, 306; Carol Coogan: pages 15, 18, 59, 62, 119, 120, 225, 228, 271, 273, 276, 321, 323, 326; © Chris Down: pages 20, 25, 65, 68, 71, 124, 126, 131, 218, 223, 281, 283, 286; © Kathleen Edwards: pages 27, 31, 75, 77, 81, 133, 136, 233, 236, 319; © Wen Hsu: pages 13, 35, 36, 83, 94, 97, 101, 217, 241, 279, 309, 311, 313; © Mickie Mueller: pages 41, 45, 85, 90, 139, 141, 247, 250, 253, 296, 298, 330, 333, 334; © Amber Zoellner: pages 54, 107, 111, 114, 263, 266, 267, 289, 291, 292.

Clip Art Illustrations: Dover Publications

Special thanks to Amber Wolfe for the use of daily color and incense correspondences. For more detailed information, please see *Personal Alchemy* by Amber Wolfe.

You can order Llewellyn annuals and books from *New Worlds*, Llewellyn's catalog. To request a free copy of the catalog, call toll-free 1-877-NEW-WRLD or visit our website: www.llewellyn.com

Astrological data compiled and programmed by Rique Pottenger. Based on the earlier work of Neil F. Michelsen.

Llewellyn Worldwide Ltd.
2143 Wooddale Drive
Woodbury, MN 55125

About the Authors

BARBARA ARDINGER, PHD, (www.barbaraardinger.com) is the author of *Secret Lives*, a novel about a circle of crones, mothers, and maidens, plus goddesses, a talking cat, and the Green Man. Her earlier books include *Pagan Every Day*, *Goddess Meditations*, *Finding New Goddesses* (a parody of goddess encyclopedias), and *Quicksilver Moon* (a realistic novel except for the vampire). As a freelance editor, she has edited more than 250 books of fiction and nonfiction. Barbara lives in Southern California with two rescued Maine coon cats, Heisenberg and Schroedinger.

ELIZABETH BARRETTE was the managing editor of *PanGaia* and has been involved with the Pagan community for twenty-four years, actively networking via coffeehouse meetings and open sabbats. Her other writings include speculative fiction and gender studies. Her 2011 poem "The Cathedral of the Michaelangelines" earned a nomination for the Rhysling Award. She lives in central Illinois and enjoys herbal landscaping and gardening for wildlife.

PENNY BILLINGTON is the editor of *Touchstone*, the monthly magazine of the Order of Bards, Ovates, and Druids. As a Druid celebrant, she has organized ritual and ceremony for over ten years, and regularly gives workshops throughout the UK. Her published work includes three Druid Detective novels, magazine articles on Druidry and Dion Fortune, contributions to the OBOD Druid grade course, and research for *The Book of English Magic*. Her latest book, *The Path of Druidry: Walking the Ancient Green Way*, is a practical study guide published by Llewellyn. pennybillington.co.uk.

BLAKE OCTAVIAN BLAIR (Carrboro, NC) is an Eclectic Pagan Witch, ordained minister, psychic, tarot reader, freelance writer, Usui Reiki Master-Teacher, musical artist, and a devotee of Lord Ganesha. He holds a degree in English and Religion from the Univer-

sity of Florida. In his spare time he enjoys beading jewelry, knitting, and is an avid reader. Blake lives in the Piedmont Region of North Carolina with his beloved husband, an aquarium full of fish, and an indoor jungle of houseplants. Visit www.blakeoctavianblair.com or write him at blake@blakeoctavianblair.com.

DEBORAH BLAKE is a Wiccan High Priestess who has been leading Blue Moon Circle for many years. She is the author of *Circle, Coven and Grove, Everyday Witch A to Z, The Goddess is in the Details,* and *The Everyday Witch A to Z Spellbook,* all from Llewellyn. She is also working on a number of novels. Deborah also runs The Artisans' Guild and works as a jewelry maker, a tarot reader, and an Intuitive Energy Healer. She lives in rural upstate New York with five cats who supervise all her activities, both magickal and mundane.

LISA ALLEN/CALANTIRNIEL has practiced many forms of natural spirituality since the early 1990s. She is a professional astrologer, tarot card reader, dowser, flower essence creator, Usiu Reiki Master, a ULC Reverend, and a Master Herbalist. She has an organic garden, crochets professionally, and is co-creating Tië eldaliéva, "the Elven Path," a spiritual practice based on J. R. R. Tolkien's Middle-Earth stories. http://astroherbalist.com.

EMILY CARDING (Cornwall, United Kingdom) is an author, priestess, and artist. An initiate of Alexandrian Wicca and a member of the Starstone network, Carding has been working with inner world Faery contacts since childhood. She has been trained in techniques of Celtic shamanism by John and Caitlin Matthews, and has worked with renowned Faery teachers R. J. Stewart and Brian and Wendy Froud. A respected and active member of the Faery and Tarot community worldwide, Carding's work has received international recognition. Visit her online at ChildOfAvalon.com.

DALLAS JENNIFER COBB practices gratitude magic, giving thanks for her magical life, happy and healthy family, meaningful and

flexible work, and joyous life. She believes the Goddess will provide time, energy, wisdom, and money to accomplish all her deepest desires. She lives in paradise, in a waterfront village in rural Ontario. Contact her at jennifer.cobb@live.com.

AUTUMN DAMIANA is a writer, artist, crafter, and amateur photographer, and has been a mostly solitary eclectic Witch for fourteen years. She is passionate about eco-friendly living, and writes about this and her day-to-day walk on the Pagan path in her blog, "Sacred Survival in a Mundane World" at http://autumndamiana.blogspot.com/. When not writing or making art, you can find her outside enjoying nature or investigating local history in her hometown of San Jose, California. Contact her at autumndamiana@gmail.com.

RAVEN DIGITALIS is the author of *Planetary Spells & Rituals*, *Shadow Magick Compendium*, and *Goth Craft*, all from Llewellyn. He is a Neopagan Priest, cofounder of the "disciplined eclectic" tradition and training coven Opus Aima Obscuræ, and is a DJ. Also trained in Georgian Witchcraft and Buddhist philosophy, Raven is a Witch, Priest, and Empath. He holds a degree in anthropology and is also an animal rights activist, photographic artist, tarot reader, and co-owner of Twigs & Brews Herbs. www.ravendigitalis.com, www.myspace.com/oakraven, www.facebook.com/ravendigitalisauthor.

ELLEN DUGAN, the "Garden Witch," is an award-winning author and psychic-clairvoyant. A practicing Witch for more than twenty-seven years, she is the author of many Llewellyn books; her newest are *A Garden Witch's Herbal* and *Book of Witchery*. Ellen encourages folks to personalize their spellcraft, to go outside and get their hands dirty, so they can discover the wonder and magick of the natural world. Ellen and her family live in Missouri. www.ellendugan.com.

DENISE "DION-ISIS" DUMARS is a writer of nonfiction, fiction, poetry, and screenplays. She has authored two books on magic and spirituality, including *Be Blesséd: Daily Devotions for Busy Wiccans and Pagans*

(New Page 2006). She also wrote a book of poetry, *Paranormal/ Romance: Poems Romancing the Paranormal* (Sam's Dot, 2012). She is a founder of the Iseum of Isis Paedusis, which holds public rituals at Pacific Unitarian Church in Rancho Palos Verdes, California. She lives in Los Angeles County, but her heart is in New Orleans.

ELI EFFINGER-WEINTRAUB is a writer and editor in the Twin Cities Watershed. She writes prose fiction, stage plays, creative nonfiction, and spoken-word memoir. Eli has written for the Minnesota Fringe Festival, Theatre Unbound, Patrick's Cabaret, Seal Press, Alyson Books, *Electric Velocipede,* and *Witches & Pagans* magazine and blogs at No Unsacred Space and PaganSquare. She has a special interest in urban cycling, sustainable living and dying, and steampunk.

EMYME is a solitary practitioner who resides in a multigenerational, multicat household in southern New Jersey. Hobbies that renew her are: gardening, sewing and crafts, and home care and repair. Emyme has self-published a children's book about mending families after divorce and remarriage. She is an avid diarist; dabbles in poetry; creates her own blessings, incantations, and spells; and is currently writing a series of fantasy fiction stories set in the twenty-fifth century. Her personal mantra is summed up in four words: Curiosity, Objectivity, Quality, Integrity. catsmeow24@verizon.net.

SYBIL FOGG has been a practicing Witch for more than twenty years. She is also known as Sybil Wilen. She uses her mother's maiden name in Pagan circles to honor her grandparents. She's also a wife, mother, writer, teacher, and belly dancer. She lives in Portland, Maine, with her husband and children. www.sybilwilen.com.

KAREN GLASGOW-FOLLETT has been practicing witchcraft since 1972. Karen lives in the Midwest with her husband. Her résumé includes Reiki healer, psychic medium, craft designer, writer, psychic development educator, and obstetrical nurse. Karen does spend some of her spare time trying to figure out what to be when she grows up.

EMBER GRANT is a poet and freelance writer and has been contributing to the Llewellyn Annuals for ten years. Her first book from Llewellyn, *Magical Candle Crafting*, was published in March 2011.

JAMES KAMBOS is a writer and artist living in the beautiful hill country of southern Ohio. His interest in magic began in boyhood watching his Greek grandmother perform spells based on Greek folk magic. An avid gardener, he raises herbs, vegetables, and wild flowers.

SANDRA KYNES, an explorer of Celtic history, myth, and magic, is a member of the Order of Bards, Ovates, and Druids. She has lived in New York City, Europe, England, and New England. Spiritually, her inquisitiveness has led her to investigate the roots of Pagan belief. Besides leading healing circles and women's rituals, she is a yoga instructor, massage therapist, and Reiki practitioner. Sandra's writing has been featured in several Llewellyn annuals under the name Sedwyn. Her books include: *Gemstone Feng Shui* (2002), *A Year of Ritual* (2004), *Whispers from the Woods* (2006), and *The Altar: Place of Meditation and Transformation* (2007).

MARY PAT LYNCH, PHD explores the realms of dreams, astrology, the Tarot and shamanic journeying, and loves writing about her explorations. Life is a magical story, lived across many dimensions, and wonderful to share.

LISA MC SHERRY is a priestess and author living in the Pacific Northwest with her husband and three fur-children. She blogs at www .cybercoven.org, leads the JaguarMoon coven (www.jaguarmoon .org), and is the editor of Facing North (www.FacingNorth.net), which publishes reviews of books, music, and tools of the craft.

MICKIE MUELLER is an award-winning and critically acclaimed artist of fantasy, fairy, and myth. She is an ordained Pagan minister and has studied natural magic, fairy magic, and Celtic tradition. She is also a Reiki healing master/teacher in the Usui Shiki Royoho tradition. She works primarily in a mix of colored pencil and watercolor

infused with corresponding magical herbs. Mickie is the illustrator of *The Well Worn Path* and *The Hidden Path* decks and the writer/illustrator of *The Voice of the Trees, A Celtic Divination Oracle*, and the illustrator of the upcoming *The Mystical Cats Tarot*, coming in 2014.

SUSAN PESZNECKER is a writer, college English teacher, and hearth Pagan/Druid living in northwest Oregon. Her magickal roots include Pictish Scot and eastern European/Native American traditions. She holds a master's in nonfiction writing and loves to read, stargaze, camp with her wonder poodle, and play in her biodynamic garden. She's cofounder of the Druid Grove of Two Coasts and teaches nature studies and herbology for the online Grey School. Sue has authored *Crafting Magick with Pen and Ink* and *The Magickal Retreat* (both with Llewellyn). www.susanpesznecker.com.

DIANA RAJCHEL serves as the executive editor for PNC-News, and is the author of *Divorcing a Real Witch: for Pagans and Those Who Used to Love Them*. She is a third-degree Wiccan priestess in the Shadowmoon tradition, with seventeen years of practical experience as a witch. Visit her at http://dianarajchel.com.

SUZANNE RESS has been writing nonfiction and fiction for more than twenty-five years. She is an accomplished self-taught gardener, beekeeper, silversmith, and mosaicist. She lives in the woods at the foot of the Alps in northern Italy with her husband, daughter, two dogs, three horses, and an elusive red stag.

MARION SIPE is a New Orleanian at heart and a traveler by nature. She has been a writer for eleven years and a practicing Witch for seventeen. A devotee of Hekate, she's served as a priestess, leading rituals with both private covens and public churches. She also teaches classes and writes about various aspects of paganism.

CASSIUS SPARROW an Eclectic Pagan Witch, tarot reader, author, and garden enthusiast. He is a devotee of both Hermes and Dionysos, and a practicing Pagan for over ten years. He currently lives

on the Gulf Coast of Florida with his darling wife and their cat, Zucca. In his free time, he can be found writing, baking, or working in his herb garden. Contact him at cassiussparrow@gmail.com.

KELLY SURTEES is the editor of the *Wellbeing Astrology Guide* in Australia and a blogger for astrology.com. Besides her regular horoscope columns, Kelly has had more than seventy feature articles (on astrology, spirituality, paganism, alternative practices, food, health, and lifestyle), published in magazines and books around the globe, including in the UK, Canada, Australia, Europe, and the U.S. She also gives lectures at astrology conferences and has been teaching online since 2008. https://kellysurteesastrology.wordpress.com/

ELLEN COUTTS WAFF is a professed dilettante, enjoying serving as her town treasurer, performing at the Maryland Renaissance Festival, caring for her 1742 home, and writing. She is a founder of the Druid Grove of Two Coasts, and treasurer of the Druid Order of the White Oak. A witch since 1979, she is a founder of Synergy, a celebratory coven, in 1984. She is a fellow of the Society of Antiquaries of Scotland. She owns Laurel Brook Studios, art clothiers.

CHARLYNN WALLS is an active member of the St. Louis Pagan Community. Driven toward community service, she works on the St. Louis Pagan Picnic and St. Louis Witches Ball Committees. She is a member of two covens and she has written articles for *Witches and Pagans* magazine and is pursuing other writing opportunities.

CHARLIE RAINBOW WOLF is of Cherokee and English heritage. She is happiest when creating something. Knowledgeable in many aspects of healing, particularly using meditation as "medicine," Charlie is the Dean of Faculty at the Grey School. However, tarot has captivated her for more than two decades. She has a flair for recycling and enjoys organic gardening and cooking. She feeds her creative muse with writing, pottery, knitting, and soap-making. She lives in the Midwest with her husband and special-needs Great Danes.

Table of Contents

Water Magic

Earth Magic

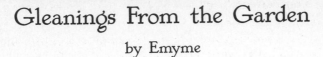

Gleanings From the Garden

by Emyme

For the solitary witch, spellwork can be an extremely personal and private endeavor. The usual basic form is this: ingredients are gathered, cleansed if need be, and set aside for mixture. Tools are brought to the altar, intentions prepared, and the casting follows. Afterward, it's time for cleaning up and refreshments. Earth-based religions are flexible and the actual process may take many forms—it can be as simple as carving a few words on a chime candle or it can be an elaborate ritual with ceremonial robes, ground and center, honor the elements and directions, cast the spell, cakes and ale. Many castings fall somewhere in between.

Intention is the most important part of any spell—do what you wish, but harm no one. Ingredients run a close second on the importance scale. Many supplies—fruits, vegetables, grains, herbs, spices, powders, and various liquids—can be found at the supermarket, farmers' market, or roadside stand. For those in a cosmopolitan area, all ingredients might be found at a Wiccan supply store. Websites and mail-order opportunities abound. However, and I think all will agree, the very best and most potent supplies and ingredients are homegrown.

Much as the veil between worlds can be thin at certain times of the year, the line between earth-based beliefs and gardening can be faded and fleeting. Being close to the earth, being part of changing the earth, brings gardeners closer to the elements and the creator—whatever creator is honored. Look at your yard and garden, your little bit of earth, and see what can be used in future spellwork. All ingredients from your own garden are more potent for having been personally grown and/or gathered—always with the best of intentions.

I am a novice witch and a slightly-less-than intermediate gardener. To all those in the same place on their journey—please indulge me in sharing some of my experiences and practices. The obvious choices for any witches garden, indoors or out, are the herbs and spices. My strength lies in other directions. I offer the following:

Everyday Offerings

Marigolds come in a variety of colors and sizes. Planted in a southern exposure bed that receives full sun, they will thrive. Water and the occasional deadheading (the removal of spent blossoms to make way for more) are all that is required. They are a natural insect repellent. In spellwork, marigolds symbolize the sun and power, abundance and plenty. Before the flowers die off, collect as many petals as may be needed. Place on a cookie sheet lined with foil and

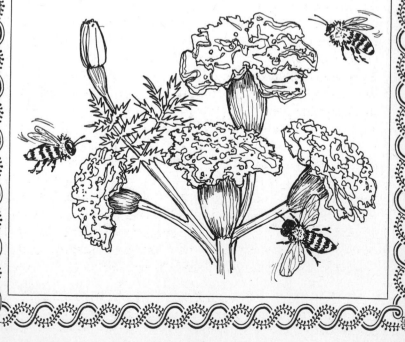

bake at the low oven setting (about 100 to 180 degrees) for about twenty minutes, or until completely dry. You may have to "stir" them once or twice. Prepared this way, and kept in airtight containers, they will last for years for use in prosperity and healing spells, as a decoration, or in potpourri.

Roses are another flower essential to many spells, especially those for relationships and romance. Again, southern exposure and plenty of sun help grow a healthy plant. I inherited a rose bush when I bought my current home. It is spindly and not so very attractive as bushes go; however, the flowers are a fine, rich shade of pink. No amount of pruning has harmed this bush, and it blooms well into November. After the cut flowers have passed their peak, remove the petals from the hip and allow to air-dry completely in an open-weave basket, stirring occasionally, then store in glass jars. They will last for months. Petals from roses received as gifts or purchased specifically for drying are perfectly fine. Just remember to cleanse the petals of any outside influence. (Sea salt, sage, even a well-intentioned breath will negate foreign energy.) Color may play a part in the type of spell cast. There are many books and references available to determine which color is best for any particular purpose.

While flower petals can be integral to spellcasting, other parts of the plant can also be employed in the creation of tools. **Day lilies** were also already growing in abundance when I purchased my home. In full sun, day lilies will bloom at least twice. Most bloom once, but at variable times, so there are always several blossoms available. After the growing season, when the flowers have dropped off, the stalk remains. When completely dry, it will pull out of the base plant with ease. My besom began life as a bunch of dry day lily stems culled from the prosperity corner of my property. The bundle of stalks is light and manageable, and tied with a purple ribbon for added power.

Depending on where you live, trees may play a part in your home's landscaping. My backyard boasted several large **trees** including oak, a maple, and a hickory. Sadly, I was forced to remove some due to disease, inconvenient placement, and weather damage. (In keeping with green awareness, try to plant a new tree for every one cut down.) Some trees were cut to the ground and the mulch was used in other parts of the yard. Others were cut down, leaving a stump that offered the possibility of a platform or altar. A wealth of magickal tools has come from the branches and limbs—including wands and walking sticks and dowsers. The hickory provided several sturdy "Y" shaped sections, which appear representative of the torsos of the Lord and Lady. These potent talismans now decorate my flower gardens and infuse fertility to inspire growth. I also salvaged a wedge and a slice from the hickory for some future use. Every year, acorns rain down from the oaks. What the squirrels do not hoard are collected and used for spells that call for masculine power. Dried leaves can be crumbled into powder and safely stored indefinitely. A fascinating side note: every time we contracted for professional tree removal; each worker took a branch of whatever was cut down. Superstition … tradition … magick.

A Special Connection

Similar to the way we all embrace a spirit animal, plants often hold special meaning. **Holly** is such a plant for me. Every place I have ever lived has been blessed with holly, either in the form of a living, growing bush or as decoration during Yuletide. My affinity for this beautiful and varied plant makes it the perfect addition to any spell in which I need an extra boost of personal power. In the

happy circumstance that you feel attracted to certain flowers, bushes, or trees—plants of any sort—make sure to attempt the growing of it.

Not all spells call for a mixture of flower petals, herbs, leaves, or twigs. Where there are gardens and trees there are almost always birds—birds that shed feathers, build and abandon nests, and sadly, on occasion, lose eggs. These are all useful items to have in your store of supplies. The carcasses of bees, butterflies, and moths; and empty cocoons also can be saved for spellwork. Remember, nothing must ever be destroyed or disturbed for a spell. The consequences would hardly be worth it.

Finally, a word about the inanimate. A few years back, I attempted to lure the Fey Folk with a fairy ring of granite rocks. My purpose was to add extra magic to my back yard space, to encourage visits and good luck. All I managed to do was trip over the rocks whenever I mowed the grass in that area. I swear I heard wee fairy laughter every time.

The ring was finally dismantled for truck access during a tree removal, and I never replaced it. As compensation, toadstool fairy rings appeared. Lesson learned—it is usually best to let the Fey create their own magical spaces.

~

Solitary eclectic, hedge, or kitchen—no matter which path you choose on your Wiccan journey, I hope this personal composition inspires you to take a closer look at your own yards, gardens, patios, or windowsills and what they have to offer.

For Further Study:

Greenaway, Kate, and Jean Marsh. *The Illuminated Language of Flowers: Over 700 Flowers and Plants listed Alphabetically With Their Meanings.* New York: Henry Holt and Co., 1978.

The Magic Feats of Clay
by Charlie Rainbow Wolf

I think that I always knew I was destined to work with clay. From the time I was a young child in art class at school, I always had to get my hands into my work. Brushes didn't appeal to me when painting—I had to get in there with my fingers. It frustrated me that the canvas was only two-dimensional. Finally, the sympathetic art teacher let me start to add things like sand and string and wallpaper paste to my work. We both realized then that I needed clay.

The appeal of clay is not just getting my hands into it. It goes far deeper than that. When I start working with clay, a sympathetic relationship is born. I know that I am working with the body of the Earth herself, and that seems somehow sacred to me. There is a connection between my hands, the clay, and what is taking form. It is movement frozen in time. Now, that's magic.

However, clay has to be understood before it can transform. Just as different people have different personalities—and we're not always all going to get along!—different clays have different personalities, too. The right clay has to be chosen for the right job. Clay with grog in it (a gritty substance added to the clay to reduce shrinkage and the risk of breakage) stands up great in a raku kiln, but it will tear the skin on the potter's hands when thrown on the wheel if he or she is not used to handling the rough texture. Great sculptures might be made with most clays, but they must be fired at the proper temperatures for both the clay and the glazes to be successful finished items. Take my word for it—I've learned a lot from my mistakes.

The colors of the clay will differ, too. Most of us are familiar with the beautiful terra cotta red of flowerpots. If a glaze is to be applied, the outcome will be different if it is applied to red clay, or buff clay, or white clay. Remember, just as our own personalities shine through whether we're in jeans or a suit, the personality of the clay is going to shine through the glaze.

Tools and Techniques

There are many ways of working with clay. Some potters are very adept at throwing on a wheel. This takes time and skill to master, and the potter has to be one with the clay in order to make the project throw well. I have found that using a kickwheel is a more connected way to throw than using an electric wheel. An electric wheel will automatically spin at a set number of rotations per second. The potter then raises the pot with the hands. A kickwheel is a wheel connected to a base that the potter "kicks" in rotation to make it spin—not unlike an old-fashioned treadle sewing machine. The potter controls the wheel's speed with the kicks. It is a very connected process, and one that takes much more discipline than throwing on the wheel.

A Fluid Form

Clay can be used as a near-solid when working with slabs, a near-liquid when throwing on the wheel, or even as a liquid. Some people will pour liquid clay into molds to make their pottery shapes. To me, this process removes much of the magic of working with clay because these molds are usually mass-produced. All the ceramics worker is doing in this instance is making a replica of someone else's work. Yes, while this requires time and skill and discipline, the finished product can't really be called unique.

Of course, potters can make their own molds. These are called sprigs. I use them myself when I want lots of little amulets for a specific event. The figure is made and fired, then a plaster or clay mold is made from the original. After that, it is very easy to quickly replicate little brooches, pendants, and other items while still capturing the original energy of the first piece.

Clay can be used to create a multitude of designs, from the smallest brooch to the largest statue. I am a big fan of using **slabs**. These are pieces of clay rolled flat to a desired width and thickness, then draped over a bowl or other object for shape. Lovely bowls and platters can be created in this manner.

Slabs can also be used to hand build, another technique I favor. Many quaint boxes and containers can be made using a basic slab, perhaps with little sprigs from self-made molds attached to them. This is a very quick way for the potter to make something totally unique and personable, in a reasonably short time.

Coiling is yet another way to create unique items. The coils can be hand rolled for a rustic and organic appearance or they can be made with symmetry by putting the clay into an extruder. Like a giant cookie press, an extruder will squash the clay out of a patterned hole at the base of the press. These holes can be made in any shape the potter wishes. They give lovely uniform shapes, but in the process lose a bit of the clay's energy. I've found that the less "machinery" involved with the process, the more magical the finished item.

Delightful pieces can be made using **pinchpots**, little clay cups that start as a ball of clay and then are pinched into shape. These can be used either on their own or stuck together to form an egg, which can then be made into numerous things. I use this technique a lot when making whimsical totem animal figures. It lends itself beautifully to any animal that could have a chubby body. As with all creations, the only limitation is the potter's imagination.

~

Clay has a memory, and while all of the above methods will display that memory, the pinchpot or the slab methods will reveal the clay's memory the most. Clay will shrink up to 12.5 percent in the kiln. I've lost count of how many times I have worked and worked and worked to get a bulge out of a pinchpot or a kink out of a slab. It looks fine when it goes into the kiln, but after firing; there it is again! The way to avoid this is to discipline oneself to work with the clay, rather than fight against it.

When working with the clay on a metaphysical level, much can be learned by melding with it and asking it what it wants to be. I've heard that this is what sculptors do with their pieces of marble. I have found it best to approach the clay the same way. The pinchpot totem animals? I've learned that if one tells me it is a fish, not to try to force it to be a bird. The end product just doesn't work.

Shaping Up

At this point, before it goes into the kiln, the clay is very fragile. Great discipline (There's that word again. See how the clay can be a teacher?) and care needs to be taken when handling the clay—called greenware—at this stage. Like dried mud, it can crack and break very easily, and all your work literally turn to dust. In order to turn the greenware to something more durable, it has to be fired. Kilns can be set to nearly any temperature, but the most popular ones usually range from 1,800 degrees F up to 2,300 degrees F. The firing temperatures will be determined by the type of clay used. Just as there is a symbiotic relationship between the potter and the clay, there's a relationship between the clay and the firing temperature. There is alchemy involved in the process of turning the greenware to the bisqueware.

Once the clay has been fired, it needs to be glazed. There are many different ways of coloring the item. Several manufacturers sell ready-made glazes that can be brushed or sprayed on the piece of fired pottery (known as bisqueware), or the bisque can be dipped into the glazes. While these methods work very well, there's little room for personal expression. The colors are the colors they are, and they are created for firing on a particular clay at a particular temperature. Subtle color variations will occur depending on the hue of the base clay. White clay gives a more true representation, while buff clay will soften the color and make it more muted and earthy. Terra cotta can change the color altogether. Trial and error is the best way to see what works best for the intended outcome. It's also half the fun of potting!

Making the glazes yourself is another option, and the raw chemicals can be purchased at most pottery supply stores. This is not a good idea for completely inexperienced potters, but it does give a wonderful opportunity to learn how the heat of the kiln creates the fused color. Even ground colored glass can be used as glaze—I've seen many wonderful fountains made from buff clay, with ground blue glass where the water lies. The heat of the kiln melts the glass and fuse it to the clay.

Organic Firing Methods

Just as there are many different ways to shape the clay, there are more organic ways of firing and coloring the pots beyond just applying glaze. Here are three common alternatives.

Raku

One of the most popular methods is called "raku." A certain clay has be used for this. It has grog in it, and fires to a particular temperature. The grog is added so that the piece will withstand the rough treatment it is to receive as the smoke and flames from the reduction process paint the patterns onto the surface of the pot.

Raku pottery has a long history. Originating in Japan, this pottery is most recognized for its tea bowls. Taking tea was very ceremonial for the Japanese, and thus the vessel in which the tea was poured was also very ceremonial. The tea bowls were shaped by hand, glazed, and removed from the kiln while still glowing hot. The item would then be placed in a barrel or some other open (and fireproof!) container, filled with combustible materials. Once the materials caught fire from the heat of the piece of pottery, the container would be covered, and the fire would have to draw oxygen from the clay, rather than the air. It is this process that gives every piece of raku pottery a unique pattern. Some call this "flame-painted pottery." I have heard of potters using a raku glaze, and just taking the pots out of the kiln and letting the air crackle the glazes, but that is not how I was taught.

Raku pottery has evolved through the centuries into many different techniques, which all produce slightly different results. However, they all use the combustible materials. For the magician who wants to make a ceremonial bowl, this is a method that brings the potter and the creation process in very close harmony. After all, the shape of the bowl is the dance of the potter's hands with the clay. The specially chosen raku glaze would be the potter's choice. The finished pattern is the shape of the flames on the clay as they discolor the surface and crackle the glaze.

Pit Firing

Pit firing differs from raku in that the bisqueware is buried under a huge bonfire, which is then set alight. Pit firing is a very ancient—perhaps the oldest—form of firing. The temperatures must be kept very hot and the fire must burn for quite some time to fire the pot correctly. This is a very simple method, but also one that is time consuming and takes a great deal of attention to fire a successful pot. The pots are not glazed, but rather, they are burnished after they have been fired and cooled to get their unique finishes. I like it because it's a natural process working directly with the fire.

Smokers

Some potters use smokers, and this also is very natural and lets the flame do most of the decorating. The pottery is packed with combustible materials in a fireproof container. Ventilation is the key to the successful firing. Most of the smokers I have seen have holes drilled in them at various intervals. The top and the bottom of the combustible materials are set alight. Once they are burning well, the lid is applied, and the pots left to smoke.

Experiment, But Don't Play with Fire

These are the basics, but it is possible to experiment with many different combustibles. Dried leaves will not only impart a different color than old straw or sawdust, but also a different energy—if the potter is attuned to this vibration. Another option is adding things to the item being fired to create different patterns in the finish. I know potters who have touched the red-hot piece with feathers, who have wrapped a piece in hair or fine wire before placing it in the kiln, even those who have put pots painted with Pepto Bismol into their smokers! Truly the only limitation is where we are led to experiment—provided, of course, the safety factor is maintained! I should also mention that because of the porous nature of some of these methods, most of these "flame painted" pots will not hold water and are going to be for decorative purposes only.

A final note on safety: check the glazes and any chemicals used for many of the substances used in these techniques could be harmful if ingested.

~

Hopefully, it is now easy to appreciate that working with clay involves working with all of the elements. The clay is the belly of Mother Earth herself. It has to be moistened with water to make it pliable for the potter to fashion. It has to be dried by the air before it can be placed in the kiln. The fire in the kiln turns the brittle greenware into robust bisqueware. Should raku or one of the other techniques be used to finish the piece, the fire becomes part of the item's very design. The finished piece is something of which the potter can be proud, and which honors all the elements every step of the way. When we connect with the clay, pottery is truly an alchemical adventure.

Lakshmi:
Goddess of Prosperity

By Ellen Dugan

Lakshmi is the Hindu goddess of both material and spiritual prosperity. She is the goddess of abundance, wealth, light, wisdom, fortune, fertility, generosity, courage, and good luck. Wow, that's one busy deity! Lakshmi is actively worshiped by millions of devotees today and is one of the most popular goddesses of the Hindu pantheon. She is considered to be the embodiment of grace and charm. Typically portrayed as a smiling and beautiful woman dressed in a red sari, Lakshmi has four arms and long, dark wavy hair. Her four arms, which are always in motion, represent each of the four directions, showing that she is always busy distributing wealth and to illustrate the omnipotence of the goddess.

The word "Lakshmi" is taken from the Sanskrit word *Laksya*, which means "goal." She is known as a household goddess or as a domestic deity. In some provinces, Lakshmi's festival occurs in autumn when the full moon is the brightest—in other words, the harvest moon. On this night, she is believed to fly down on her sacred white owl to remove any poverty or stagnation from our lives. Lakshmi also uses her nighttime flights with the owl to shower her followers with abundance and wealth. Furthermore, October is generally considered to be sacred to Lakshmi, and at her Festival of Light, *Diwali*, flowers such as marigolds, foods, and sweets are left as offerings.

This goddess of prosperity is different from other deities, as Lakshmi is associated with the element of water. Yes, you read that correctly, not the element of earth, but actually water. While this may be surprising to folks, considering her iconography, it shouldn't be. You simply need to wrap your mind around a different pantheon. Water is life. Water brings fertility to the land and helps the crops grow and the plants to bear fruit. Riches can be interpreted in many, many ways. For me, the water elemental association for Lakshmi works. After all according to mythology she was born from the "milky ocean," which helps explain her links to fertility magick, and Lakshmi is typically portrayed surrounded by water, standing upon a mystical floating lotus blossom.

The lotus is a classic fertility symbol as this blossom takes its strength from the water. This flower also represents spiritual power and personal growth. Plus the lotus has a mystery to share. You will notice that while the lotus floats upon the water, it is not wet. This is her spiritual lesson: Enjoy the wealth she brings, but do not drown in any obsession with the obtainment of it.

Lakshmi is associated with two different creatures. The white owl, of course, for its vision and intelligence while traveling at night, and white elephants. In India, elephants are a symbol of royal power and a white elephant represents purity. Often Lakshmi is portrayed as flanked by a total of four white elephants. The pachyderms symbolize the four directions, sovereignty, and best of all they attracted rain.

According to Hindu mythology, at one time all white elephants flew, up in the sky like clouds, and they were filled with water. Then one day, a few accidentally fell to earth, losing their wings. These earthbound elephants have always wanted to rejoin their brothers up in the sky who shower the earth below with life-giving rain. So the most the landbound elephants could do now was to use their trunks and to spray water into the air to simulate rain. This is why when they are portrayed with the goddess Lakshmi they often have their trunks raised and are showering water/rain behind the goddess in a kind of salute.

For modern witches, Lakshmi is technically a mother goddess and is associated with the full moon phase. Personally, when I have worked magick with Lakshmi I have found that her magick manifests in a soft, gentle way. Her influence is felt quickly, especially when you are generous to others.

As for how her magick manifests, think gentle nudges, good luck, and positive energy and magick that smoothly fills you up and brings prosperity into your life. She has a comforting presence and a gentle demeanor. Lakshmi responds particularly well to honest and honorable magickal requests concerning matters of prosperity and abundance that involve the well-being of the family.

For a witch wanting to learn more about Lakshmi's magickal correspondences, all you have to do is take a look at the art and how she is represented. To begin with, her sari is red, a color that represents activity. Her costume has golden embroidery, which signifies fulfillment as well as material wealth. Lakshmi has a royal golden crown with rubies, strings of pearls, and golden jewelry.

Lakshmi holds the promise of material fulfillment and contentment, and to prove that traditionally golden coins are always shown falling from her left hand. This gesture demonstrates that she provides wealth, prosperity, and contentment to all of her devotees.

Magickal Correspondences for Lakshmi
Goddess aspect: Mother
Moon phase: Full moon
Planet: Venus
Element: Water
Colors: Red and gold
Flower: Lotus and marigold
Crystals and gems: Low-grade rubies or pearls (Pearl jewelry works well.)
Metal: Gold
Animals: White owl and white elephant
Other items: Coins, especially gold coins
Magickal goals: Prosperity, abundance, fertility, and generosity.

A Spell for Prosperity with Lakshmi

Work the spell during a waxing moon or on the night of a full moon.

Suggested Supplies: For this spell, get a picture of the goddess Lakshmi. Do an image search and print a picture of Lakshmi that appeals to you. I found a pretty one, printed it out, and put it in a small frame so I could use it as a focal point on my magickal workspace. You will want to add a golden coin, or a dollar bill to the spell. Also, you'll need a small red and a small gold candle with two coordinating candle holders to keep the spell candles secure, along with small dish of water, and a few marigold flowers from the garden or a dried lotus blossom. (Lotus pods are easily found at the arts and crafts store.)

Refer to the correspondence chart above for more ideas and put some effort into making the altar setup as pretty as you can. Arrange the accoutrements around the central image of Lakshmi in a way that pleases you.

Please note: Traditionally any requests made to Lakshmi are started by repeating the phase "Om Ganesha" three times. Ganesha is the elephant-headed deity and interestingly, a remover of obstacles. He is honored at the opening of rituals and ceremonies. Then after Ganesha's invocation, you may proceed with the spell. Also in ritual, Lakshmi is addressed as "Maha Lakshmi."

To begin, ground and center yourself and study her image carefully. Allow her smiling face to fill you up with warmth and happiness. Then light the red and the gold candle. Now repeat the invocation and spell verse.

Om Ganesha
Om Ganesha
Om Ganesha
Beautiful dancing Goddess of wealth, luck, and prosperity,
Grant to me good fortune, I request your help, Maha-Lakshmi.
Please let golden coins, extra cash and abundance flow
my way,
Surround me with your loving presence, blessing me
night and day.
I will return this gentle kindness, that you have shown to me,
By helping others when I can, as I will so mote it be.

Allow the spell candles to burn until they go out on their own. Be sure to keep an eye on them. Leave the altar set up and her picture in place for one week, freshening flowers and water as you need to. If you like, you may relight new small candles to her everyday during the week. When the abundance starts to flow into your life, remember to be generous in turn to others.

Blessed be!

Engaging All Five Senses in Spellwork

by Marion Sipe

Spellwork is the practice of bringing the possible into reality whether the spells are for better health, a new job, or tastier garden tomatoes. All of these goals, and most others, work on the principle that the worker uses their own will to shape reality, and because of this, the worker must be able to form a clear picture of the intended outcome. You can't create what you can't imagine, so the more clearly the goal is identified, the more likely the desired outcome. Engaging all of our senses in spellwork can help us define that goal and give it aspects that appeal to our need to interact with something to prove to ourselves it is real. Additionally, sometimes we need to define goals that aren't concrete, but rather involve abstractions such as emotions and memories. Such goals can be hard to represent, but by using our other senses, we can find representation for them, and manifest even the most abstract goals into reality.

While visualization is a much praised and important part of spellwork, each of our four other senses has the potential to connect us to our spellwork in deeper and more intense ways. Human beings are primarily visual creatures, but that does not mean that the visual sense is the strongest for everyone. Nor does it mean that our other senses have less to offer. Many of us already use cues for our other senses in ritual; a drumbeat or music in the background, incense in the air, cakes and ale. However, we don't always bring these elements into the spellwork itself. We can use smells, tastes, sounds, and textures in spellcraft to create a deeper link with the magic as well as a more complete representation of the desired result.

For instance, smells provide a powerful trigger for memory and emotion. As an example, you can improve a spell to relieve insomnia by using the smell of fresh linen, applying the scent to a small sachet tucked into your pillow. The scent becomes another part of the spell whether it's the use of baby powder in a sachet meant to aid in fertility or using a vial of oil as the focus for a calm flying spell.

We can also use scents to bring a spell to mind again after the casting, strengthening the magic or its effect on you. Additionally, spells that you can taste can have a huge impact on the body, and make a great vehicle for workings such as health spells or other purposes involving the body. The sense of touch plays a large role in our interaction with others, but is also the medium through which we interact with and manipulate the world. When we think of something as material, we think of being able to touch it; therefore, giving a texture and feel to the goals of our spellwork lends a quality of realism that brings them closer to manifestation.

Smell

Taste and smell are closely linked, but they do have different aspects. Smell is very portable, something you can wear to continually remind yourself of your spellwork. Spells for courage, confidence, and other emotion-linked outcomes can be kept close, and when something is worn on your skin, it becomes a part of you. A vial of oil used as the focus for a calming spell can be a great way to get through a long flight, and the scents we use in our home can be integrated into protection and cleansing spells for when the place needs a quick touch-up.

However, you can also use scents to evoke memory and, through that memory, the results you wish to attain. Drawing on memories of a loved one, for example, can strengthen spells for that person, aid in contacting a loved one who has passed on, or help you access emotions tied to those memories. Emotions can be particularly hard to define in spellwork, but the way a result makes us feel can be an important

aspect of the working. In this way, finding the right scent to produce that emotion can make your goal more solid, bringing it just a little further into reality.

Taste

While made up largely of smell, taste has different useful properties—just ask any kitchen witch. For instance, it can provide a particularly useful vehicle for health spells, either through using food as a focus for your spell and then using that food to season others, or by ingesting edible oils or foods during the spell itself. We often speak of things so close we can almost taste them, and this literally allows us to give a taste to our desired results by linking them to something we can experience through our senses. For instance, a spell integrated into your favorite vinaigrette can turn your lunchtime salad into a working to help lower your blood pressure. The taste becomes associated with the spell itself, and each time you taste it, you refresh the spell's influence.

Tastes can also conjure up feelings of home and comfort and family. After a bad day, some tastes have the power to comfort us, or pick up our mood. You can tap into this natural power with magic, or use it to strengthen your magic.

Hearing

We readily acknowledge that our sense of hearing has power over us, but we often don't realize how much. A drumbeat simulating an increasing heart rate can create feelings of tension and anxiety, while we all find certain music soothing or energizing. We can use this effect on our emotions in spellwork as a means of representing our goals, both concrete and abstract. A spell to calm anxiety, for example, may incorporate a drumbeat with an increasing cadence, which you then incrementally slow. Not only does it replicate the results that you're looking to be able to reproduce, but it pulls them from potential into reality.

You can also play the sounds back later, helping to remind you of the spell and its intended effects. Moreover, linking the

spell and the sound makes the sound a part of the spell. Every time you listen to the sound, it triggers the same process and the results are now something you can hear and with which you can interact. Additionally, using sounds in rituals can take on many forms, from music that encompasses the emotional message you wish to create to simple sound effects that simulate your reaction to the desired result.

Touch

Despite being the one we most use to interact with the world, touch is perhaps the most underrated sense. In the material world, we use it to manipulate objects, to create desired results, much as spellworkers use their wills to create magical results. For this reason, touch can be a tremendous help to spellwork, though it may require stepping outside of our general perceptions in order to use it effectively. Having a book in one's hands feels a certain way, and you would recognize a book in your hands even if you couldn't see it. In the same way, we can use our sense of touch to give texture, depth, and solidity to our spells. Often, we judge more real that which we can touch. Giving texture to our workings, and the results for which we're aiming, creates in us a sense of realism that establishes it firmly in our minds as real, material, touchable.

While you can use any texture, it is best to use as a focus or a material something that reminds you of the goal. You probably wouldn't use rough burlap for a sleep sachet or fragile cotton to represent protective armor. It's also important to be inventive when it comes to touch. Water has a feel all its own when you submerge your fingertips in it, and the feel of still water is completely different to that of moving water, but both lend reality to a working and create a certain feeling within us.

Sight

While I have been touting the use of other senses, visualization remains a very important part of spellwork. Being able to visualize a result brings it closer to reality, but augmenting that with information for your other senses completes the experience, making it more than just a picture. If you can represent the emotional content with sound or touch or smell, if you can create a complete an in-depth representation of your result, you are much closer to reaching that goal.

Even if you can't create a perfect image in your mind, the other senses can help fill in the blanks left by visualization. Smells, sounds, and textures allow you to expand that picture, and the more real you make it, the more real it is.

⁓

When all five senses are engaged in our spellwork, we are taking steps toward bringing our goal a deeper sense of reality. While different senses may be more or less suited to different types of spells, all spells benefit from this added realism. When we can vividly imagine our results in detail, they are already closer to being manifest. Using each of our senses, and finding ways to combine them, can make our spellwork more powerful, add depth to the representations of our goals, and add power to our workings. Combining hearing, smell, taste, and touch with sight allows us to imagine it in greater detail and to put more power behind it.

Enlightened Eats

by Dallas Jennifer Cobb

Eating can raise your energy, imbue you with spiritual properties, uplift and heal you. Yes, we're supposed to eat well, drink lots of water and take vitamins, but little is taught about foods' essential energy. When we eat, we don't just digest nutrients. While nutritional quality is important, an even greater effect depends on how "enlightened," or energized, food is.

Foods have their own natural energy, which can be depleted or enhanced by human intervention. We can raise food's vibration, producing "enlightened eats," and enhance both its physical and spiritual nutrition. Learn about the natural energy in food, how food is constructed molecularly, and how we can influence the energy of food so that you can enlighten everything you eat. You have the power to enlighten or deplete foods' energy.

Simple Science

Like all matter, food is made up of cells that contain mild electromagnetic charges. As we chew, swallow, and digest, food provides us with nutrients and energy.

Fruits and vegetables are composed of nearly 70 percent water. Water is one of the most miraculous substances known because its composition of two hydrogen atoms plus one oxygen atom make it a three-cell molecule with a slightly unstable bond. This means that hydrogen atoms are easily separated and become free radicals that carry a negative charge. These negative ions can then bond with positive ions, neutralizing their often-damaging effect.

We often hear that fruits and vegetables are high in antioxidants, also called "free radicals." Antioxidants have miraculous positive effects such as slowing the rate of cellular aging, reducing wrinkling, repairing mild skin damage from solar radiation, and neutralizing the harmful effects of smoking, drinking alcohol, and taking drugs.

Essential Energy

While we learn all about the caloric and nutritional content of food, too little is taught about the energetic content. In its natural state, food has a vibrational frequency that is measured in Hertz, an energy measurement related to electromagnetic energy. This electromagnetic energy is also called *prana* or life force.

Different foods have different vibrational levels. An easy way to "enlighten" your eats is to choose from the higher vibrating foods:

- Live foods like sprouts vibrate between 15 and 27 Hertz;
- Fresh herbs vibrate between 12 and 27 Hertz;
- Dried herbs vibrate between 2 and 27 Hertz;
- Fresh produce (fruit and vegetables) vibrate between 1 and 15 Hertz, with organic produce consistently vibrating at a higher rate than conventionally produced fruits and vegetables;
- Canned foods, processed foods, and genetically modified foods vibrate at 0 Hertz.

Consider the effect of ingesting these different foods—some with a significant amount of enlightened energy, and others entirely devoid of energy. Which do you think promote and maintain optimum health? Dr. Bernard Jensen identified the foods that heal, the majority of them being raw, live foods. [1]

When possible, consume locally produced, in-season, fruits and vegetables. Eat them raw as much as possible.

1. Jensen, Bernard. *Foods that Heal.* New York, New York: Avery Trade, 2002.

Choose foods that are vine- or tree-ripened so they have naturally developed their full complement of nutrients. Fresh food tastes better, has better texture, and is better for you. And that is enlightened.

Depleting Energy

Too often, good quality, natural food becomes depleted of energy. Many techniques used to preserve food negatively affect its energy. The following techniques lower, or eliminate the natural energy of food: overcooking, irradiation, canning, processing, pasteurization, and picking fruits and vegetables before they are naturally ripened.

People Power

We know what affects our personal energy. I need 9.5 hours of sleep, a good breakfast, lots of water, and daily exercise to feel well. I avoid sweets. Sure, they taste good, but I crash a little while later and feel awful. I gave up recreational alcohol use because it took me several days to recover from even "light drinking."

With focus, we can tune in to the cycles and needs of our bodies, minds, and spirits, and learn what elevates our personal energy, and what depletes it. Sure, there are people, places, and things that negatively affect us, but we can't control them. However, we can control what we eat, and how we eat it.

Notice what foods make you feel better—not just in the moment, but afterward. Notice the lingering vibration of the food. I love fresh-baked bread, but realized that wheat played havoc on my digestion. My stomach would rumble and become bloated, eventually producing nasty gas. Not only did wheat deplete my energy, but my family didn't want to be near me either. When I switched to spelt or oat flour bread, I noticed an immediate change in how I felt. These grains haven't been genetically modified as much as wheat has, so they retain more of their natural energy.

By paying attention to what I ate, when I ate it, and how I felt as a result, I've learned how to enhance (or deplete) my own energy. After I added protein to my previously carbohydrate-heavy breakfast, switching from cereal to eggs and toast, I felt more even-keeled and my energy lasted longer. I was clearheaded and didn't experience any midmorning slump. When I make smoothies with fruit, spirulina, nuts containing essential fatty acids, and protein, I positively vibrate, feeling the direct physical effect of the nutrients in my system. I feel good.

"Enlighten" Your Eats

So you've chosen food with abundant natural energy. You've assessed your energy levels to see how you are affected by different foods and eating patterns. Now you can enlighten these eats to further enhance their energy levels.

Spiritually uplifting food is a universally practiced tradition that crosses all cultures. While it's mostly done ritualistically by a spiritual or religious leader, anyone can learn techniques to raise the energy of food in community, at home or out in public.

Many traditions practice prayer before eating. It helps create reverence and gratitude for food and uplift its vibration. Learn a few simple blessings to use when you're in the community to raise the energy of the people you're breaking bread with and enlighten the eats. Prayers from any denomination will focus uplifting intentions.

Raising the energy of the people coming together to eat also affects the vibration of the food. Even a pantheistic group can come together for a moment of silent thanks or to join hands before eating, easily uniting the group.

In public, I use several portable techniques. Whether at a café or restaurant, casual dinner at a friends' house, or a big family gathering, I always raise the energy of anything I am going to consume. The practice of enlightening my eats simultaneously raises my energy, producing gratitude and awareness. No matter where I am, it takes just a moment, and in that moment I become more aware of, and thankful for, the nourishment I am about to consume.

Quick Ways to Enlighten Your Eats:

Eat your favorite food. No, I don't mean eat only chocolate, I mean know what your absolute favorite fruits, vegetables, nuts, seeds, and legumes are, and make sure you always have these in your home. Not only will you be getting more natural energy and nutrition, but you will feel great joy and appreciation for your favorite foods.

Prepare food with love. As you chop, mix, or assemble food, cultivate a feeling of love for the food, for the people you will share it with, for the farmers who produced the food, or even for the sun and rain that went into growing the food. The vibration of love will alter the electromagnetic frequency of the food, and raise its energy signature.

Gratitude will uplift you and enlighten your eats. Wrap your hands around your plate and, while looking what you are about to consume, feel pure gratitude for the food and drink. Say *"Thank you, thank you, thank you"* silently or aloud. The Law of Attraction states that what you will receive more of what you give thanks for.

Sound waves change foods' vibration. Chant "Om," or hum over food to uplift it.

Reverently say (silently or aloud) *I bless this food with love and light.*

Sacred geometry focuses energy, so placing food within a sacred pyramid will uplift it.

Blessing food will alter its essential energy. The simplest technique is to place hands reverently around a vessel containing food. Breathe deeply, close your eyes, feel pure joy emanating from your heart, and send it into the food.

Send light into what you are about to consume. Hold one hand on either side of the food and visualize a translucent white light flowing from your hands and into your food, uplifting its vibration. Alternatively, set food in the sun or moonlight and let planetary energy uplift the food.

Seek out ethically raised animals and poultry. An animal that's lived a good life, enjoyed the outdoors, eaten grass, and enjoyed the sun, has a higher *prana* or life force than factory-raised animals. Know your local producers and see for yourself how your food was raised. Usually, a happy farmer produces happy food.

The vibration of your voice will uplift fluids. Hold the vessel in your hands, lean close, and whisper *"Blessings,"* *"Love"* or *"Thank you."* As your breath makes ripples in the fluid, know that your energy has affected it. Research has shown that words actually change the physical structure of water crystals.[2]

---

2 Emoto, Masaru. *The Hidden Messages in Water.* Hillsboro, Oregon: Beyond Words Publishing Company, 2004.

Even if food is dead, uplift your energy before consuming it. I learned long ago, it's better to indulge in a treat and feel good about it than to feel guilty. Good feelings can overcome the emptiness of food with no natural energy. Guilt is far more harmful than a small amount of junk food.

～

Now when you go to the grocery store, don't just read nutritional labels, but seek out foods that vibrate highly, possess high levels of natural energy, and then, as you put them in your shopping basket, bless them. Later when you get home, use some of these techniques to further enlighten your eats.

Folk Clothing

by Ellen Coutts Waff

It is accepted knowledge that Witches often perform their rites skyclad. Doreen Valiente, the mother of Gardnerian Witchcraft, stated "the traditional attire of witches is generally believed to be nudity." Gerald Gardner, being a "naturist," or nudist, "maintained that witches *always* worked in the nude." Nudity is both freeing and equalizing, but often needs getting used to… "…one can in a sense cast off one's everyday self with one's everyday clothing." But, what of practical concerns? What of the weather, the location, the neighbors? What of just plain discomfort about doing ritual in the altogether? Are there appropriate, even pleasing alternatives?

Robe Rules

The prime directive for any ritual garb is to allow for movement, both *of* the body and for energy *through* the body, as if one were naked. Looseness of the robe is therefore important to choosing what to wear in circle. Arms must be able to be raised freely, room must be allowed for dancing, so nothing tight in the leg. When making one's first robe, just a long piece of fabric with a hole cut out for the head, and maybe two slits for the cords to go through is a common solution. Sometimes color choice is dictated by the individual tradition, but black reigns supreme. Going barefoot is advised to enable earth currents to move upward into and through the covener's body. If baring the feet is not possible, thin-soled moccasins, slippers, sandals, or just socks are worn.

Is this all there is then? What if a simple unconstructed garment is not really pleasing to the wearer? Within the requirement for looseness in ritual garb, any and every earthly choice available. There have been witches who possessed sumptuous Parisian silk robes embellished with pearls and gold lace. Others use folk garb from lands with which they identify. Ritual garb should, above all, give pleasure to its owner. It can be simple, complex, dramatic, symbolic, very personal, or an emblem of hierarchy within an order.

Folk-Clothing Options Abound

Folk clothing offers a most interesting variety. Undergarments such as chemises or long shirts, such as the Irish/Scottish *leine* are comfortable and loose. They can be belted easily. Egyptians, as a warm-climate people, wore beautifully pleated, loose, see-through garments. The Greek or Roman toga, or other draped garment such as an Indian sari, are quite dramatic and can be colorful as well. The Japanese kimono is a glorious garment to wear for ritual. Belly dance clothing can be fun to wear, too. One of the best sources for constructing these items is Folkwear Patterns, www.folkwear.com. Folkwear has patterns, with extensive documentation included, on any to-be-constructed garment. The choices are many and varied. Research must be done for draped clothing, such as togas. It is not unusual for folk clothing to be quite simple in construction, as the garments needed to fit traditional widths of handwoven fabric. There was little waste. A common width was an "el" or the measure from fingertip to elbow, about 27 inches. Even now, many sewers use an arm's length plus shoulder and face to the nose tip to measure one yard of fabric.

Layering is advised for outdoor rituals in cold or inclement weather. Traditionally, a cloak or *brat* covers

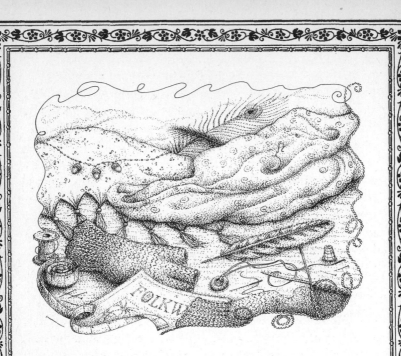

clothing, with or without a hood. A hood can also be made separately of a more waterproof material, such as leather. Fur could be worn depending on the philosophy of the wearer. Knitting or crocheting can be employed to make wonderful caps, shoulder coverings, mittens, or fingerless mitts. *Piecework* magazine has great patterns, as do other knitting or crocheting magazines, such as *Jane Austen Knits*. Colors can be chosen to suit the wearer or to suit the ritual occasion. Spring Equinox/Eostara calls for light colors, whereas Samhain could be quite Goth. The deity of the season could be honored with some special color or detail, as could the *genius loci*, the spirit of place. Even wearing "camo" might be quite appropriate to a God or Goddess of the Hunt…. Never forget that green has always been known to be the Faeries' color!

Fabric

Each fabric possesses its own energy signature. This, too, should be taken into consideration. Silk is an energetic fabric, which can transmit readily. Wool, also, is "alive" and remains warming even when wet. Cotton, conversely, can make the wearer cold if it gets wet, but it is very comfortable in hot weather. Linen is most comfortable for the heat. Silk and wool are animal fibers; cotton and linen are from plants. Natural fibers are best for ritual use. Synthetics have different characteristics that vary based on the individual fiber. Special fabrics can be used for folk garb in the same manner as in their country of origin. Kente cloth and Mud cloth should be wrapped or made into a simple garment, hanging from the shoulders. Bark and feather cloth probably should not be worn, but might be used as a cloaklike covering. Tartan lengths can be constructed into garments, but are probably best used as the belted plaid for men, or its counterpart, the *airisead* for women. Look for instructions on pleating and wrapping on the Internet. A belt is required.

Accessories

Traditionally, necklaces are worn, both with robes and with folk garb. Many societies have unique expectations about what is worn with their clothing. The Norwegian *bunad* is worn with silver brooches and chest pieces unique to that garb. Each area in Norway has its own variation on the *bunad* both in color and design. In general, it is a woman's chemise, skirt, apron, and jacket, worn with the jewelry and a headpiece specific to that area. Amber and jet have traditionally comprised the necklaces worn in traditional witchcraft. Druids' necklaces are made of acorns. The Lord Mayor of London wears a heavy gold chain and pendant... there are infinite variations for infinite rituals.

Headgear and hair arrangements can also accent garb. Some insist that hair be worn down and loose for women, and long-haired men in circle. This requirement stems from the belief that the spells done can be "tied up" in hair that is done up, or knotted. Others expect that their members wear circlets, or chaplets of silver, metal, leather, or other material on their heads, with perhaps some symbol of their position or their person inscribed on it. Some wear flower wreaths, some hats, some hoods. Some bearded men tie flowers, bones, or braids into the beard. All of these variations serve as embellishment, and can make a ritual the unique and "out of the ordinary" experience it should be.

One ancient technique for altering perception in a ritual context is that of mask-wearing. The Lascaux cave paintings show a man, usually termed a shaman, dancing in a stag mask. The mask not only changes the way others in ritual see the wearer, but also changes his/her persona.

Masks may lead to experiences that can only be described as "possession." It is best, if one is assuming a masked persona, to act with forethought and full responsibility, as if engaged in trancework. In Scotland in the seventeenth and eighteenth centuries, "guising" was common at the hinge-points of the year, when masked fellows appeared with much noise and fanfare at folks' doors demanding food, drink, and coin! They were feared and respected, even though the folks knew that the guisers were their young neighbors. They were a bit more than human when wearing those disguises.

~

The saying goes: "clothing makes the man," and that carries into the ritual circle. One can create the persona one wishes, by the choices made in garb. Folk clothing allows infinite possibilities for that creation. One still is able to "cast off one's everyday self with one's everyday clothing."

The Magic of Metals

by Ember Grant

Imagine life in the Stone Age. Humans discovered that certain stones, such as flint, could be chipped and shaped into tools and weapons, even made into pottery. For more than two million years, our ancestors relied on stones for life. But then, sometime around 4500 BC, somewhere on the continent we now call Asia, people learned to extract copper from malachite, melt it, and pour it into molds. Bronze (copper reinforced with tin) soon followed, then iron. A new age dawned—the age of metals.

In magical practice, your choice of metal can aid the flow of your energy, so it's important to consider the various types available. The most ancient metals used by civilization are gold, copper, silver, lead, tin, iron, and mercury—all naturally occurring metals. (However, since mercury is toxic, it will not be explored here.) In addition, blends of metals such as brass and pewter are popular, so we'll look at them as well and also a more "modern" metal, platinum (discovered in the 1500s). You will most likely find metals in jewelry, decorative items such as statues and candleholders, and sometimes wands.

Brass, a mixture of copper and zinc, is associated with the Sun. Due to its golden color, brass has long been used as a substitute for gold. Brass is often confused with bronze, which is a mixture of copper and tin (other metals that are copper alloys are sometimes called bronze). Metaphysically, brass is used for healing, attracting wealth, and protection. Brass items such as candleholders and incense burners can be lovely additions to your altar and are excellent symbols of the fire element.

Copper is a popular magical metal and is associated with the planet Venus and the element of water. Discovery of copper ushered in the Bronze Age, but the Egyptians made bronze as early as 3900 BC. Copper is an abundant metal and an excellent conductor of electricity—consider purchasing a wand made of copper to aid your energy flow. Metaphysically, copper promotes positive self-esteem and can be used to enhance mental and emotional states. For these reasons, copper is also an excellent choice for pieces of magical jewelry.

Gold has long been considered the most noble of metals, representing the Sun and the element of fire. Of the precious metals (gold, silver, and platinum), gold is the most popular for jewelry and ornamentation—it doesn't tarnish or corrode, and it's easy to work with. Since pure gold is often too soft for jewelry, it's often mixed with other metals like silver or copper. The oldest gold jewelry dated in the world is from Bulgaria—and is more than 6,000 years old. Since gold is the ultimate symbol of wealth, it's often used in spells for prosperity and success, and also healing. Its energy is said to be especially projective. Try wearing gold jewelry on your projective hand to assist the sending of energy during spellwork.

Iron corresponds with the planet Mars and the element of fire. All the iron in the earth (and the other native elements) came from exploding stars. While it's the most common element in the planet Earth, it's actually rarely found on the surface in pure form (due to its tendency to oxidize, or rust). The Earth's core is believed to be comprised mainly of iron and nickel. Because pure iron is actually soft, it's most commonly used in the form of steel (by adding carbon, manganese, or other substances in order to harden it). Iron is mainly mined from oxides like hematite, magnetite, and pyrite, so these minerals can be utilized for their associations with iron. Wrought iron, an iron alloy, has been used to create decorative items that you may wish to incorporate into your practice. The word *wrought* means "to be worked," such as by a smith. Genuine wrought iron is rare and now mainly a technique pursued by artists. Today, much of what is called wrought iron is actually cast from a mold. Magically, iron is used for protection, strength, grounding, and healing.

Since **lead** is toxic, use galena (lead ore) for magic. Lead is associated with Saturn and the earth element and is very heavy. Historically, lead has been used in protective and defensive magic; the Romans used lead for sewer pipes. Galena is comprised of lead and sulfur and also represents the element of earth. The main ore of lead, galena also yields silver as a byproduct. Galena is an excellent stone for grounding and centering. It was once used as kohl; the ancient Egyptians smeared this powder around their eyes to reduce the glare of the desert sun and keep flies away. Pure galena looks like silver and is often found with pyrite and calcite—many specimens are a lovely combination of these minerals.

Pewter is made mostly of tin, with copper and small amounts of other metals (older pieces may contain lead) mixed in, so the properties of tin apply to pewter. Tin is associated with the planet Jupiter and the element of air. Like many of the other metals described here, tin has been used by humans for thousands of years. Tin is a chemical element and does not occur by itself—it is extracted from other compounds. It is often used to coat other metals because it can resist several types of corrosion. Pewter has been in use since 1450 BC, with the oldest piece was found in an Egyptian tomb. Metaphysically, it can be used for divination, luck, and drawing money. Many ritual chalices and cups are made of pewter, and pewter jewelry is common as well. You may also find some lovely pewter statues to decorate your altar.

Platinum's value is twice that of gold. The name comes from the Spanish word *plata* meaning silver, since its color is similar. Unlike silver, it does not tarnish. Platinum is associated with Neptune and the water element—it's emotionally cleansing and balancing, and also enhances intuition.

Silver, possibly the most popular metal used in magic, represents the Moon and the water element. Since silver, like gold, is malleable, it has been used for ages in coins, jewelry, and for other practical and decorative purposes. Of all the metals, silver is the best conductor of energy—one reason it's so popular in magical practice. Silver is considered to have receptive energy, which is useful for intuition. Wear silver on your receptive hand during magical practice to draw energy toward you. In addition to jewelry, you may find other silver items, such as goblets or plates, that you can use during ritual.

～

The freedom of movement of electrons makes metals excellent conductors of energy. The best conductors from those mentioned here are: silver, copper, gold, iron/steel, brass, and bronze. Whichever metal you choose, remember you can add an extra boost to your magic by considering the metaphysical properties of these beautiful energy conductors.

Earth-Based Spirituality in a City Setting

by Raven Digitalis

As we stand on the Earth, all cosmic bodies are either gravitationally or energetically influencing our experience, and we theirs. As magical practitioners, it's our duty to do our part in maintaining our own planet through Earth consciousness and servitude. This is especially true considering that the very word *Pagan* comes from the Latin *paganus*, basically meaning "rural" or "country-dwelling." In this day and age, Pagan spirituality has greatly mingled with more formerly "elite" forms of ceremonial magic, most of which are based in Hermetics and ancient grimoires that tend to be highly based in astrology and mysticism. I believe that while there will always be separate schools of magic, the Earth is the No. 1 planet in our cosmos and deserves to be mindfully worked with in *all* spiritual schools—including academic-based or science-based "high" magical schools of occultism.

Personally, I seem to be observing more and more non-Wiccan occultists taking a deeper interest in Earth-based spirituality. For some people, this is expressed in Druidry or another Neopagan system alongside a person's Lodge work or personal occult practice. Keep in mind that Wicca, the most prominent expression of modern witchcraft, is a mixture of "rural" folk charmery and mythology, alongside the more monotheistic-centric ritual magic traditions. Wicca, especially within the original Gardnerian tradition, has plenty of elements of ceremonial systems, including Thelema, Freemasonry, Hermeticism, and even Enochian magic. For this reason, Wiccans and "ceremonialists" are not quite as different as practitioners may believe.

Earth-worship is not restricted to Witches, Wiccans, and Neopagans. Occultists who may be more prone to studying the Qlippoth than the chakras—even those who are vehemently non-Wiccan—are *allowed* to be interested in Earth issues, and damn well should be, in my opinion. This Earth is our home. The purpose of magic is not just to get what we want—it's to help our world, which includes ourselves, those around us, surrounding ecosystems, and the very soil that supports us.

Magic in the City

To the Earth-based spiritualist raised in a smaller area, the city may seem lacking in magical energy, but it's there. It's just a different type of magic; it's the magic of society, science, high art, and technology. If a person is more partial to Wicca or Druidry, the city may seem more magically empty than it does to, say, a chaos magician or a ritual Thelemite. For some, it can be spiritually disturbing to see the natural world reduced to park settings.

City life can seem hopeless because of the sheer number of people and the perception that the majority aren't making conscious choices or acting with love. It's disappointing and saddening, but one mustn't internalize it too deeply, and instead seek to actively and respectfully educate—and to lead by setting a good example! If the emotional pressure gets too tough, remember that you can take action and get help, either in the form of counseling or by moving to a quieter area if possible.

Though there is so much culture and so many beautiful things about city life, cities can sometimes seem suffocating to those who are particularly energetically sensitive. People like this may choose to live in a quieter outskirt of a city, relocate to a small city or big town, or create other means of tuning out the masses. Living from paycheck to paycheck, or living at the whim of a corporation can make many people feel trapped, but it's not the only factor. The city itself plays a role because cities have their own vibration—their own consciousness. Many cities, especially larger cities and those that have rough weather patterns or are located in valleys, have a denser energetic feel to them. When a city evokes these feelings, ideas of moving or escaping the concrete jungle (if that's what one desires) may seem more futile or impossible than they really are. Realistically, change is possible if it's what one desires: there is always a way to create more satisfaction and fulfillment in life. If a magical person has decided that big-city life is for them, they have the option of making the most of the city and work their magic toward sustainability on a consistent basis, even if it means being a bit more on guard and having an increased need to separate oneself from magical drama and infighting!

Sustainability, which encompasses one's private, personal relationship with Gaia, can occur much more easily in a rural or country setting. Still, it's certainly possible to take active steps toward sustainable or low-impact living when residing in a city.

A City-dweller's Checklist

The following is a list for city-dwelling Pagans and occultists to reference for making more progressive, ecocentric lifestyle changes. May your journey toward consciousness dance ever in hand with the land!

Recycle everything you possibly can, even if it means bringing it down to the recycling center yourself.

If you feel that it's important for you to live in a city, consider going to college if you haven't already or aren't

SEEDLINGS

currently enrolled. Earth consciousnesses can be acutely learned by way of scientific education. Many assistance programs and individuals exist to help a person get started in the educational system—and don't worry about those student loans; they'll get paid back eventually—probably!

If you live in an apartment, organically grow tomatoes (they're easy to grow), as well as flowers and other vegetable. Use planters on your balcony or rooftop. Otherwise, create or purchase an indoor greenhouse and any necessary lighting or heating to accompany the plant operation. Buy books and do research on indoor growing!

If you have a bit of yard space, consider creating a small organic garden—it's extremely fun and rewarding and is relatively inexpensive.

Reuse bottles, containers, and packaging to give materials a longer life.

Buy organic or expressly sustainable products at literally all times—let's phase out the earth-killing, genetically modified (GMO) industry.

Buy your produce, dairy, meat, and other foods locally at farmers' markets and privately owned grocery stores and cooperatives (co-ops).

Do away with shopping at giant chain stores, super-centers, and big-box stores whenever possible.

Boycott any and all factory-farmed meat (including that served in restaurants) and research the horrors of the industry. If you eat meat, choose to support only local farmers, hunters, and fishers.

If you get seafood in a restaurant or store, keep an informative Seafood Watch pocket guide handy, available free of charge at www.montereybayaquarium.org.

Buy or sell items secondhand through avenues like thrift stores, yard sales, and local listings such as www.craigslist.org and www.freecycle.org.

Donate unwanted or unused items to nonprofit organizations.

Try to *see through* the advertising around you, as an exercise for increasing awareness. Advertisers use magic on a consistent basis. Consider the "speed" of the colors used on billboards, company logos, or magazine spreads: Why are they using the color scheme they are, and what energy does it evoke? Also consider the styles and expressions of the models in advertisements: what's being said? In other words, what spells are advertisers trying to cast on the audience?

Use reusable cups, plates, silverware, and cloth napkins instead of the paper or plastic varieties.

Pick up and throw away litter whenever you see it.

Contemplate joining a local, national, or international environmental "eco-activism" network and getting involved with protests, rallies, and taking measures to influence political change. Many of these networks also follow earth-based spiritual paths, including the interconnected trinity of Feri Witchcraft, Reclaiming, and Dianic Wicca.

If you buy gemstones, check the source to see if it's chemically or naturally mined, and what the working conditions are like in the country of origin.

If you buy oils, candles, or anything scented (including soaps and hygiene products), vow to only purchase essential oils rather than "fragrant" oil, simply because of the amount of toxic chemical waste byproducts that often constitute the latter.

Rarely or never buy single-use bottled water; the bottles are bad for the environment and many varieties are nothing more than purified tap water.

Switch all of your light bulbs to energy-efficient bulbs. Turn off lights in rooms that aren't in use.

If you have a dishwasher, only run it when the washer is completely full.

Air-dry clothing whenever possible.

Insulate your hot water heater and pipes to conserve heat and save moolah.

Put a brick or a stone-filled half-gallon jug in the tank (back) of your toilet to help conserve water usage.

Try to buy durable, all-natural items rather than cheap, imported plastic crap.

Utilize your local environmental compost agency for any fallen or dead greenery on your property.

Start a compost bucket for all of your food waste—you can even add worms! But beware of the fruit flies in the summertime.

Instead of buying chemical or synthesized toiletries, try buying only all-natural products to put in or on your body. It's better for your health and the earth.

Use white vinegar or Himalayan crystal salt for deodorant instead of chemical antiperspirants.

Try using baking soda and vinegar as effective all natural cleaners, as opposed to nasty chemical cleaners.

Contemplate your impact on the Earth with every single purchase you make. Every … single … purchase … literally!

If you live on a small plot of land within a city, consider raising a handful of chickens. Chickens are actually quite easy to raise if their needs are met and they're consistently tended to. Talk to your landlords, neighbors, and city officials (you might need a permit, even if you own the property) to gather their thoughts on a small, well-cared-for flock of egg-laying hens—and offer to share the eggs! Remember, hens start laying eggs at six months old. Also, be sure to do some research, as there are a variety of factors to consider, including the breed, the coop, the setup (including protection from dogs), winterizing, ranging space, cleaning, bedding, and the cost of startup.

Use organic materials to build up the health of soil for gardening.

Do away with pesticides on your lawn or garden.

Research and explore permaculture and organic gardening methods.

Bring your own reusable bags to the grocery store; if you forget your reusable bags at home, get paper or plastic bags and just recycle them!

If you can't pronounce ingredients on food you purchase, research the ingredient names and the company's sustainability reputation.

Try bicycling, walking, skateboarding, rollerblading, or something nonmotorized instead of using a car.

When using oil-based transportation, try carpooling or using public transport whenever possible.

Buy items, including food, that have a small carbon footprint (i.e., are not imported from God-knows-where).

Use all-natural cleaning products for your house and home—they really do work!

Positively influence your workplace or corporation to make more conscious, Earth-based choices in their daily operations.

Use recycled paper products whenever possible.

Write to your congressman, politicians, and submit letters to the editor of both local and mass media enterprises. They really do listen and count your voice as "one of hundreds (or thousands)!"

Use all-natural soap and dishwashing liquid instead of toxic products.

Eat what's *in season* in your area and research locavorism.

To conserve water, take shorter showers or a bath instead, turn off the faucet when you brush your teeth, and don't flush after every pee.

Support local environmental protection agencies; maybe even participate in protests!

Buy fair trade and shade-grown coffee instead of massively-produced plantation coffee. Fair trade ensures good work conditions for laborers, and shade-grown coffee varieties encourage much-needed bird habitat.

Support local and nearby breweries and wineries instead of only buying imported liquor or spirits.

Contemplate how to live "off the grid" and find alternative energy resources.

If you use tobacco and live in the States, try buying American Spirit tobacco (particularly their American-grown varieties) instead of something produced by one of "the giants." (Also, never throw a cig butt out the window!)

If you have cats or dogs, do some much-needed research into the wet and dry food you're giving them. Research brands online to discover their stances on environmental standards, as well as researching their true ingredient information. The vast majority of pet food is not sustainable and are not wise purchases for Earth-worshipers. Inexpensive, all-natural, sustainable pet food is becoming more widely available every day.

Finally, discover the reality of peak oil and humanity's dependency on fossil fuel. My suggestion is to read *The Long Descent: A User's Guide to the End of the Industrial Age* by our brilliant Archdruid comrade John Michael Greer.

Walking the Veil: Death Work and Funerary Rites

By: Charlynn Walls

Death is one of those delicate topics that people too often avoid until it directly affects their lives. For me, that has happened on more than one occasion, and as much as I would have liked to bury my head in the sand, it was something I had to confront head-on. When I was still a very young adult, I lived with my grandma, grandpa, and great-grandma. They were in poor health, and I was happy to help with anything that they needed. Unfortunately, that included making funeral arrangements. At the time, I did not know exactly what I had gotten myself into.

As Pagans, we have a responsibility to be advocates for those living within our communities and to be able to deal with issues that arise during our most vulnerable moments.

Our communities, though, tend to focus on occasions of celebration and education, such as rites of passage, holidays, festivals, and outreach programs. Even as practitioners of earth-based faiths who know death is an integral part of life, it can be a difficult subject to tackle. Death work and funerary services are areas we often taken for granted. However, as the baby boomer generation continues to age, our communities will be forced to face the issue of mortality. And addressing it now is important, so that we'll be prepared to adequately provide the necessary support.

Our communities need access to resources that educate our pastoral care workers in death working and funerary services. Death work involves all aspects of planning prior to death, working with the terminally ill and helping ease the transition during an individual's final moment. Funerary services encompass carrying out the final wishes of the recently deceased and their families. Together, these aspects bring about closure and make sure that the individual's final moments on the physical plane are respected. Priests and priestesses need to learn their traditional rites from local elders. They also have to be available for these services and make accessibility known to their communities through local stores, newsletters, and online resources.

So what should we be doing in order to address the needs of the people within our communities? There are several areas to be taken into consideration:

What is the person's personal belief structure?

Does the person have a living will that expresses their wishes or a power of attorney?

Is there a need for a formal or informal clergy?

Belief Structure

Finding two or more Wiccans, Witches, or Pagans with an identical belief structure is rare. As such, it is difficult to make broad generalizations about death work and funerary services for Pagans as a whole. But, that's okay, as I believe the focus should be on the individual. Take the time to get to know their personal beliefs and work with them to ensure that you are living up to their concepts surrounding death. So, as someone providing these services, you'll have a lot to work through. I suggest taking notes to get a good grasp on the overall picture and to note any important details.

First, knowing an individual's support system is important. Do they work with a group or coven, or are they solitary? Are they close to their family? And is the family aware they are Pagan?

Those who work with a group or coven already have a built-in support system. These members of their extended family may already have a good idea of the individual's wishes, so you will want to include them in any memorials or rituals presented for the person you are working with. They can also work closely with the family to help oversee the arrangements.

Those following a solitary path have probably approached you to seek out someone they can connect with and can start an open dialogue on this difficult subject. The major topics of concern should include hospice, service, and burial. Since these are sensitive matters, you will need to find out how they want to involve their family. Expectations should be made clear at this time. This would also be an important time to communicate the need for an advance medical directive or living will. In those documents, you can outline your wishes and who you want to oversee your wishes. It is important these are not one-time conversations—you will want to follow up with those in your care so that things can be adjusted over time.

My grandmother had several conversations with me about what to do if something should happen to her. I knew almost all the details of the service that she wanted. So when the time came to make arrangements, I was able to assist my great-grandma with the planning, taking a lot of the burden off of her. Likewise, when my father passed on, I took the reins and helped my stepmother. I arranged for the music, the service, the type of casket, and grave marker. For instance, I knew my father did not want a traditional service where he would be subjected to a preacher's vision of heaven and hell. He had

told the entire family he wanted a Masonic service. Based on those frank conversations, I was able to push for that and make sure we honored his last wishes.

Living Will

Living wills are directives that detail your desires to pass naturally if you are diagnosed with a terminal illness or injury. These types of medical directives have become increasingly popular over the years and explicitly state under what circumstances the person no longer wishes to receive medical treatment that will prolong their life if death is inevitable. Along these lines, a power of attorney can be established, giving control of your medical decisions to another person if you become incapacitated.

These forms are available through each state's medical association, which can be completed and notarized. If you have specific questions, a lawyer is a good resource. Prices are usually reasonable for these services, and they can ensure that your wishes will be respected regardless of your location.

A living will and power of attorney need to be readily available in order to be effective. Make certain that your physician has a copy on record. Anyone who could potentially become an advocate should have a copy, as should a person designated as a power of attorney.

My grandmother had both documents and they proved invaluable. I was able to advocate on her behalf after the hospital had already violated her directives upon admittance. Once I was able to produce the documentation, we were able to let her pass on with the dignity and respect that she wanted. It was hard, but ultimately she had already made all the difficult decisions. All I had to do was carry them out.

Informal vs. Formal Clergy

Depending on the situation, a person may desire informal or formal clergy to be present and preside over a service. Informal clergy is any priest or priestess that the person normally seeks advice or services from, even though they may only have education through their coven or group. Often, informal clergy are sought out because of the relationships that have formed over time.

When one of my good friends passed away a few years ago, we arranged an informal clergy available to minister to her during her final days. Our community elders came together and sat with her, journeyed with her, and helped her come to terms with what was happening to her. They were also available to sit with her daughter; even though she did not share her mother's path, they were people she trusted, so, in the end, she was better able to deal with her mother's untimely passing.

Formal clergy is anyone with a degree in Theology, Divinity, or other recognized pastoral training. Those with formalized education can often participate in chaplain services often offered through hospitals. This is an aspect that we as a community lack the most. Since my friend was Pagan, there was no one to minister to her from the hospital's chaplain service. Those on staff were understanding, but really unable to deal with her needs. Elibility requirements to become a chaplain are easily found on any hospital website. I would encourage anyone is interested in serving their community to explore this option if you think that this is your calling.

Be There

Though it is often a difficult topic, those who work with the terminally ill and dying can find it very rewarding. It certainly is not for the faint of heart. The best advice I can give is that if you decide to work with anyone is to be available.

Be available to sit for a while. Sometimes you do not have to do anything but just be there. It is comforting to know that you are not alone and will not be alone in your final moments. Be available to talk. Do not be afraid to discuss the tough questions. They will be grateful that you took the time to hear them out and to offer your advice. Be available to listen. When someone is confronting their mortality, they want to be heard. They want to know that someone has their best interests at heart. Be there in their time of need. If you make the commitment to work with someone, make sure you can follow through on your promises to be there. When someone puts their trust in you to walk them to the other side, you need to be there with your hand outstretched. It is a great responsibility and one that requires the ultimate trust.

Walking the Veil Meditation

The guided meditation that follows is derived from the work I did when my own grandmother was on life support. As her advocate, I was responsible not only for making sure her wishes were fulfilled to the letter of her living will, but also for doing anything within my ability to make sure she passed as peacefully as possible. The design of the meditation is simple and created so you can ease the transition of the person you are working with from one plane to another.

To walk the veil between the worlds is difficult, and it is not for everyone. If you feel compelled to take up this calling, you need to prepare yourself. This endeavor will be mentally, physically, and emotionally exhausting. You need to steel yourself before beginning and take time afterward to wind down and decompress.

To begin, take a moment to ground and center. Call out to the Earth to provide stable ground for you to walk upon. Feel the strength of stone to give you strength to help you shoulder the pressure and responsibility you are undertaking. Feel the pulse of the earth beneath your feet, and start pulling that energy into you. You will feel it start to enter your feet and start working up your legs. Feel the weight of the earth—the weight of solid stone. Feel it move up your body and into your torso. Any butterflies you may be experiencing are replaced with the warmth of earth on a sunny day. Let its stabilizing influence quiet any anxiety or worry. Feel the strength pulse in you as it moves through your arms and out into your hands. They are steady and sure; feel the calm as

it moves up and out of the top of your head. Feel the earth energy flow out and over the outside of your body giving you the strength of the standing stones of old. With this shield surrounding you, you are able to withstand anything that comes your way. Once you feel you are ready, let the pulsing of the earth's energy slow to a steady rhythm. Now you are ready to undertake the walk to the veil.

Enter the room you will be working in. If you feel the need to create sacred space, now is the time to do so. Speaking out loud is not necessary, and silence may actually be preferred if the family is skittish about Wicca or Paganism. All you need to do is to extend your arm toward the floor and walk around the room picturing a soft blue-white light surround the area. You can call to the quarters if it falls in line with the belief structure of the person you are working with.

Next, sit down next to the bed of the person you're walking with. Establishing a physical connection may be helpful. Take their hand in yours and close your eyes. Once your connection is stable, you can feel your body become weightless. Now you will be able to move to the astral plane. There you can meet the person you are working with. You can gesture for them to follow you or extend your hand for them to take.

The transition is not easy for some, and they may experience a wellspring of emotion. You will feel it pull at your solar plexus. Allow the emotion to flow off the protective barrier you put on prior to meeting and flow down into the earth. Walk next to them when they are ready to continue the journey. Depending on their level of acceptance, this may happen quickly or it may take a while. Be patient. Depending on their belief structure, a doorway or a bridge may appear in the distance. This will be the crossing in the veil to the Summerland. At this time, they may have messages to convey to you. The messages may come to you in words, phrases, or as pictures. Note anything that they relay to you. Be there, reassure them, and when they are ready, they will cross over. Once the threshold has been passed, the gap in the veil will close itself. Take some time in this place to process. When you are ready, you can return to your body.

Remembrance Altar

Remembering their life is another way we can process and deal with the grief of losing a friend or relative. Creating a space that honors their memory has the added benefit of being a great way to involve all the family and friends. You can build an altar at the memorial service or in the home of the deceased, and ask each person to bring a photo or an item that reminds them of that person.

Build the altar by placing small stones, flowers, petals, shells, candles, and incense (if well ventilated!) around the area where the remembrance items will be placed. Take the season into account, as well as the personal likes of the honoree. Choose a good photo and place it in the center of the altar. Next to the photo place a basket, set some small pieces of parchment, and a few pens.

When the people begin to arrive for the service, show them the remembrance table and have them place their photo or item on it. Then encourage them to write a memory of their loved one down on paper and place it in the basket. Take some photos of the altar before and after the additions. You can then offer those photos to the immediate family, so they can see what an impact their loved one had on those around them.

The memories can be read during a point in the service. It will be a celebration of the person's life and their effect on those around them. It also takes the pressure off those that want to say something about the person but are too emotional or too embarrassed to stand up in a room full of people.

Once the service is completed you can take the notes and burn them in a fire-safe container, the smoke carrying the messages to the other world. That process can be a whole ritual of its own. The ashes can then be mixed into the soil at the gravesite or can be scattered with the ashes if cremation was performed.

The Earth Magic of Iona
by Mary Pat Lynch, PhD

The Isle of Iona holds a place in history and legend all out of proportion to its size. This tiny island off the west coast of Scotland, five miles long and a mile and a half wide, echoes through the ages like a Celtic harp on a clear night.

Traveling to Iona is a challenge; you won't get there by accident. Part of the Inner Hebrides, Iona is to the west of Mull. Travel first to the town of Oban, gateway to the Isles and home to a ferry terminal as well as tea shops, a single-malt distillery, great seafood, a castle, and men in kilts. Take the CalMac ferry to the Isle of Mull, then board Bowman's bus for a ride across Mull's long southern arm to the pier at Fionnphort. There, board the sturdy ferry for a ten-minute ride across the sound.

You can see Iona from Fionnphort unless there's a real gale blowing. It's only a mile across. Something happens on the way, though. A shimmer in the air, a shift in the light, and you've entered another dimension. Standing on Iona's pier looking back, Mull seems to be drifting away.

Old Irish tales speak of the "stray sod," a bit of ground with the power to transport the unwary, making the ordinary into the uncanny. It's possible Iona herself is a stray sod, carrying all who set foot on her shores into other worlds.

Magic in Stone

Stepping onto Iona puts you in touch with some of the oldest rocks exposed on the face of the earth. Nearby Mull and the adjacent mainland are vigorously volcanic, full of basalts and lavas. Iona is something else entirely, layers of incredibly ancient gneisses folded and compressed for billions of years.

When Iona's rocks were forming, the Earth was hot and empty. There was little free oxygen, and life had yet to emerge from the seas. Part of a supercontinent resting south of the equator, Iona traveled far before coming to rest on Scotland's Atlantic coast.

Place a hand on the black face of a cliff, glistening under a sheen of water falling from a hidden source, or rest yourself on banded red boulders as the surf rolls in, and reach back to a time before people, before mammals, before reptiles, before plants—when only the stones were there. What stories they have to tell!

Iona's most magical stone is a white marble shot through with translucent green, one of the only native marbles in the British Isles. Mostly calcite, the green tints are created by traces of serpentines, olivines, and pyroxenes, the minerals of peridot and chrysolite. They give Iona marble delicate shading and magical depth.

Iona marble was quarried for a time, although the challenges of wresting stone from so remote a location were great. The machines of the last attempt, in the early 1900s, can still be seen in a narrow bay on the island's southeast corner. As always, small chunks of marble roll into the sea, are polished in the surf, and tossed up again, to be found, then made into jewelry, or carried as talismans.

It's said no one carrying an Iona stone will ever drown, a literal comfort at the ocean's edge and perhaps a metaphoric promise for those on inner journeys. The smallest Iona stones are called mermaid's tears, from a mermaid who fell in love with a monk who loved his Church more than he did her.

The best places to find Iona stones are to the south, as the currents carry stones from the quarry out and around to the beaches. The most popular is Columba's Bay, said to be the landing place of the saint who brought Christianity to the island, building a place for the monk who broke a mermaid's heart.

Center of Power

Iona is widely known today as a place of Christian pilgrimage, home to an ecumenical community that supports social justice as well as spiritual exploration. The Christian history of Iona began with Columba, also known as Columcille, son of a noble lineage in northern Ireland who became a monk, abbot, founder of monastic houses, missionary to the Picts, worker of miracles, and saint.

Celebrated today as a simple pilgrim of peace, he was rather a commanding man of the Church whose achievements were made possible by his high status. He founded twenty-five monasteries, including the houses at Derry, Durrow, and Kells as well as Iona. The eminence of his monasteries is reflected in the fact that two of the most beautiful illustrated manuscripts known, the Book of Durrow and the Book of Kells, are thought to have been begun on Iona, then removed inland as protection from Viking raiders.

In Columba's time, the 600s, the Celts of northern Ireland had established a foothold in western Scotland. The kingdom of Dal Riata, in present-day Argyll, Bute, and Lochaber, was reaching its height, extending the influence of Gaelic language, customs and religion into Scotland. Stories tell of Columba landing on Iona in a coracle accompanied by twelve monks, having reached a place of exile from which his native Ireland could not be seen. This image of monks traveling to a strange, uninhabited isle is beguiling, but far from the realities of the day.

Columba left Ireland on a mission to Scotland, and also to atone for, and possibly escape, the consequences of his own actions. These could relate to the unlawful copying of a manuscript he very much desired, or involvement in a dynastic war, or a combination of reasons shrouded in time.

He first visited the king of Dal Riata, who granted Iona to Columba. It's possible the island was uninhabited at the time, although this seems unlikely, given the presence of an Iron Age hill fort and the fertility of Iona's soil. What is most certainly true is that the grant of land was given because Iona was already recognized as a place of power.

In Celtic tradition, power comes from the land. Kings and chieftains must be consecrated to the land to lead the people in times of peace and plenty, a relationship celebrated as a sacred marriage. It is therefore significant that Iona is the burial places of kings. An inventory from 1549 lists forty-eight Scottish, eight Viking, and four Irish kings interred in the ancient Rèilig Odhrain, including Pictish kings, Macbeth and Duncan, and most recently, Labour Party leader John Smith.

Power is also reflected in names, and Iona's is so ancient its origins and meaning are unknown. The name appears in ancient manuscripts as Eo, Eu, Hi, or Hy, and relate to Hy-Breasil, mystical land of Celtic legend where fortunate spirits dwelt after death. Hy-Breasil has been linked with Avalon and Atlantis, other lands of peace and plenty where immortal beings rest. An alternate interpretation links Iona with the yew tree, which brings us back to Hy-Breasil, as the yew has ties with death, divination, and immortality.

Another approach is to suggest that Iona is simply called "island" or "she" because she needs no other name, or perhaps because the true name is not spoken.

Iona is a thin place, where the veils between the worlds are more easily moved aside to allow passage from one to another. On Iona, multiple realities are always and simultaneously present.

Wondrous Exploration

On a bright, cold May morning, I sat alone with my drum on Iona's Isle of Protection overlooking the Bay at the Back of the Ocean. I had come to journey, hoping, on the shoulders of this magical place, to travel farther than I had before.

Sitting with the spray in my face, oyster catchers skimming the rocky surf to my right, and a rock pipit circling and parachuting above me, I thought, How can I close my eyes and journey when I am already surrounded by wonders? Setting aside my drum, I settled back against the rock to enjoy the morning.

Immediately a chorus of voices sounded in my ears, coming from spirits of rock and moss and salt water as well as beings I could neither see nor name. "We want to hear the drum!" they said. "It's not all about you, you know," they chided. "You are here to drum, now drum." And so I did, drumming with eyes open to please the spirits of that place, and celebrate the day with them. As the drum vibrated through my ears and hand and arm, I found myself journeying with eyes open, entering into conversation and song with the voices around me, who told me things I needed to know and showed me scenes from past, or perhaps parallel, times.

This became my practice on Iona, to drum and journey with eyes open, inviting and allowing the spirits of place to lead me across to other worlds I was happy to explore, in a place of power and mystery.

Women, Cows, and Clerics

Sovereignty, the right to rule, is given by the land, not taken by force. Sovereignty is in the gift of the Goddess. So it was in the old times, until some came who sought—and still seek—to take what they want without respect or recompense.

The coming of Columba, seen today as a man of peace and Dove of the Church, was part of a larger pattern of uprooting ancient traditions that honored the Earth, and gods and goddesses of land and tribe, to replace them with patriarchal Christianity.

Columba was a man of his time, a monk in the Celtic Church that gave women a larger place than Rome. He is said to have supported the old bardic schools, saying "it is right to buy the poems of the poets, and keep the poets in Ireland."

He may have known and practiced some of the old ways, being a "crane cleric" who kept a foot in both camps. One of the eerier stories of Columba's time on Iona is the tale of Oran, a monk, it is said, buried alive in the foundations of the first chapel.

Echoing other Celtic legends, when Columba first built on Iona, the chapel walls crumbled again and again. Keeping vigil one night, Columba was visited by an unearthly woman who said the chapel walls would fall until a man was buried alive at their base. Oran volunteered, or was chosen by lot, and so was buried, and sturdy walls raised over him.

After three days and nights, Columba, curious, dug into the soil near Oran's head, uncovering the face of his brother, whose eyes opened. The buried brother spoke, saying heaven and hell were not as scripture said, nor was God as we imagined. Aghast at the blasphemy, Columba ordered the monks to throw earth on Oran's mouth and eyes. And so he was buried a second time, and forever.

Support for bards who sang praise songs to the nobility, and continuing practices that brought power, are not the same as honoring the Goddess in the land.

It's told that one of Columba's first actions in reaching Iona was to ban women and cows, saying "Where there are cows, there are women, and where there are women, there is mischief."

Links between women, cows, and goddesses in Celtic tradition are strong. Cattle were the wealth and sustenance of the tribes. Boann, creatrix of the Boyne, goddess of flowing waters, wife of Nechtan, consort of the Dagda, mother of Aengus, is, by name, the Cow Goddess. Boann is also known as the Roof of the Ocean, and the Milky Way is named in Irish *Bealach na Bó Finne*, "the Way of the White Cow."

So women and cows moved to a nearby island still called Eilean na Ban, Island of the Women, and returned to Iona, it is said, after Columba's death. Banishing women is one thing, removing goddess energy from the land is not so easily accomplished.

The highest point in Iona is the summit of Dun I, Iona's Hill Fort. Iona being low-lying ground, the summit rises only 328 feet, and yet it's a good stiff walk, especially with a strong wind blowing in off the water and the rain in your face.

At the top, the modern cairn is easy to find. Turn away to the northeast and walk down a gentle slope toward the edge that looks north to Staffa. Up against a rocky face, you'll see a deep, still pool. You've found The Well of Eternal Youth, sacred to Brigid. Come to this well at sunrise, splash your head with a handful of water, and magic happens.

Such wells, found throughout Celtic lands, are part of a tradition of goddesses and seasons in which Brigid, or Bríde as she's called in Scotland, is the youthful and lovely Queen of Spring. Her opposite is the aged crone known as the Cailleach, the Hag of Beara, and Black Annis, who reigns over cold, stony winter.

These two are Sun goddesses, the bright Sun of summer and the little Sun of winter, who vanquish each other at the turnings of the year. We can imagine how the lovely maiden Brigid becomes the wizened Cailleach as the year wanes, but how is the shriveled hag made young again?

Some tales speak of magical wells. As the first rays of the Spring Sun strike the water, the old woman dissolves and the young maiden rises in her place. This is the eternal cycle of the kairos, sacred time spiraling again and again through ancient patterns.

Just below the Well on Dun I is a place called Sloc na Caillich Oidhche. Caillich oidhche is the owl, making this the Gully of the Owl. And yet another cailleach is also invoked. As winter loses her grip, we picture the ancient one waiting in the gully, hidden from view. Reluctantly she makes her way to the well as the sun climbs over the lip of the world, surrendering herself once more to Spring.

Shining Ones and Fairy Realms

Thin places in Celtic lands are home to the gentle folk, the Shining Ones of Faery, and Iona is no exception. The best-known tale speaks of the Hill of Angels, on the edge of the machair, the raised grassy plain next to the Bay at the Back of the Ocean.

A monk out walking one night saw Columba standing on a rounded hill surrounded by golden light. Coming nearer, the monk heard voices, saw white-robed forms descending from the sky, and realized Columba was speaking with angels.

So the story is told, and the Hill is an important stop on the modern pilgrim trail, but we can notice that the angel's hill is found on a farmstead called Sithean, the Fairy Mound, across the road

from the smaller hill known as Sithean Beag, the little Fairy Mound.

In some tellings, the fairies are angels caught between heaven and hell. Following Lucifer out of heaven, then quickly realizing their mistake, they turned to see God already shutting the gates against them. Neither one nor the other, they live close to Earth, but hidden, sometimes helping, sometimes mischievous, always exiled.

Iona place names suggest other haunts of the Folk: the Hill of the Brownie, the Well of the North Wind, Manannan's Fort, the Sacred Hollow. This last is intriguing because its Gaelic name is Coire Sianta, and while *coire* can be translated as "hollow," it also means "whirlpool" and "cauldron," carrying more numinous connotations than a simple low place in the ground.

The ancient rocks of Iona are divided into gneisses and pegmatites and subdivided by the minerals found within them. Rocks this old are very complex, having been folded, compressed, intruded upon by other rocks, and shifted over and over again.

The scientific names are equally complex, but the geological map of the island shows an interesting pattern: within the gneiss formation that makes up the bulk of Iona, we see a long spur of pegmatite running from the marble quarry in the southeast to the Sithean, the fairy mound, near the machair.

A close look at the topographical map shows another mound, Sithean Mor na h'Aird, the Big Fairy Mound of the Height, close to the marble quarry. So the pegmatite spur runs from the Hill of Angels and Little Fairy Mound on the plain, to another Fairy Mound on the coast.

~

Carrying my drum as well as the map, I went to see what I might find. There are several paths to the quarry; mine was along the east coast, through upland moors, past the Porpoise Inlet, the Gully of the Chimney, and the Port of the Young Lad's Rock. Walking down into a narrow valley, I passed the stone foundations of the House of the Lowlanders, and began looking for the Sithean. Seeing no rounded, grassy hill like the ones near the machair. I wondered if the mound was still there, or had washed away.

In the area marked on the map, there were some large rocks, similar to others along the coast, that looked to have some small trees among the grasses and heather. It didn't look promising from where I stood, but I wanted to explore the area thoroughly before giving up. Walking around to the left, where a more gradual slope allowed access, I saw there was a hollow on the top that hid a more complex landscape than could be seen from below.

Despite walking slowly, or maybe because I had my nose in the map, I almost stepped into a cleft in the ground. A rush of air and the echoing sound of wings brought me up short. I looked down into darkness, past stone walls with ferns clinging to narrow ledges. I sat at the edge of the cleft long enough to realize the beating wings belonged to doves, and that the cleft reached right through the rock to the shore, as I could hear surf echoing up to where I sat.

The feel of magic was strong. I explored further, finding another, wider cleft with twisting trees clustered over a cavelike opening. A garden warbler landed in the branches above me, singing beautifully, undisturbed by my presence. Finding a seat on the rocks at the edge of the opening, I unpacked my drum and offered a soft beat to the warbler's song. Here I experienced the most powerful journeys of my time on Iona, eyes open, accompanied by birdsong, with the power of the land rising beneath me.

Iona is a small island, yet I have barely begun to explore her mysteries. I cannot wait to return.

Air Magic

Your Fairy Garden: A Place For Nature

By Mickie Mueller

When we work with fairy energy, we are working with the spirits of the land and the plants and animals that thrive in nature. Sorry, fairies aren't all purple sparkles in pretty dresses; they are actually primal beings, part of the land in a very real way. As witches, we can work with the energies of the Fey folk to benefit our magic and our spirit, but to gain the trust of these spiritual nature beings, it can be beneficial to create a space where they feel comfortable, safe and honored. I like to call this space a fairy garden.

A fairy garden can be an area that you've selected in your yard, or it can even be a large pot on a deck or porch. It can be a miniature garden or full-sized—it can even be a planter inside your home if you don't have an outdoor area. If your garden is outdoors, no matter where it is, the first thing you'll want to do is select an area in your yard that you can dedicate to the fairies. Pay attention to what kind of light it gets. Does it get full sun, shade, or a little of both? This will help you determine what kinds of plants to put in your garden. To begin with, you'll have to clear the area, and if you can manage it without chemicals, all the better. One of the best ways we've found for clearing out grass to put in a garden is to cover the area with something like plywood or landscaping fabric for a while. This keeps light from getting to the grass and allows it to die off naturally and begin to decompose. Then you can turn over the soil and you have something to start with. Fairies will not be offended by this; they understand the concept of life, death, and rebirth, and that's a good start for a fairy garden.

Fairy Plants: Bought, Borrowed, Rescued

The next things you'll need are some plants, of course. You can plant seeds if you wish or purchase plants in pots. Don't discount the idea of using some native plants as well. Plantains, wild violets, clover, or wood sorrel may be considered weeds by some, but they are quite beautiful and can add beauty to your fairy garden while letting the fairies know that you have respect for all life. I have all of these plants growing in my fairy garden. A wildflower is just a weed that you happen to like. Plus, they're free!

Native plants can be easier to grow, too. They usually manage well in the climate no matter the weather. If you are looking for native plants that aren't already growing in your yard, you can usually find nurseries (check those sponsored by the state) that have native wildflowers. Using native plants in your fairy garden can help appeal to the natural spirits of the land and honor them by giving them a place to grow. In addition, your local fairies are most likely strongly tied to the native plants as part of the local ecology, so drawing spirits of the land into an area filled with native plants makes a lot of sense. As a bonus, local plants can also be good attractors of local wildlife like butterflies and birds. However, you should never try to transplant wildflowers that you find growing in public areas; this is usually illegal and they are an important part of the natural ecosystem and should not be removed.

Many fairy-friendly plants and flowers can be easily found at your local nursery or in seed catalogs. I try to look for perennials, so I don't have to buy buy new flowers every year, although there are a few annuals that I love and invest in every year. Herbs are always a good choice, as herbs grown in your fairy garden are full of extra magic, but be sure to ask the fairies permission before harvesting them.

I've learned over the years that a plant will only grow where it wants to grow, not necessarily where you want it to grow. You can create a beautiful magical garden in shade or sun that the fairy folk will love, just be sure to choose the right plants. Another great way to bring new plants into your fairy garden is to wait for plants in your local garden center to go on clearance. You can pick up plants for a song and you'll be rescuing them, so the fairies will be very pleased. Often the most scraggly looking plants from the clearance aisle end up looking gorgeous with a little TLC. Don't forget to mulch, mulch, and mulch. Lots of mulch helps keep grass and unwanted weeds from popping up and maintain moisture in the soil. Here is a list fairy plants that would be lovely to get your fairy garden started; however, this is by no means all of the fairy plants.

Fairy Garden Plants: lilac, honeysuckle, ferns, moss, thyme, rosemary, primrose, roses, foxglove, violets, pansies, cowslips, lavender, sweet pea, heather, poppies, peony

Fairy Garden Trees: oak, ash, hawthorn, willow, apple, holly, elder, hazel, rowan

Baubles and Whimsy

Plants aren't the only additions for your fairy garden to attract and honor fairy spirits. Adding other kinds of outdoor décor can bring extra magical energy into your fairy garden. There are many beautiful additions you can make to your fairy garden. For example, a glass gazing ball can make a really elegant and magical statement. Try to avoid iron ornaments in the fairy garden—as iron was traditionally used to ward off fairies—but you may use them in other areas of your yard. Iron can be very protective, especially near your front door.

You can add items to represent the natural elements. For the element of air, wind chimes are an easy addition. The tones of wind chimes can raise the vibration of the area as well as drown out street noise, making the garden more tranquil. A garden flag or any ornament that moves in the wind is good for the air element as well.

For the element of fire, try adding some lights. I find that for a magical garden, solar lights that harness the natural energy of the sun are perfect. The simple stake lights are very pretty, and now there are even solar powered small "fairy" lights on strings available.

The water element is easy. A simple birdbath is a great addition in your fairy garden because all kinds of creatures will love it. We get a large variety of birds, and even squirrels. Be sure to keep it clean and full. If you want to get really fancy, you can add a small solar-powered fountain. If you have a bigger budget, you could even add a fancy fountain or in-ground pond.

In addition to the obvious earth element representation of the plants, statuary can be great earth element anchoring pieces. Statues of fairies can help to become a real statement and give the garden a very magical feel. Mushrooms, frogs, and gnomes will look enchanting and communicate a "fairy garden" vision in garden. Adding a birdfeeder to your fairy garden combines the elements of earth in the birdseed and the element of air as birds flock to your garden. Another combination of elements could be adding a hummingbird feeder, a meeting of air and water.

Now we come to the element of spirit. The perfect thing to honor the spirit of a fairy garden is a fairy house. There are lots of ways to create a really cool fairy house. A fairy house can be as simple or elaborate as you wish. You can purchase a birdhouse and redecorate it for your needs. Maybe build one using scrap wood and natural items found on a walk in the woods. Why not create a Hobbit-style house, modeling it after an earth home. You can even build small furniture if you're so inclined. The idea of a fairy house is all about spirit. It's a symbol of hospitality and reverence to the spirits of nature that we call fairies. The fairy house is an altar of sorts, a place between the realms of the material world and the spiritual world where the lines of the two blur. This is the perfect place to leave an offering to the fairies, release a moth that got in your house, or place a found feather.

Leaving gifts for the fairies is a great way to make friends with these nature spirits and they'll be more willing to add some of their energy to your magical workings if you honor them with fitting tribute. The fairy garden is, of course, both a blessing to your property and a gift to the fairy folk. But there are other kinds of offerings you can make. When you hold a magical circle for sabbats, esbats, or anytime, save a small portion of your cakes and wine from the ritual and leave it in your fairy garden. This simple action makes an automatic connection between your magical workings and the local spirits of the land. They are often called by different name such as the Good Folk, Good Neighbors, or People of Peace. This is done out of respect so as to remind us as humans to never speak ill of them—remember the many tales in folklore of those who did, much to their detriment. It's very important when dealing with fairy folk to always act with the utmost respect and care.

Other offerings that are traditional fairy favorites are milk, honey, bread, butter, and cake. Any combination make a wonderful fairy offering and will be appreciated. I often leave a sampling of the first vegetables we harvest and use in a meal. You can even leave them on a small plate on the ground—the location doesn't really matter, but it should be done with respect and proper solemnity. Also, when leaving an offering, be sure to make a statement—one from the heart—announcing that what you're leaving is a gift for the fairies. On evenings of specific fairy nights like Beltane, Midsummer, and Samhain, I like to light a tealight candle in a jar and leave it in my fairy garden near the fairy house. I make an offering too, along with an announcement that the house and garden are open to fairy tribes that may be traveling the land on this sacred evening. I always keep an eye on the candle until it

burns out. When you leave a fairy offering, remember it's the exchange of energy and the intention that's important. The spirits of the land will soak up the positive intention and the essence of the food or drink even if an animal comes by and eats the physical food. So rest assured that no matter what becomes of the physical offering, the fairy folk have appreciated it fully.

Fairy Garden Dedication

Once you have your fairy garden planted, you may like to bless it and dedicate it to the fairies. Here is a ritual you can do to let the local fairies know that you created this garden in their honor as a natural habitat. You don't have to invite them, as they are the spirits of nature and they exist everywhere and go where they please. With this ritual, you're just letting them know that you have created a space where you personally welcome their energy. This is best done at either dawn or dusk, as these are both magical "in between" times. You'll need a fairy offering of some kind, cake, bread with butter and honey (no margarine, please). Walk clockwise around your fairy garden three times. Then place the offering in a spot in the garden you have reserved for such offerings, on a flat stone, near your fairy house, or wherever you wish. After you have placed the offering, sit down in or near your garden and close your eyes. Feel the energy of nature all around you as it swirls through the air. Feel life pulsing in the ground below you, feel the life force of every plant, tree, and stone. Once you are at one with the land, open your eyes and make the following statement:

> *I come here amongst the Good Neighbors that laugh within*
> *woods,*
> *This garden space I dedicate to you for the greatest good.*
> *May we meet here in good faith and peace, our magic wild*
> *and free,*
> *Amongst the blossoms, rain, wind, or snow, dear friends, so*
> *shall it be!*

You may sit there as long as you like and see if you hear a message in your heart or spot a sign that the Fey have agreed that your fairy garden is a blessed place to meet with you. This can be anything from a warm feeling inside to a leaf falling from a tree to land in your lap. You'll know it when you sense it. Make it a regular place to commune with nature, leave offerings from time to time, and allow the magic of nature to express beauty and mysteries through your enchanted space.

∼

On a final note, a fairy garden doesn't need to be the perfect weed-free, bug-free garden. You may be growing vegetables in other areas and using some form of pest control, but you should try to keep the areas distinct. We try to grow our vegetable and flower gardens without toxic chemicals. At my house, we experiment with our own organic forms of pest control. But no matter what you do to keep destructive insects out of your other gardens, tread lightly in your fairy garden when dealing with anything you might refer to as a pest elsewhere. I even try not to get angry if the squirrels occasionally topple the fairy house. I do pluck the stray grass out, but if a weed pops up and it's pretty and not causing any harm, I let it stay. The bugs, rabbits, squirrels, and other critters aren't pests in a fairy garden—they are guests! It should be a place that's a little wilder, a natural haven in the city or suburbs for the beings of nature. If you're going to spray your fairy garden down with pesticides, the spirits of the fairies won't feel very welcome, and it will merely be a pretty garden with fairy statues instead of one where you can feel the presence of nature at its fullest—and perhaps catch a glimpse of a leaf or flower dancing in the still air and wonder: could that be a fairy?

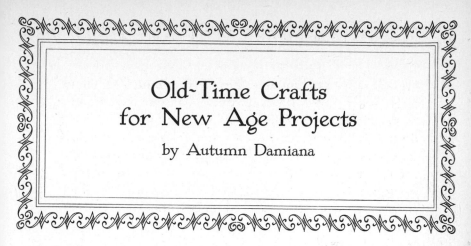

Old-Time Crafts for New Age Projects

by Autumn Damiana

Crafts that were popular during the Georgian, Victorian, Edwardian, and other overlapping eras (such as La Belle Époque or the Gilded Age) have never entirely lost their popularity. However, activities as fads come and go, and these have been no exception. Only recently have the crafts of this era as a whole been seen in a new light. A renaissance of crafting circles and clubs dedicated to these arts, from sewing and quilting to making scrapbooks or Christmas crafts, as well as a rekindled interest in the eighteenth and nineteenth centuries by collectors, cosplayers, historical reenactors, Steampunk enthusiasts, and others have made these crafts trendy and popular again. In addition, modern methods and materials have also made the same crafting techniques cheaper, easier, and less time-consuming, and therefore less intimidating to tackle. Here is an introduction to these old-time crafts, with suggestions on how they can be brought into the New Age.

A Leisurely Pursuit

Some lucky individuals out there are able to make and sell crafts for a living, but in general, crafting is regarded as a hobby or part-time venture. This casual attitude toward crafts also dates back to the Victorian era when the Industrial Revolution made the newly emerging middle-class families wealthy enough to afford to hire domestic help, which created plenty of free time for the women of the house. As the Victorian mindset frowned upon idleness, women passed the hours making elaborate and highly ornamental arts and crafts that both challenged and showcased their skills.

Most of what they made was functional as well as decorative, and when the completed projects were displayed throughout the home, they were a credit to both the artist and her family. Back then, it was almost exclusively women who engaged in these activities, although today there are more and more men who enjoy crafting and are learning these arts for themselves.

Crafts from Days of Old

When people think of Victorian-era crafts, needlework is one of the first things that comes to mind. The term "needlework" encompasses any craft done using a needle, such as various types of sewing, embroidery, and sometimes other related arts like knitting and crochet. Also included are cross-stitch, crewel (a type of free-form embroidery), needlepoint (tapestry-type embroidery on canvas), tatting (lace-making), and whitework (embroidery used to decorate linens that is the same color as the fabric—usually white). Needlepoint was perhaps the most popular craft, and is still the most common craft associated with the Victorians, although sewing was also quite common.

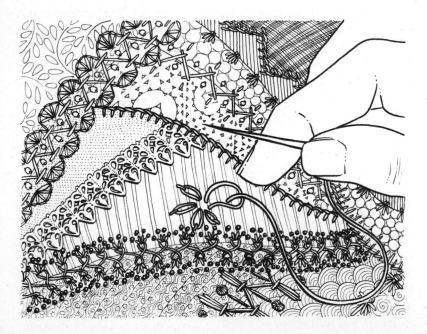

Almost every woman during this era knew at least the basics of how to sew, but only the poor or working class had to know how to make their own clothes. The rich (and later on even the middle class) employed servants and dressmakers and had their clothes tailor-made. Therefore, sewing was a diversion or was limited to the simple mending of existing clothes. However, patchwork and other forms of quilting were widespread, especially the technique known as "crazy quilting." This method involved piecing together all sorts of scrap or recycled fabrics, and then lavishly adorning the patchwork with embroidery and stitched borders along each of the seams, sometimes adding beads, ribbon, lace, buttons, etc. The result was a remarkably individual quilt: a creative mode of expression that used up odds and ends that might otherwise go to waste.

Another way that creativity could be expressed was in the form of Victorian paper crafts. These included decoupage, papier mâché, the making of scrapbooks, and quilling. Due to the increase of available printed materials, paper crafts took off. Books with hundreds of images specifically made for cutting out and decoupaging, as well as doilies in paper form appeared at this time. Papier mâché became an alternative to the impressive and expensive laquerware of the Chinese, since it was cheaper and could be made at home. Scrapbooks, which have been around in some form or another since time immemorial, began to truly take shape in the myriad decorative journals and keepsakes that abounded in this era. And quilling (or paper filigree) which uses tightly coiled paper shapes for decoration, is also still practiced today.

Victorians were also deeply interested in the natural world and loved to collect or make keepsakes from shells and flowers. While shellwork was initally only done by the upper classes, the increase in sea travel made shells more common, and shell art was used to decorate trinket boxes, vases, picture frames, mirrors, and even horseshoes, crosses, and other ornamental objects. These shell art pieces were often extremely complex and may have had flowers, hearts, or other images worked into them in mosaic-like form. Flowers collected in the summer months were then dried or pressed to preserve them. The pressed flowers were used to make cards, or were decoupaged onto a surface, such as a lampshade.

Dried flowers could be used to make arrangements, wreaths, and potpourri, as they lent both beauty and fragrance.

Finally, we have the Christmas crafts of the era. Most of our modern Christmas traditions were borrowed from the Victorian age, like giving gifts, decorating a Christmas tree, hanging stockings, caroling, and eating Christmas dinner. Tree-trimming crafts and handmade gifts and cards were very fashionable then, and were made using all of the above crafting techniques. Victorian women also would frequently make extra crafts (especially blankets and quilts) to give to the poor or to sell for charity fundraising.

The New Age of Crafting

Most crafts from the Victorian era are still in use today. Witches, Pagans, and other New Age folk in particular seem to be contributing to the survival of these traditions, as many of us love to make crafts and have an affinity for things from times past. (I know that every time I go to a Pagan festival, I almost always see someone crocheting or doing cross-stitch!) Not surprisingly, it is often projects with a spiritual function or aspect that are being created. Here are some other ideas along the same lines.

Knitting/Crochet: The basics for either one of these arts are not hard to learn, and because so many people still knit and crochet, supplies are also inexpensive and available everywhere. You can easily create pouches for amulets, crystals, runes, tarot cards, or mojo bags, reusable eco-friendly totes, even crocheted yarn, wire, or beaded jewelry. As an alternative to traditional knitting, I bought a circular loom and taught myself to loom knit (which makes a long tube of fabric) in one afternoon by watching YouTube videos. After that, it was no problem to make drawstring pouches for all my magical items.

Sewing/Quilting: It's less common to see anything entirely hand-sewn anymore. Most people add to or makeover existing clothes and other projects, or use one of the many modern shortcuts to sewing available, such as fusible webbing, fabric glue or tape, Velcro, snaps, rivets, or even grommets and/or lacing instead. However, this makes it much easier for anyone to "sew" their own ritual robes, altar cloths, poppets, bags of all kinds, yoga or meditation mats, prayer flags, and, of course, all those fun banners and costumes for your upcoming festivals!

Other Needlecrafts: I'm constantly amazed by how many embroidery, needlepoint, and cross-stitch patterns have been created with specifically New Age designs. This means that if you want to take up one of these crafts, you will have an abundance of ready-made mystical and magical projects to choose from. Simple embroidery stitches are also not hard to teach yourself with a good book, and you can use these to decorate just about anything, including your sewing projects. Try learning the Couching, Overcast, or Stem Stitches to outline simple pentacles, runes, or other symbols. Or, try your hand at a witchy-themed cross-stitch sampler.

Paper Crafts: Since paper manufacturing is much more prevalent today than in the past, all of the same paper crafts popular then are even more so now (except perhaps quilling). I personally like to give new life to all the wonderful metaphysical catalogues and magazines I receive, by cutting out pictures that I use to decoupage with or paste into my Book of Shadows, which has become a kind of witchy scrapbook! I also use papier mâché to make devotional/altar bowls, rattles, masks, costume accessories, and even wands.

Shells/Flowers: Shells are both plentiful and inexpensive. They can be glued onto the edges of scrying bowls, magic mirrors, crystal ball holders, and any other fortune-telling device, since

clairvoyance and divination are ruled by the element of water. Or you can make shell-studded boxes and other vessels, or even a water-themed pentacle plaque. Pressed flowers can be used to decorate all the same items as paper cutouts or shells for an earthy vibe or for that particular flower's attributes. And dried flowers are still essential to make potpourri, wreaths, and other arrangements, or can be used as altar decorations or even offerings.

Christmas Crafts: Most Christmas symbolism, while celebrated both today and in the Victorian era, actually has its origins in ancient Pagan festivals. This means that not only is it acceptable to use much of the Christmas finery to celebrate Yule and the Winter Solstice, it may be even more appropriate! A tree decorated with natural items such as pine cones, nuts, dried fruit and flowers, and the like appeal to both the Victorian and New Age sensibilities. And for good karma, why not donate a few useful crafts or the money from selling them to those less fortunate, like the Victorians did?

Two Projects to Try:

New Age Crazy Quilting:

Making a crazy quilt used to be extremely time-consuming, but using these directions, you can achieve a similar effect in half the time, and you don't need to know how to sew a stitch! You can use your finished crazy quilt as an altar cloth, banner, table cloth, wall hanging, or bed covering, depending on the piece of fabric you start with. It can even be an actual quilt if you add batting and a quilt backing! Just keep in mind that that the more you embellish the finished piece, the less serviceable it will be to lay flat.

Materials Needed:
Plain cloth with finished edges
Fabric glue or fusible webbing
Assortment of fabric scraps
Scissors
3 or 4 colors of dimensional fabric paint
Chalk or wash-out fabric pen or pencil
Premade pattern (optional)
Iron (optional)
Ribbons, buttons, beads, lace, etc. (optional)

1. Decide on the motif you want for your cloth, using a pre-made pattern if you wish. You can also freehand a triple moon, ankh, Celtic knot, border, mountain scene, or whatever with the chalk or fabric pen. An abstract design or a random pattern of different fabrics and shapes scattered every which way also looks nice. It is not necessary to cover the entire cloth with fabric scraps unless you want to. Whatever pattern you decide, try to make it simple; details can be added later through decoration.

2. Using your guidelines as a template, cut out shapes from fabric scraps to approximate the shapes of the areas marked (it is okay if they are not exact). With either fabric glue or fusible webbing, secure the shapes to the fabric (you will need to use an iron if you are using fusible webbing).

3. Draw stitched or embroidered borders between the fabric pieces with the dimensional fabric paint and/or draw further stitching or other embroidery designs on the cloth or cloth pieces. Ribbon can also be adhered over the edges between fabric pieces as a border, especially if you want to cover up spaces between the patches. Buttons, beads, lace, and other embellishments should be added last, using either fabric glue or the dimensional fabric paint. You now have a beautiful New Age crazy quilt!

Gilded Walnut Favors

This is an old Victorian Christmas project for making ornaments that consists of no more than a walnut shell with the nut removed, glued back together with a tiny present inside and painted gold. You can hang the decorated walnut on the Yule tree until it is time for a gift exchange, or give it to the recipient as an ornament for his/her tree, which can be opened later. You can even display the walnuts in a bowl, as part of an arrangement, or hide them as described below. Not only are these ornaments easy and inexpensive to make, but this craft is a lot of fun to do with a group.

Materials Needed:
A bag of unshelled walnuts
Nutcracker or similar tools
White glue
Gold acrylic paint
Paper towels

Scissors
"Filler goodies" (see step 2)
Masking tape (optional)
Small paint brush (optional)
Spool of one-eighth inch ribbon (optional)

1. Split the walnut shell in half and remove the nut. Try to split the shell along the seam because the two halves need to fit back together again, so any crushed or shattered shells will not work. (Try using a dull knife or a flat-head screwdriver and a hammer instead of a nutcracker.) This takes practice, so be patient. Set aside the nuts, as they are not needed for the project. Eat them as you go (unless they are black walnuts, which are poisonous), if you like!

2. Place a "filler goodie" inside one half of the shell. Dab a few small dots of white glue on the edge of the shell, and press the two shell halves together to glue it shut again. Wipe off any excess glue with a paper towel. Allow it to dry at least an hour or two—you may also want to wrap the shell with masking tape to hold it together while it dries. Try to keep the glue on the shells to a minimum, as the shell must eventually be broken to get the filler goodie out, hopefully without crushing it.

"Filler Goodies" refer to any gift small enough to fit into a walnut shell. Examples include pendants, rings, earrings, charms, crystals, tumbled stones, beads, friendship bracelets, marbles, and dice. With each gift, you can include a short written or printed message as to what each treasure is or how to use it. Or, let the ornaments become a tool of divination by hiding fortunes inside. These can be runes, written fortunes, symbols (a thimble, a button, a coin, etc.), or anything else you can think of. Get creative!

3. Paint the shell with gold acrylic paint. You can use the paintbrush to paint the walnut solid, or dab your finger in a bit of the paint and use it to gild just the raised edges of the shell for a more natural effect. When the paint is completely dry, the walnut can be put into a stocking or nestled into a gift basket. If you want, you can start a new tradition by staging a "Yule walnut hunt" with a handful of these hidden throughout the house. Or, to make it into an ornament:

4. Before step 2, cut 6 to 8 in. of the ribbon. Fold the ribbon in half, making the two ends of the ribbon meet. Tie an overhand knot with both ends of the ribbon, making a loop. Trim the ends just below the knot. After inserting the "filler goodie" into one half of the walnut, place the knotted end of the ribbon loop into the shell as well. Sandwich the ribbon between the two shell halves when gluing them together. The knot inside the shell will keep the ribbon from pulling out of the ornament, leaving a protruding loop at the top for hanging.

13 Meditations for a Short Attention Span

by Diana Rajchel

Ultimately, meditation has only one rule: you must turn communication within yourself. For most people, this means not communicating with others during meditative time. Even if you can only cut off the world for fifteen seconds, do it—outside input is NOT meditation. While the meditation may come in stolen moments, it is a cumulative skill, and even those tiny meditations make you better at it.

There are, ultimately, many reasons why traditional deep meditation might not work. People with jobs and families just don't have much time to meditate. Others suffer from ADHD or other neurological dysfunctions, and between corporate life and traditional schooling, it's very easy to fall into the trap of the "more, better, faster" mentality.

For people in these situations who want to use meditation to break out of them, small present-moment techniques work best. You may not be able to step entirely out of the flow of life, but you can take a single moment and make it yours. A moment as tiny as pushing the off button on your computer monitor to savor a sip of coffee can count as an act of meditation.

The following thirteen techniques are indeed meditation methods; each one can, with practice, train your brain to reach a meditative state. For beginners, it's more important that you know how to get to that state than it is that you stay in it for any particular amount of time.

Count to two, and repeat. Seriously, that's it. You don't need to count slowly. Count at the natural speed of your own mind. Do so without timing it to your breath for as long as you can stand it. It's about directing your attention and giving your mind something to do at a time when it might fight you with excessive boredom or stress signals. You may also try counting to 100 at any natural speed. This is a popular and effective technique in anger management, too.

Find your achy body parts and **breathe into them**. Identify an area that has tension and picture every breath you inhale entering through your pores where the ache is, and each exhalation as the pain leaving. If your attention shifts, move on to a different spot on your body, or stop—you've worked your attention as far as it can go for the time being.

Pick an image and see how long you can hold it in your mind. For example, you could choose a tarot card and continue to picture it as you go about other business. At the end of the day, you can stop to evaluate what you learned. You may receive insights into the card, object, or person that you can write about.

Walk. The simple act of walking alone is a type of meditation. You are not communicating with others, but you are paying attention to the world around you. To advance the walking meditation, walk and count. You can count the steps to a tree ahead of you on the path. Count how many steps to your car from your doorway. Count how many steps to the coffee maker from your desk. It keeps you focused entirely on what you are doing—and that is in itself a meditative state.

Stack or line up some items, and then deliberately scatter them. The act of clearing space and positioning items like pencils, paperclips, or shoes, is actually a meditative practice. You can find yourself engaged with making things line up just right, and just as Buddhist monks scatter their sand mandalas when finished, you scatter your tidy stacks in an exercise of nonattachment/enjoying mild chaos. You will still need to sweep up. Playful meditation has as much value as serious

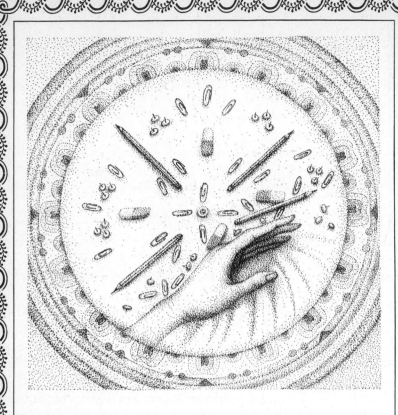

meditation—perhaps even more, as it can stimulate creativity in ways that gigantic revelations rarely can.

Close your eyes and **listen to all ambient noise**. Meditation does not require you to ignore everyone and everything around you—it requires you to focus your attention on specific things without engaging with them. Rather than trying to shut out the noises of traffic, chatty neighbors, or the children, close your eyes and simply listen as though they are static or other low-meaning noise.

Name objects in front of you. You can do this anywhere—at work, during a long car ride, even at home. Look at one object, and say its name to yourself: "book," "wall art," "carpet," and so on. Simply name every item immediately before you.

Keep a small bottle of a favorite fragrance on hand. Sniff every so often—this alters your mood, and brings your attention fully to one thing in your environment. Clary sage and lemongrass are both wonderful fragrances for meditative clarity.

Use your **sense of touch**. Comparing the textures of your clothing can give you a brief meditative timeout. Run your hands over your legs and over your abdomen. Notice the differences in how the fabric of different pieces of clothing feels.

Try **stretching your hands.** Touch each one of your fingers to the thumb on the same hand. Press down with each connection. In some cases, it may take some practice stretching your fingers.

Visualize as many colors as you can in one sitting. This pulls together the right and left hemispheres of your brain and is a key skill for most chakra work. Notice which colors you dwell on, and which you have trouble picturing.

Tell yourself a story. If you are alone, speak that story aloud. It can be about something as simple as a chicken crossing the road, or involve monks and dragons. The point is to engage yourself on your own power, not with the input of a book or television. Do not write these stories down—they are for you in your moment. They need not be long—two or three sentences, maybe even just one sentence.

Practice the slow version of **what dancers call spotting.** Turn your head and focus on one point of the wall. Stay there for two to three seconds, then look up and focus on the ceiling for two to three seconds. Then focus on another spot on the wall, then the carpet, etc. This is all about directing attention and only takes seconds to practice.

~

Beginners often overcomplicate meditation. When we let go of our expectations, it becomes easier to engage as a life tool because we can have a little fun with it. As long as you fulfill the basic requirements of going within, observing, and engaging wholly with yourself, you can concoct scores of your own creative meditation methods. Just adjust your expectations a little—the point of meditation is that its benefits happen slowly. Not only does it require practice, it is rarely an instantaneous state. You may never feel "meditative" even though your brain responds to the practice. You may find that the relaxation sneaks up on you. You might not feel relaxed, but you don't stress out more at trouble as you go through your daily life calmer and more centered, even if you only meditate in stolen seconds throughout the day.

Energetic Attunement for the Garage Saling Witch

by Karen Glasgow-Follett

My home is decorated in a masterful blend of "early parent's basement" and "eclectic garage saling." I have been making that statement, or some version of it, for well over thirty years. While the content of the statement has remained a constant; other people's spoken attitude about that statement has undergone a considerable upcycle.

Attitudinal words, such as, "used, secondhand, and preowned" have been replaced with "recycled, repurposed, upcycled, and rediscovered." Instead of using words like, "old, worn, and outdated," we use words such as "vintage, antique, and shabby chic." The old thinking would see us as thrift-sale shoppers who obviously can't afford new. New thinking recognizes us as ecologically conscious and financially savvy treasure seekers who can ferret out the chaff and purchase value and quality.

Of course, I can't speak for all practitioners, but I know that many of my magical cohorts ardently engage in the act of treasure seeking. There are many crossover interests that would attract the Witch to the world of object rediscovering, reclaiming, and repurposing. Many of my magical cohorts and I have also discovered that we rarely bring home just the object; we also bring home its history.

All people interact on both a physical and an energetic level with the elements of their world—and most of us know it. We consciously recognize the appeal of beauty and quality at a very value-conscious price. We may get that adrenaline rush at the thrill of the quest. We may have that desire to decrease our carbon footprint by recycling. We may have the creative desire to turn that "sow's ear into that silk purse." These are many of the physical attractors that cause us to unpredictably cross lanes of traffic and do the erratic brake slam/sliding turn combo in order to follow a "Garage Sale–This Way" sign.

The underlying essence of any physical state is the energetic imprint that reflects the item's manufacture, intent of use, and the characteristics of its environment and the people possessing it. These energy vibrations, subtle to most people, are often the visceral force that draws our attention, invests us in the desire to possess the item, and prompts us to start digging through our purses and pockets for some cash.

Attraction and Intent

As Witches, we typically are more aware of and sensitive to the vibration of energy attraction and imprints, which often heralds an inherent attraction to items bearing strong energy vibration. Energy attractions may develop as we connect with pieces that rouse our cell memory of another incarnation's era or environment. Attraction also occurs when an item's symbolic energy resonates with our intent. That wonderful desk may be speaking your energetic language as an office desk for a new business endeavor. Imprints can be more inconspicuous at the initial encounter, but then grow in intensity as they interact in our home environment. Imprints can be virtually unfelt until we begin a process of stripping, polishing, and otherwise rehabbing the item. The energetic release people feel as they rehab a house can also be unveiled as we rehab an item.

These imprinting energies can be pleasant and vibrationally in tune with us and our home. However, not all pleasant imprints are vibrationally in tune with our home. Finally, and unfortunately, there are those cases where imprints are quite problematic. Their energies may range from energetic attachments to imprints of illness, sorrow, depression, or abuse.

Personalize and Align Energy

Regardless of the energy imprint, most of us want to introduce items to our home that are energetically clear and ready to be energetically "ours." But no matter how complex, the energetic clearing process primarily consists of working with the current core of our selves and home, the containment of the new item and its current energy, clearing and allowing any energy to recharge its resonation, and (if desired) charging the energy toward a specific purpose (or purposes). Note that while I make suggestions based on my experience, there are other methods. Magic and working with energy is as individual and as unique as your very thumbprint. Your intuition is usually your best guide.

Energy will always have an affinity to other energy of like vibration. This affinity, coupled with the magical understanding that all things begin with the energy core, tells us that we will begin at your inner core (spiritual, mental, emotional, and physical self) and your outer core (your home environment and the situations and patterns in your immediate life). These two cores intermingle and reflect each other. We are, indeed, the centers of our universe. What we see on the outside has been attracted to us by the energy of our feelings, our expectations, and our beliefs. Energy is never static, so we can either shift our energy to change troublesome situations or we can reinforce our flow of energy to maintain our inner and outer core harmony.

Working within Your Core Self

We are rippling vibrational beams of energy. We have the ability to vibrationally align ourselves at any level that we choose. We can align ourselves to receive very little that nourishes us. We can align ourselves to our Highest Divine Self vibration that creates the situations and events that are in harmony with our highest desires. Since our energy pattern ripples, we set up a web of energy that influences every object and every situation in our lives.

Aligning to your Highest Self Vibration begins with visualizing that you are a beam of pure vibrational energy. Allow yourself and this energy to securely ground. With each breath, feel the energy glow and grow within you and shimmering around you. As you feel the energy grow, state these or similar words:

As I honor my Creator with my creation,
I align my energy with my Highest vibration.

As you release those words, feel your energy raise and align with your Highest Self. Visualize your face and body within this energy to symbolically ground it as yours.

As you take your deep breath in, affirm that your energy is aligned. As you release your breath, allow your energy beam to flow to the earth to ground and to allow for the circulating flow of "As above, so below" magical energy.

Contain the Item's Vibration

Now that the energy is attuned in your core, you'll want to preserve your core's vibration by containing the item that you are introducing in a magical circle. Some frequent magical treasure seekers keep a containing circle always erected, which is a good idea to adopt. They use salt, candles, symbols, smudging, and pure energy shields to define the space for working with their new item. Personally I am a hoarder...ahem, collector...of jewelry, books, and dolls. I have a box prepared for the items of "iffy" energy. Some people even place their hands around an item and visualize a cocoon surrounding their treasures, keeping the energy contained in a given space.

Regardless of the ceremony executed or the space allotted, you will want to keep in mind and "intend" the purposes for this enclosed circle. The first and foremost intent is to keep the energy

of your new "find" from mingling with the energy of your own possessions and home. The second, and equally important, intent is to create an area that transmutes all energy into pure (neutral) energy that is without any pretense of negative or positive. The third, and again, equally important, intent is to create an area where you will feel comfortable working with your new item.

One method of "intending" the purposes is to again recognize yourself as being that beam of energy channel. Allow yourself to ground. Feel yourself with the earth and her strength. At the same time, feel the gentle flow of Divine Energy enter your crown and move through you in a stream of power. Center this power within you. Most people feel this centering occur in their upper abdomen (or solar plexus) as this is the energetic vortex where Divine Source energy is receive and intended for use on the physical plane.

State these or similar words;

> *From skies above—To earth below,*
> *I channel this circle of Divine flow (encompassing your item or space)*
> *An energy cocoon form containment and protection,*
> *All energy within transcends to its highest vibration.*
> *So below and as above, So mote it be,*
> *In perfect trust and perfect love.*

Clear Away Imprinted Energy

With your containment secure, the next step is to clear the item of any imprinted energy. The first step is to allow your treasure to "tell you its story." Tuning into the story of your item is to psychically tune it to its vibrational language and history.

Either touch the item to tune in to the tactile vibrations (as in psychometry) or focus on the item. Energetically or verbally invite the item to tell you its story. Allow your thoughts to flow as you tune it to your item. You may be generating the account of your purchase of your item. You may be generating the physical nuances of your item. You may be generating the intended use and new home of your item. Allow this generated story to flow as long as needed.

You will notice that the flow will shift from generating information to receiving information. This shift is your cue that you have now psychically tuned in and are now receiving the story of your treasure. As you psychically receive the story, allow for the "first flow" of information to be recognized as the pure flow of story. You can question and allow the energy to answer, but still trust the first flowing answer to be the one recognized as reality. When you feel the energy recede, you will completely know the energetic history of your item and you will know how to work with its imprint.

Clearing is a process of allowing the energy imprint to release and transform to its highest vibration. All too often, we clear an object by focusing on the negative imprint. While this does historically work, some people (particularly those who are very energetically sensitive) notice that this focus on the negative may inadvertently create a "like energy vibration" that attracts other negative energy. Another "pro" to focusing on the high vibration is that, unless you want to charge your item for a specific intent, you can clear and charge within the same working.

Ways to Charging Items for a Goal or the Highest Vibration

We will focus on common methods and the tools that raise vibration. Please note that there are no rights or wrongs here. If it works; it works. Your choice of tools and methods may vary based on your item (materials of manufacture, use, intent, and discovered vibrational history and imprint) and your intuitive response.

Again, remember that the first step in charging and tranforming an item's energy is to clear it first.

Begin any clearing with your statement and raised energy of intent. In this instance, ground and center your energy and state these or similar words;

> *Currents of Divine Energy direct your course—*
> *All energy within transforms to Highest Source.*

Herbs and essential oils, such as sage, mint, frankincense, sandalwood, balsam fir, anise, and ash have long been used as a wrap on in a censer or diffuser to raise vibration. Allow the herb to smolder or the oil to steam. Circle the item visualizing the release of the imprinted energy moving toward and being transformed by Source vibration.

Herbs, elixirs, and/or herbal essential oils can be used with great success. Using a porous paper (like a folded coffee filter or teabag), place herbs in water (boiled or placed in sunlight) until "cooked" or sprinkle essential oil in water and allow it to cure in the sun or the moon. My favorite is peppermint as a clearing and high-vibration oil mixed with lavender for its harmonizing and balancing love qualities. Then either bathe, wipe down, or spray the item. Visualize the releasing energy being bathed and transmuted back to its purity.

Earth is a wonderful, nourishing purifier. The blessed soil from the Mother Earth can remove any energy and change its polarity to one of nourishment, stability, and security. If needed, gather a pot or other vessel of earth. Either cover the item with earth or visualize the energy moving from the item into the earth. Visualize the nourishing elements of the earth clearing your item.

The dual nature of "fire destroys and fire creates" has long been understood in the magical community. Using **fire** to attract and remove and energy while transforming the energy in creative light and warmth is a wonderful method of clearing. Your choice of candles will depend on the story imprint of your item. For general clearing, many practitioners use white, black, silver, and/or gold. Taking fire precautions, light your candle near or on your item. Visualize and affirm that the imprinted energy is flowing through the flames, purified by the flame's warmth and light.

Brooms have long been used to manipulate and energetically protect. A small broom can be very useful in the direction of energy toward or away from any point. You can use your brooms to define an area of protection.

Crystals and crystal elixirs are incredible tools of clearing. Crystals like quartz, rose quartz, citrine, tourmaline, and amethyst can all be used to allow the item to release any untoward energy and have this energy transmuted to highest vibration. If the item allows, the use of gem elixir can be fabulous. I love working with emerald energy. This wonderful crystal of heart chakra bears the energy of divinity manifesting in the world; the constant love of the Divine source. Cover the crystal with pure water that ideally has been charged in the moon or the sun. Ground yourself and once again become that channel of Divine energy. Place your hand over the crystal and water and feel the flow of intent flow through your hands and into the crystal water. Place the energized water in an atomizer or other special bottle. You can then either immerse your item wipe down your item or spray your item. Visualize the molecules of water and crystal bathing and recrystalizing the energy for Highest source.

Holy water is a wonderful tool to protect, clear, and raise energy. To create holy water, stand in the light of the full moon. Form a triangle using the thumbs and the forefingers of both hands. Call on the divine energy to flow through you and your hands, visualize the energy flowing in to the water. Allow the water to cure during the full moon energies.

You can give your item a **lunar or a solar bath**. In direct line with the sun or moon, form a triangle with your thumbs and forefingers. Focus the transmuting clearing energy through the triangle to the object. Affirm that this light is lifting the vibration of the item that you hold.

Evaluating Your Charges

Regardless of the clearing manner, you will want to make sure that all imprinting energy has been released. There are two excellent ways to determine if you have met your clearing goal. The first is to trust your gut feelings. Again, allow your item to give you the story of how it now feels. You can also pay attention to how the environment feels as your item "lives" there. A perhaps more tangible method employs the use of a pendulum. Pendulums have long been associated with "tangible" language to the messages of our Highest Source Energy. Predetermine with your pendulum what movement will indicate an item that is cleared and what movement will indicate an item that still has "issues." Hold the pendulum over the item and watch the movement pattern. If the pattern indicates that some imprint is left over, repeat the "telling of the story process" and then choose a clearing method that might be best suited for the residual.

While the clearing process that focused intent of Higher vibration has already balanced the energy imprint for most every environment, we often purchase items with a specific intent in mind. In this situation we will want to "charge" or create a new imprinting energy on our item.

Even if we don't have a specific intent, we may want to further tune our treasure in to us so that it speaks our language and knows our desires. While we can create a ritual to consecrate an item, and if this item is to be used as a part of magic or of ritual, that may be what we would want to do. But for most items, the flow of energy from everyday use is a great charger. For specific charging of intent, we work with our Higher Self energy.

Your Higher/Divine Self energy is always in harmony with your greater good. Allow yourself to ground. Create a self-conduit from the infinite Divine Self into the earth. Take a deep breath in and as you exhale; visualize a stream of energy flowing from your divine source through your crown. As you visualize the energy, affirm that this is your Higher Self flow. Visualize your face, your body, and your current clothing to further affix your impression as this being your Higher Self. With each breath, feel the flow of energy flow through you from crown through the base of your spine. Allow the energy to flow through the soles of your feet and into the earth. Each breath that you take conducts the flow of Higher self. Place your hands over the item (or hold the item) visualize the flow from Higher Self through your hands infusing the item. State these or similar words;

"State intent" energy flows through thee,
With Divine Vibration so mote it be.

When you feel the energy is filled (you may get a sensation of energy bouncing back to you), thank Higher Self, take a deep breath in, and as you exhale, allow the excess energy to flow into the earth.

Continue to fine-tune the energy to your vibration by using your treasure. This is like getting to know a new friend. As you spend time together, you get to know each other's little nuances.

～

You have now learned the skills (or added in new skills) that will enable you to quest in the confidence of knowing that each new object will blend in to your home with balance and comfort. You have the confidence of knowing that the greatest and most treasured "find" is that you can, and will always be able to, create harmony and balance within your home and hearth.

Finding True Abundance:
A Visit with the Dragon

by Barbara Ardinger, PhD

Abundance, which means "fullness to overflowing," can take many forms. It's more than just money. The metaphysical prosperity authors, for example, commonly write about can mean health and relationships as well as money. Stop a minute and make some notes about what abundance means to you. What has to come into your life to help you feel that you're finding abundance? I'm self-employed, so what I see as abundance is authors who hire me to edit their books. They pay me, of course, so I'm seeing an abundance of work plus money, which creates other elements of abundance in my life.

What we need to recognize—and you already know this— is that abundance already exists. It doesn't suddenly and mysteriously manifest from nothing and pop into our hands and checkbooks because, following the metaphysical authors' advice, we have reprogrammed our minds and made a treasure map. (Do they still tell us to make treasure maps?)

Abundance is energy. It's creativity and inventiveness. It's recycling and reusing, saving and spending. It's the inspiration and loving-kindness that move from person to person as we pay it forward. It's also political in the sense that although the planet is rich and abundant enough to enrich everyone, a tiny percentage of the world's population (most of them white men in business suits) own about 90 percent of its resources. There is, in fact, enough for all the hungry children and their mothers to have enough to eat and to have safe and clean places to live. Abundance in the political sense might mean

117

a redistribution of resources. Poverty must be nonfeminized and nonchild-ized. It's a kindergarten lesson we seem to have forgotten. We need to remember how to share.

Visualize and Remember

This visit with the Dragon—guardian of the treasure and age-old symbol of wisdom and eternal life—will help us clarify our ideas about the Earth's abundance and our share of it. Note that the dragon I describe is a dragon I bought at a metaphysical bookstore perhaps thirty years ago. Her wings were faded and chipped, so I painted them a brighter gold. She has always sat in the room where I write.

Sit comfortably, take several deep, easy breaths, and enter your alpha state. Take another deep, easy breath and imagine that you are in the antechamber of the queen's palace. The walls, floor, and ceiling of this room sparkle with quartz crystals of many colors and large Herkimer diamonds, which are quartz crystals that often contain rainbows of crushed ice inside them. This crystalline energy gives us peace, courage, and strength.

Take another deep, easy breath. In your imagination, step forward and walk through the door in the eastern wall of the room. Now you are in the second antechamber. Here the walls, floor, and ceiling are carved kunzite, which is a smooth, soft, pinkish mineral. Kunzite energy opens our hearts to peace and love. Feel this energy flowing around you.

Take another deep, easy breath and step through another door. Now you are standing in the third antechamber. This room is made of sacred pipestone (the most sacred stone known to the Native Americans), agates and jaspers of every color, and petrified wood. Pipestone is a soft, red mineral. Like agates and jaspers, its energy brings us the peace and power of the earth itself. The petrified wood is likewise grounded and grounding.

Take another deep, easy breath and imagine yourself walking into the fourth antechamber. This room is made of

black tourmaline, which deflects negativity both from other people and from within yourself.

Now you're facing a huge, grand, beautifully carved door in the eastern wall of this antechamber. This door opens by itself. Walk into the throne room of the queen. The walls, floor, and ceiling of the throne room are encrusted with gems set in patterns like the constellations of stars in the sky. Look around. Look up. You can see alchemical symbols, the astrological glyphs, and mysterious sigils. Spend as much time as you want to studying the symbols you see. The throne room of the queen is filled with wisdom and magic.

Now you hear a rumbling sound coming from the far end of the room. It's time to meet the queen.

The queen is a Dragon! She is a dignified reptile who is as ancient as the earth and as wise as time. Look at this ancient animal, the personification of regeneration. She is about twice the size of an adult human and is covered with emerald-green scales from her head to the tip of her tail. See her golden wings, folded back along her sleek body. See her five-clawed feet and the puffs of steam that come out of her mouth when she speaks. Note her calm, impressive demeanor. You feel no fear or horror, only respectful awe. You could become friends with this Dragon ... if such forwardness were permitted.

"Welcome, my human friend," you hear her say. "Welcome to my realm. Who are you, and why have you come here?"

Approach the throne. Tell the Dragon your name. Give her your birth name and your magical name if you have one. Tell her you are seeking your abundance and a better understanding of the Earth's abundance.

"Good," she says. "You are welcome here. Be at ease."

Unlike the dragons of myths, legends, and long novels, the queen is not sitting on her hoard. No, she's sitting on a huge diamond throne, and the hoard lies around her. Notice the heaps of diamonds and rubies, the agates and petrified wood, the gold and silver. See the precious jewels, the earth stones, and the precious metals twinkling and gleaming. You can feel the wealth of the queen's throne room.

The abundance lies here for you and every other person on Earth. You see models and miniatures, pictures, photos, symbols of every kind of earthly abundance. Look more care-

fully. You also see corn and wheat and rice and other good food, raw and cooked. Books and magazines. Comfortable clothing. Symbols of good health and disease-free bodies. High-tech goodies like smartphones and tablets and computers. In a niche off to the side, you can see pairs of endangered animals, fish, birds, and insects. There are also thousands of heirloom seeds and growing plants. There are huge amphorae of clean water and pure air. Everything here is beautiful. The beauty and abundance of the earth and the treasures of civilization are stored here for safekeeping.

The Dragon speaks again. "You see the abundance of the Earth. This abundance is inexhaustible. There's enough for the children of the slums of every city, enough for mothers who must walk across deserts to find food or healthcare, enough for the starving children of every nation. I am witness to the abundance of the Earth," she says. "I'm the guardian. I've seen it all."

Now you notice that the Dragon guards additional treasure—your own abundance. It's waiting for you to claim it. You feel comfortable with this Dragon. She seems to be able to read your mind.

"You may ask three questions," she says. "Ask me about what you see here. I will answer your questions truthfully."

Here are three questions you can ask the Dragon:

In what parts of my life is my abundance already manifesting?

How do I distinguish between what I want and what I need?

How can I best use my share to take care of myself and others who live on the planet?

Be silent now as the Dragon considers your questions. When she speaks, listen carefully. Know that you will receive the answers you require. If you don't remember what she says immediately, know that the information will come to you in its proper time. It may come in unusual ways, like you "just happen" to read an article in a magazine or "just happen" to find an app with ideas or suggestions. You will receive what you need, now and in the future.

When the Dragon falls silent, thank her. Now you can inspect the treasures of the earth again. Is there anything you specifically want? How can you get it? Keep in mind the wisdom of an old bumper sticker: Ask the Goddess and do your own homework. Here, perhaps we should rephrase it slightly: Ask the Dragon and do your own homework.

You already know what this means. Don't just sit and wait for a mobile device, a fancy new car, a new job or new clients, or some spiffy new clothes to come wafting in through your front door. Let people know what you're looking for and ask for leads. Find the best prices. Work hard and save your money. Plan ahead.

Take another deep, easy breath, and when you come back to your consensual reality, make some useful plans to find the part of the earth's abundance that belongs to you. But don't cheat to get it! This is your Mother—er, the Dragon speaking.

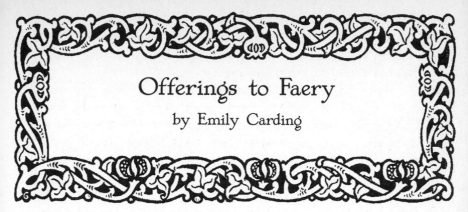

Offerings to Faery

by Emily Carding

Fascination with the Faery realm may be more widespread in the twenty-first century than ever before, with gatherings and festivals happening throughout the globe and a huge variety of books available on the subject. However, when such material is so abundant, it can be difficult to extract the truth from the dross. Many popular authors and "teachers" encourage a consumerist and self-oriented approach to connecting with otherworldly beings, portraying them as invisible helpers rather than independent beings that are powerful in their own right. Connecting with Faery can only truly be undertaken with a pure heart and selfless intent, remembering that there are things we can and should do for them with no thought of reward for ourselves.

One of the simplest and most effective ways we can build this cooperative connection with our faery cousins is through regular offerings, which not only honor the spirits of the land and our otherworldly allies, but build a bridge through the energetic exchange that takes place. Unfortunately, there is much misinformation on this subject and far less sound and practical advice. Within this short article, I hope to give you some of the latter and set you on a clear, unmuddied path forward in your work with faery beings.

Why?

So, before we begin in earnest, it is important to consider why we may want to leave offerings to Faery and, indeed, why we choose to seek a connection with them at all. We live in a time of great and accelerated change in the world around us. Technology develops at an unfathomable pace, whilst the natural world

appears to be spiraling toward disaster. Many are now awakening to the fact that these may well be the last days we have to renew our respect for the planet and reverse destructive patterns before it's too late. Those who are spiritually aware understand that just as we all carry a spark of the infinite divine within us, so such sparks also dwell within nature. When our inner light connects with the inner light of the world, or Faery, then both realms become stronger as part of the Whole. This is the essence of true Faery work, and good offerings can be a simple yet powerful part of strengthening this connection.

When inspiration has struck, it can be tempting to leap into Faery work with both feet, but remember that true connection takes time. Eagerness to "see faeries" or experience magic, coupled with impatience, can sadly lead to a slippery spiral path of illusion, with the mind creating the experiences that it so desperately seeks. True Faery work involves connection experienced through the whole self and is better sensed through the open heart than through any of our earthly senses. Take time to study folklore, especially that of your local area, and spend as much time on the land as you can in a natural space that calls to you.

Be sure that when you seek to greet and connect with your local beings that you have some understanding of their nature. These days, "Faery" is a label that covers a vast variety of beings including elementals, plant spirits, spirits of place right through to the god-like Sidhe and Faery Kings and Queens. Of course, all lands and areas have their variants, so try to be sure that you are using the right mode of address for the beings dwelling in your landscape. Remember that however valuable intuition is, knowledge forms a strong foundation for all magical and spiritual work. If you still wish to build connection with Faery after taking an honest look at your motivations and spending some time getting to know the land that you live on, then it's time to start making offerings.

What?

A sentiment that is encountered too often in modern spiritual and magical teachings is "just do what feels right," especially in regard to offerings. This is of little use to those starting off and looking for guidance, and equally (if not more) harmful to those who are experienced but have never had anybody point out if they have been doing anything wrong over the years. A key principle worth remembering is that an offering should be something of intrinsic value that you have in some way invested energy. Here are some suggestions for appropriate offerings to the Faery realm, as well as some bad habits that should be avoided and the reasoning behind them:

Traditional

There is a reason certain things become traditional—generations of folks before have tried and tested methods and found what works. Although it is certainly possible to be more personal and creative with offerings, traditional choices are often best to begin with and can provide a continuing dependable thread, like the bass note or drumbeat of your workings.

Baked goods are an excellent traditional offering in most cultures. Remember that offerings are an exchange of energy, so the best ones are those you have made yourself. It would be worthwhile researching local recipes for bread and cakes and use homegrown, organic ingredients when possible. Of course, it is possible to use shop-bought baked goods as an offering, especially when you bear in mind that you purchased them with your money—money that you earned by expending your own energy. Do be sure, however, to put some thought into your choice, and try to limit the amount of artificial ingredients and ensure that the offering does not contain things harmful to local wildlife such as chocolate (more on that later). Fruit is acceptable, since there has been some human effort in the harvesting of it, provided it has been farmed or grown at home using natural methods.

Beverages that have undergone a fermentation process, such as wine, beer, or mead, make an excellent offering for most beings on most occasions! Again, if you are able to make your own, that is ideal, but by no means essential. A whole bottle may be offered on some special occasions, but it is worth considering giving the first share of any alcohol consumed to Faery as a sign of friendship and respect.

Another traditional offering that is widely known in folklore is a bowl of cream or milk, especially at full moon. (You will note the similarity in appearance between a bowl of milk and the shining round moon!) Again, it is considered good form when possible to give the first and best share as an offering, and it's quite

easy to develop this as a monthly routine, which keeps you in tune with the moon cycle and thus the rhythm of the natural world.

Offerings of incense are popular throughout the world, the sweet smell and the energy released through the burning of herbs and resins being very attractive to spiritual beings. If you have the space, grow and dry a selection of herbs at home for this purpose. The more thought and energy you put into your offerings the better, so you may wish to blend your own incenses, or at least find a source for your incense that you are sure uses good methods and ingredients. Loose grain incense burned on a charcoal disk is preferable, but be sure not to leave it burning unsupervised, as the ashes can stay dangerously hot for some time. Stick incense can also be used. Again, don't leave it unsupervised.

Silver coins and other gifts of precious metals have been traditionally left at certain sites in Celtic tradition. This is an offering that should be considered carefully. You may feel called at a certain time or place to leave an object of personal value. This can signify a great commitment to your Faery path, but be mindful that both the object and the location are appropriate, as sacred sites should be left pure and unpolluted by the intents of others, no matter how well intended. A gift of little material value but great personal significance is a far greater offering than something of great monetary worth that was bought from a shop the day before. It is also worth remembering that through your leaving of this offering, it may pass into the hands of another, thus passing into the greater pattern of life and connection.

Being Creative

One of the most heartfelt and beneficial offerings you can give is an act of creative expression, regardless of whether you would usually consider yourself to be a creative person. Creative acts are not only a delight to Faery beings, but they also open the heart and thus increase our own ability to sense and connect with the higher resonances of the hidden realms. When we offer an act of creation to Faery, we build a direct link between our soul and their world, opening a two-way flow of inspiration and sustenance. Even if you don't feel creative in the traditional sense, all human beings are born with the ability to create and destroy, so to consciously create is to make a choice and declare a message of positive intent to the universe—a message that the Faery realm will hear and understand.

You do not need to be a trained singer to be able to offer energy in the form of song. Wherever we may find ourselves, the voice is a magical tool that we always have with us. Whether we choose to learn songs, allow them to rise spontaneously, or simply sing a note from our soul, using the voice as an offering is an excellent and effective method of building connections and opening awareness—with the added advantage of leaving no mess to clear up afterward. The same applies to dance—it is the energy and purity of expression that makes a good offering, not the technical skill. If your heart feels the dance, the Faery beings will dance with you.

If you play a portable instrument, or choose to learn one, then take it into the green and wild spaces with you and play to the spirits of place. Music of all kinds is a wonderful offering and you may find that if you can quieten your mind that the music within the land may surface through you. Poetry, especially that which honors the beauty and grace of the Faery Queens, is also an excellent offering, and one which you can incorporate into your invocations. Beautiful words hold great power.

You may feel inspired to create something more permanent as a dedication to Faery, such as a painting, sculpture, or something with a practical use such as a chalice or wand. Such objects may become tools in your magical work or focal points for a Faery shrine. (More on shrines at the end of this article.)

Things to Avoid

As mentioned earlier, there are certain foodstuffs that are inappropriate for offerings. Avoid foods that have a high content of additives or that have in any way caused unethical suffering through their manufacture. A common misconception is that because we enjoy chocolate and candy, it makes a good offering to Faery. Unfortunately chocolate contains toxins that are harmful to a large number of animals, both domestic and wild. And while this seems too obvious to be worth stating, I have seen this done enough to mention that obviously anything in a plastic wrapper is the equivalent of littering, not a sacred offering! Another food related no-no is leftovers. Any offering of food or drink should always be the first and best share. To give what is left over is hugely insulting and will do far more harm than good.

It's also important to clear any offerings of food left before they decay, either by burying them or burning them. Quite often, the offerings may be accepted and consumed by animals on behalf of the local faery beings, but otherwise the goodness is taken from the food, leaving only the decaying husk (hence tales of faeries turning milk sour), which must be disposed of with consideration to the environment.

Opinion is divided on whether wildflowers make good offerings to Faery. I ask you merely consider whose energy—yours or theirs?—has gone into their growth, and whether cutting the life from a plant by picking it is something that would appeal as a gift to our Faery allies, and draw your own conclusions.

Another guilty culprit in the misguided offerings stakes is glitter. Glitter is fine on your body and face, but please don't leave it on the land. It is not Faery dust; most glitter is tiny bits of glass and plastic that get caught in the insides of small creatures and cause injury. Edible glitter is a more feasible option, but there are many more suitable and respectful choices for offerings.

Small stones charged with positive intent may make acceptable offerings under certain circumstances, but rocks, stones, and crystals are gifts given to us from the natural world. They may be used as tools, but to leave them as offerings is senseless when our energy has not gone into their creation. In recent decades, a misguided habit of leaving crystals on sacred sites has developed. Such well-intended gifts unfortunately pollute the pure energy lines of sacred spaces, though crystals from ethical sources are of course perfectly fine to place on your shrine or altar at home or in your garden.

Where and When?

Offerings should be made on a regular basis anywhere you wish to build a connection with the spirits of that place, or at any time and place you wish to conduct other magical work outdoors as part of asking their permission. Building an outdoor shrine in your garden or near your home where regular offerings can be made is also a good idea. Faery shrines can be indoors, where they can be excellent points of focus for meditation and devotional or other magical practice, but I highly recommend against leaving offering at indoor shrines. Faery beings are no respecters of man-made boundaries at the best of times and can cause a great deal of chaos when given free rein in the home, especially with technology! It is far better to honor them on the land, in their space.

How?

Offerings should not be made in haste, but in consideration and sanctity. There is no need for a complex and confusing ritual, but do be respectful and put time aside to tune in to the energies around you and declare yourself to them. When making offerings at home, create a shrine as a focus and sacred space. It does not need to be intricate or even obvious, and everyone's shrine is as different as they are! There are no hard and fast rules to shrine building, but you may find the following guidelines helpful.

Focal Point

Inevitably, your shrine will grow and change, accumulating interesting objects as the months and years go on. Bear in mind that a shrine should be a focal point for your connection, so put a good deal of thought into what will be the central piece of your shrine, around which the rest will evolve. For an outdoor shrine, you might choose a statue or perhaps a large stone or piece of wood with an appropriate symbol painted on it. If you choose the latter, be sure to use a good hard-wearing paint with a layer of varnish.

There is more freedom of choice for an indoor shrine, where you may choose a painting or something more delicate that might not endure outdoor weather conditions. Whilst other items on your shrine may shift and change, your focal point should remain.

Natural Materials

Objects on a Faery shrine should be made of natural materials as much as possible—wood, stone, bone, antler, ceramics, glass, fur, and leather are all acceptable.

The Elements

You may wish to incorporate objects from the natural world that represent the four elements on your shrine. For example, you can use a stone or piece of wood for earth, feathers for air, a candle for fire, and a chalice for water. If you can, try to use water from a natural source.

Tools

If you have any magical tools that you use specifically for your work with Faery, you may choose to keep those on your indoor shrine, as a dedicated sacred space. This will help them to hold their power and intent.

Blessing and Dedication

All objects placed on the shrine should be consecrated and dedicated to your work with Faery, and placed with focus on your intent to build positive relations with Faery. When you are happy that this process is complete, bless and dedicate the shrine as a whole. The dedication does not need to be complex. Light a candle and sprinkle your shrine three times with consecrated water. Ask Faery for inspiration. You may feel drawn to say some words, sing, or even dance. State out loud in your own words your intent to honor and build connections with the Faery realm and spend some time with your shrine in contemplation. This would also be an excellent time for an offering of a healthy portion of mead or wine shared between you and Faery—with the first share going to them, of course.

Continuing on the Faery Path

This has been a very brief look at one small area that can form part of a Faerycentric lifestyle. If you would like to learn more about this area or any other aspect of working with Faery as well as the worldwide Faery community, please read my book *Faery Craft*, (Llewellyn, 2012). I will leave you with some words that you may use to accompany your offerings to Faery, should you choose to do so, or adapt them as you please. May the wisdom of the silver stars illuminate your path, and the trees whisper kind songs of kinship as you walk forward in truth and beauty…

People of peace, who dwell in the hollow hills,
Spirits of tree, rock and river,
Song of the stars and drumbeat of the Earth,
I call to thee,
I bring you this, my offering, in peace and friendship,
That we may know unity between us,
That we may share from a common cup,
As travellers along the same path,
Walk with me, as I shall walk with you,
Now and always,
So mote it be.

The Two-Wheeled Witch

by Eli Effinger-Weintraub

My most cherished magical tool lives in my garage: a metallic blue bicycle I call Briar. Whether you're a weekend warrior riding centuries every Saturday, a committed transportation cyclist taking three-mile spins to the library, or a newcomer seeking your cadence, the potential of the bicycle as a spiritual and magical tool lies within easy reach and can bring incredible fulfillment.

Even without magical intent or focus in play, riding a bike is a powerful spiritual act. When we go by two wheels, we link ourselves to a century-long history of bicycling populated by risk-takers and rule-breakers who flouted convention to embrace the new. In some ways, cyclists still do this, defying expectations of car-dependence. When we choose cycling, we become change-makers.

Cycling strengthens our physical bodies, increasing energy levels and helping us move and function better in all aspects of our lives. This not only makes everyday life more enjoyable but forges us into more effective magical and spiritual vessels.

Cycling helps heal the Living Earth, reducing emissions and fossil fuel depletion while requiring fewer materials and less energy to produce and maintain than cars.

And, by gum, cycling is fun. As acts of reverence and mirth go, it's near the top of the list.

We can do plenty to up the magical power of a bike ride, turning even simple commutes into powerful magical workings. Before our pedaling adventure begins, we must prepare ourselves and our tools for the work.

Before You Ride

At the start of each "biking season," I reset and reinforce protective spells on Briar and my helmet. I've never felt cycling is as dangerous as naysayers claim, but I'm klutzy on the best of days, so it doesn't hurt to insure my trusty steed against accident and theft. My spells are simple: heartfelt words and sigils painted in clear nail polish on the bottom of the bike frame and inside the helmet, a sprig of dried protective herbs tucked into the ends of the grips, or a prayer or bind rune written on a long strip of paper and wound through the spokes can increase the juice.

Many cyclists run an "ABC quick check" before long rides, or after several short rides. It stands for "air, brakes, cranks/chain/cassette, quick release." Do your tires have sufficient air? Do your brakes work properly? Are your cranks, chain, and cassette correctly positioned, affixed, and moving smoothly? Are quick-release handles engaged and out of the way? While I do this check physically on Briar, I do it mentally on myself.

Air: Am I breathing deeply, from my center?

Brakes: Do I know my limitations? Can I listen if body or spirit says it's time to end the ride or the working?

Cranks/chain/cassette: Am I centered and connected to the Living Earth, to Mystery, and to my Highest Self? Am I present to myself as a whole being?

Quick release: I am alive, and I revel in this.

Play with this. Perhaps develop your own ABCs to spiritually prepare you to head out.

Setting intention before the first pedal stroke can make your ride smoother, more enjoyable, and more effective. Are you raising energy for Earth- or self-healing? Dispelling negativity through your feet as you pedal? Deepening your connection to Nature or Mystery? Or is this a ride for fun, no strings attached? All of these, and myriad others, are blessed intentions for a ride, and choosing beforehand helps you stay focused.

During the Ride

The bulk of the work happens during the ride. Once you build a strong, rhythmic cadence, explore the possibilities of the energetic relationship between your body and mind.

If you have a mantra or affirmation, say it to the rhythm of your pedal strokes. Does this change the energy of the words? Perhaps develop a phrase just for biking.

I sing while I bike. I have a never-ending improvisational "bicycle song" about how I'm feeling and the sights, sounds, and smells of the world around me.

Sing a song that's right for your ride as an offering to the Divine you hold dear.

Cycling offers opportunities for meditation, as Thomas Schenk (among others) points out (http://humanistic paganism.com/2011/09/25/bicycle-meditation-by-thomas -schenk/). Keeping enough awareness to stay safe as you travel, focus on the steady rhythm of your legs pumping and your wheels turning. Still your mind's idle chatter and simply be, breathing into and out of each moment.

Cycling can also be a powerful force for connection to the world. On her powerful Bicycle Meditations website (http:// www.bicyclemeditations.org/Welcome.htm), Claire Petersky recommends consciousness triggers. Pick something you'll encounter on your ride—birdsong, woodsmoke, flags snapping in the breeze—and connect a phrase to it. Whenever you encounter that trigger, say the phrase and raise your consciousness of your physical surroundings—your body, the road, the plant and animal life around you—and the way your bike connects you to these things.

Make a game of attention. On your ride, notice every flower, every smell, or every instance of a particular color. When you reach your destination, write down as much as you remember. Pick something different next time and challenge yourself to spot more.

Always remember magic. If you set out with the intention of raising energy for a specific magical end, it will gather with every pedal stroke and can be distributed as desired.

The Fun Doesn't End

When your ride ends, you'll need to do something with the energy you've built. If you've gone for a long ride on an empty road and never put your foot down, let the energy pass through your foot and into the ground, heading to the purpose you

assigned. Riders who do more stop-and-go riding may prefer to store energy elsewhere—in your hands, for instance.

After long rides, rides in inclement weather, or periodically if your rides are mostly short, clean your bike. As necessary, wipe the frame with a cloth, oil the chain, and remove debris from the tire treads. Like the pre-ride ABC Quick Check, these physical actions easily become energetic cleansings with attention and intention.

Recording emotions and impressions post-ride lets us examine our experiences from different angles, harvesting everything we can from each ride. Noting the way cycling alters our outlook on life can help us chart our trajectory over time as cyclists and as spiritual beings. Even if you're not interested in anything as involved as a bike journal, consider keeping note-taking tools on hand; thoughts blossom during rides but fade quickly out of the saddle.

Naming my bike and addressing it by that name helps me build a rapport with it. In turn, this gives me confidence that I can climb on and pedal off with ease and skill, riding a trusted friend, not an unfeeling hunk of metal. I also talk about Briar, and biking in general, to anyone willing to listen. In this way, bikes help foment another amazing magic: the magic of community and human connection.

With proper care, you and your bicycle can stay together for years, maybe even decades. Your worldview and temperament will help you determine whether you want to perform required maintenance yourself or leave that work to trained mechanics. Both are acts of devotion in their ways. Whichever you choose, know that you're taking the best possible care of this important magical implement capable of bringing such delight to every aspect of your life.

The Animistic View: Seeing the Soul of the World

by Susan Pesznecker

Many magickal folks proclaim themselves to be animists but may not be fully clear on its meaning, let alone know the related terms that attempt to explain or define one's spiritual paths. It's worth understanding these perspectives, for doing so helps focus our individual and collective belief sets and shapes the ways in which we study, practice, and interrelate.

The dictionary defines animism as a belief system that finds no difference between the physical and spiritual realms and which attributes a soul to both animate and inanimate objects. This is Obi-Wan's "everything is alive" view, seeing no separation between animated life and inanimate substance. The animistic view of the world finds life, soul, and energy existing in all things from plants to rocks to ocean to sky and uses this view to create order and interrelatedness throughout the known universe. This also implies a specific ethical position, namely that humans are not necessarily superior to plants, rocks, and so on, and that we must regard everything on this planet as worthy of reverence and respect.

Psychologists affirm that the animistic mindset is normal for all humans when we begin our lives. The change to regarding some objects as "lifeless" is an abstraction that happens as we approach adulthood and are subject to cultural influences. Sadly, most "modern" societies tend to regard the animistic view as childish and typically view cultures with persistent animistic perspectives as "savage" or "primitive."

Compare Animism to Other Paths

Comparing animism to other path definitions can help differentiate and better understand one's own spiritual vantage.

Agnosticism: The agnostic neither confirms nor denies the existence of a supreme being but believes that nothing is known or can be known of the existence or nature of a supreme being or of anything beyond material phenomena. In other words, understanding the presence or nature of a supreme being is felt to be beyond human understanding.

Atheism: A belief that supreme beings do not exist, have never existed, and have no responsibility for the universe, its inhabitants, or their behavior.

Autothesism: The idea that divinity is present in each person, with an implied responsibility for each one to become more perfectly divine. (See also immanence.)

Deism: Belief in the existence of at least one Supreme Being, specifically of a creator who made the universe but thereafter did not intervene in its functions. This relates to the "Deist" intellectual movement of the seventeenth and eighteenth centuries, which accepted the existence of a creator on the basis of reason but rejected belief in a supernatural deity who interacted with humankind. Polydeism is similar, but suggests that the universe was created by multiple supreme beings.

Dualism suggests the universe contains opposing powers of good and evil either as balanced equals or as two opposed or contrasted supreme beings—literally or metaphorically. Christianity fits this paradigm, with its figures of Jesus and Satan. Pagan traditions that have a God and Goddess at their centers are also dualistic.

Henotheism suggests that while there may be multiple supreme beings responsible for the universe, only one is correctly worshipped at a given time. (See also kathenotheism and monlatrism.)

Hylozoism proposes that all matter possesses life without necessarily possessing a "mind." For example, the ancient Greeks believed air, water, and fire were alive because they were able to move spontaneously, make sound, etc. Hylozoism is more philosophy than religion, but it's useful in understanding how the ancients regarded physical matter and how belief systems may have developed. The opposite of hylozoism is panpsychism, which says that all matter has a unique point of view or way of being—a primitive "mindset"—without possessing life.

Immanence: An immanent perspective says that divinity is internal rather than external and tells us we need look no further than within ourselves to find divine source. In animism, all things are divine or potentially divine, and all divinity is immanent rather than transcendent, i.e., beyond the range or reach of the human being.

Kathenotheism suggests that while multiple supreme beings may be responsible for the universe, and only one is correctly worshipped, others may be correctly worshipped at certain times and under set circumstances. (See also henotheism and monlatrism.)

Monolatrism argues that while multiple supreme beings may be responsible for the universe, only one is worthy of worship. (See also henotheism and kathenotheism.)

Monotheism: The doctrine or belief that there is only one Supreme Being.

Nonthesim rejects any belief system incorporating one or more supreme beings, while simultaneously supporting a naturalist view, i.e., that the universe is organized and ordered according to a set of immutable natural laws. A Pagan who follows no deities but finds spiritual direction in nature is behaving as a nontheist.

Pantheism is a term with three very distinct contextual meanings: First, it is a doctrine associating a single supreme being with the universe or regarding the universe as a manifestation of a single "responsible" supreme being. Second, one or more gods are seen as equivalent to the physical universe, with no separation between them. Third, it may refer to a form of worship that admits or tolerates the worship or adoration of all gods.

Panentheism: Like panthesism, panentheism identifies a relationship between the universe and one or more supreme beings, with little or no separation between the two. However, panentheism sees the supreme beings as greater than the whole of the physical universe.

Pantheon: This term is used to describe all the gods of a people or religion collectively, e.g., the Celtic pantheon.

Polytheism proposes that the universe includes multiple supreme beings, each with unique origins, attributes, and characteristics. Followers of Norse traditions tend to be polytheistic.

Reconstruction: A system that bases its teachings on known facts and scholarship about a set of original practices. A well-known example is that of Celtic reconstructionist Druids.

Sacred: A tradition dedicated to one or more gods and their worship or service.

Secularism: A system intended to separate the sacred from legal, political, and governmental discourse. Secularism neither accepts nor denies religious belief, but espouses individual freedom of choice and says human activities should be free of religious persuasion.

Shamanism: A shaman has access to and is able to influence the spirit world. Shamans are not supreme beings but intercede between humans and the gods, particularly in terms of divining and healing.

Syncretism: The merging or attempted merging of different religions, cultures, or schools of thought, e.g., Wiccans who include Celtic elements in their practices.

Theism: Belief in the existence of a supreme being or beings, especially a belief in one supreme entity as creator of the universe, intervening intentionally and sustaining a personal relationship to his creatures.

Totemism: A practice centered on objects, relics, locations, or ancestors believed to have sacred significance or to be a locus of origins.

Transcendence: A transcendent perspective says that divinity is external and beyond the range or reach of mortal humans. The transcendent view suggests we must specifically look outside of ourselves and "transcend" our human boundaries and constraints to reach the divine, which is typically located in a supreme being.

Let's look back at animism. First, it's an immanent spiritual path. Buddhism, Shintosim, and Paganism are three well-known examples of animistic traditions. Whether looking at the Moon, a hawthorn tree, a stone, a child, or a bird, animists recognize a divine life force, and these relationships take a central role in ritual work.

Second, animism may be theist, atheist, or nontheist. For example, a Druid polytheist and a nontheisitic naturalist may both be deeply animistic.

Third, animism is often syncretic, showing an attempt to blend or fuse two or more spiritual traditions. The Odinist polytheist who believes his ritual weapons have life force is practicing syncretism, as is the Native American who follows her tribal teachings but also brings Wiccan elements into her practices.

And fourth, animists tend to be naturalistic, deriving inspiration from and revering the natural world around them. For most animists, nature itself becomes a divine focus for study, worship, and ritual practice. Often, the animist is less focused on "calendar holidays" and more in tune with natural cycles and events.

~

Are you interested in beginning some animistic practices? Be aware of the seasons around you, and develop celebrations that honor their passing. Visit outdoor locations of importance to you or places regarded as site-sacred, like national parks and waterfalls, and attempt to feel or better understand the power and energy located in these locations. Develop rituals of thanks and gratitude for each unique, living aspect of the universe. Cultivate respect for every part of the world. Listen to the trees, the clouds, the stones, and the stars.

It's a beautiful perspective, to regard everything as divine....

A Meditation on Mary Shelley's "Frankenstein: or, The Modern Prometheus"

by Sybil Fogg

Most are familiar with the story of Dr. Frankenstein. He collected a pile of body parts, sewed them together, and then blasted the whole bit with electricity to create life. Unfortunately, he had not the forethought of what this might do to the life created and ended up with a rather unsettled, angry "monster" who wreaked havoc wherever he went, dismantling Dr. Frankenstein's happiness, which culminated in a showdown in the North Pole.

Mary Wollstonecraft Godwin Shelley began *Frankenstein* during a rainy summer in 1816. This has often been referred to as the "year without a summer" as the world was experiencing a volcanic winter brought on by the eruption of Mount Tambora (Indonesia) in 1815. The weather was often too dark and dreary to venture outdoors, so on their holiday that year, Mary Shelley, her future husband, Percy Shelley, and John Polidori visited their friend Lord Byron in Switzerland. To entertain themselves, they made up ghost stories and eventually came up with the idea to each write their own supernatural tale. Lord Byron jotted down notes of vampire legends he had heard in his travels, which later would come together in Polidori's "The Vampyre." Mary Shelley began work on a story of a Dr. Frankenstein, who was able to create life. Later, she developed her work into a full-length novel.

The subtitle of her novel, *The Modern Prometheus,* refers to the titan god of forethought, who was given the task of creating man from clay. He became so invested in his creation that he taught them how to read and write, math-

ematics, astronomy, healing arts, and much more. Eventually, he even taught them how to trick the gods. For this insult, Zeus, the king of the gods, withheld fire from man. Without this tool, man was cold, hungry, and unhappy. Prometheus decided to steal fire for his offspring. For this man was punished when the woman, Pandora, was created and sent down from Olympus with a box filled with the heartaches in the world, and Prometheus was bound to a stake where an eagle was sent to feed upon his ever-generating liver. Later, he was freed by the hero Hercules.

Like Prometheus, Mary Shelley's arrogant scientist Victor Frankenstein claimed his intentions were pure, that his experiments were for the betterment of man. Many magical practitioners are plagued with this very question. When we send forth spellworkings, are we really focusing on the betterment of all around us, or are we so caught up in the concept of what we can do that we forget what we should be doing?

At one point in the novel, the creature reads Milton's "Paradise Lost." After doing so, he compares his situation to that of Adam, the first man created by God. While God created Adam to be physically perfect, Dr. Frankenstein was unable to give his creation a beautiful exterior. He is described as being over eight feet tall with yellow skin so thin that one could see the veins throbbing beneath it. Dr. Frankenstein himself was so repulsed by his creation that he fled upon its birth and the creature was left to fend for itself.

Remember back to that first time you encountered magic. I recall stumbling upon it in the woods outside my childhood home. It was as though the trees whispered in my ears and wind caressed my face. I knew there was something there right outside of my reach. Eventually, I found books and read everything I could about casting circles and calling the quarters, and inviting the God and Goddess to hear me. I even felt the wind become more tan-

gible and the trees grew louder. Then I did my first spell. It was a simple spell to make me feel better about my teenage acne, thinness, hair. And it worked. And that made me feel even more powerful. As I grew up, I tried out success spells, focus spells, and more. And although, I never became rich and famous, I never was hurting. It seemed things had a way of working out at just the right moment. Many of those who walk this path have a similar story.

But, sometimes in our daily lives we encounter situations that anger or frustrate us. As workers of magic, we have an enhanced ability to stir up thoughts within ourselves that we did not know were present. These emotions are like monsters that can cause us to think it is okay to push the karma wheel a little to get it moving. When we have decided it is acceptable to draft these types of spells, we might not even realize we are dabbling in another type of magic. Perhaps we decide to weave a spell that sets the law of three onto another unsuspecting person. After we have cast our spell, we tell ourselves that it was all right because we only tickled the magic realm, suggested that it pay attention to a specific person, someone we are pretty certain will inevitably do something that will be their own downfall.

Similar to *Frankenstein*, the transcendent natural world offers us Pagans a chance at spiritual rejuvenation. Like Dr. Frankenstein, we often find ourselves in deep study learning all that we can about the environment around us. As Dr. Frankenstein sank deep into his studies, he unlocked the key to everlasting life. At first, this knowledge seemed like something that would benefit mankind in obvious ways. But, somehow he knew that it was something more because he kept it secret. How often are our spells and rituals secret, particularly if we are a solo practitioner? Perhaps a lesson to be taken from Shelley's Frankenstein is to hold a public ritual, invite non-Pagans to participate in our magical workings. Or in another direction, we can use what we've learned from Shelley's novel as a catalyst to grow.

The Meditation

A meditation on Mary Shelley's *Frankenstein: A Modern Prometheus*. This spell is useful for those times when we realize we are moving too far away from where we started magically.

Time: Waning Moon on a Saturday (March 29 and December 20, 2014 are both ideal).

Place: Bathroom or room nearby as a purification bath is part of this spell.

Tools:

Quarter candles and any other tools that are normally used to cast the circle and draw the quarters.

Black magical candle. Choose one that will burn down by the end of the ritual.

Mirror: Round preferred, another shape if necessary.

Oil: Pine for grounding and cleansing.

Incense: Clove to banish hostile or negative forces and clear head.

Bath Herbs: Chamomile for meditation, rosemary for protection, and lavender for purification.

Preparation:

Decorate the altar in black. Set up the quarter candles. Place the mirror, black candle, and pine oil on the altar along with the clove incense.

Fill bath and add herbs. Place a towel and a robe nearby. Burn the incense.

Cast the circle as you normally do and call the quarters. Make sure the circle extends beyond the bathroom or at least the bathtub.

Say a prayer to the Goddess asking her for the strength to remember who you are as a magical being. Then enter the tub. While soaking, focus on when you first heard the calling.

Imagine you are that person again. Think through your earliest workings with magic. What did it mean to you? How surprised were you when you saw your life change? How much have you learned since then? How strong is your knowledge? How similar are you to Prometheus? Do you feel you have a great gift to give the world? Embrace those feelings. Sit with them until the water runs cold. Before jumping out, sit with the cold water for a bit. Why do you feel you need to do this ritual? How similar do you feel to Dr. Frankenstein? Have you ever thought you knew when it was time for the karma wheel to be spun better than the Great Spirit? Why did you feel this way? What made you angry? Spend some time considering these questions, but do not stay in the cold water so long that you risk your health. When you are finished, dry off and put on your robe. Sit in front of your altar and anoint the black candle with the pine oil. If you need more incense, burn it. Take a few moments to meditate on the candle's flame. Prometheus brought fire to humankind. What would your life be like without fire? Spend some time contemplating this great gift. In *Frankenstein*, light is symbolic of knowledge, innovation, and enlightenment. The goal of Dr. Frankenstein is to discover the light in dark places, to unearth secrets, and gain access to information withheld by the gods. What secrets have you unlocked? What aspects of yourself have you kept hidden?

When you are satisfied, turn your attention to the mirror. Anoint this too with the pine oil. Meditate on your reflection. Prometheus paid a steep price for what he did for his creations. What would you be willing to sacrifice for others? Our façade is what others see first when they meet us. Dr. Frankenstein's creature was gentle and kind, inquisitive and learned. But none of this mattered when people saw him. Alternatively, Dr. Frankenstein was handsome and well bred. He gave off the appearance of wealth and success, but inside he was arrogant and insidious, abandoning his offspring upon its birth.

Spend some time comparing your outside to your inside. Once you are satisfied and the candle has burned down, close the circle and thank the quarters as you normally do.

~

Prometheus's fire not only kept us warm, it sparked our imaginations and allowed works like Mary Shelley's *Frankenstein* to be created. Dr. Frankenstein stands a symbol to remind us how powerful but dangerous an illuminated mind might be. We can weave this new knowledge into our magical workings and come out as stronger beings.

Almanac Section

Calendar

Time Changes

Lunar Phases

Moon Signs

Full Moons

Sabbats

World Holidays

Incense of the Day

Color of the Day

Almanac Listings

In these listings you will find the date, day, lunar phase, Moon sign, color, and incense for the day, as well as festivals from around the world.

The Date

The date is used in numerological calculations that govern magical rites.

The Day

Each day is ruled by a planet that possesses specific magical influences:

MONDAY (MOON): Peace, sleep, healing, compassion, friends, psychic awareness, purification, and fertility.

TUESDAY (MARS): Passion, sex, courage, aggression, and protection.

WEDNESDAY (MERCURY): The conscious mind, study, travel, divination, and wisdom.

THURSDAY (JUPITER): Expansion, money, prosperity, and generosity.

FRIDAY (VENUS): Love, friendship, reconciliation, and beauty.

SATURDAY (SATURN): Longevity, exorcism, endings, homes, and houses.

SUNDAY (SUN): Healing, spirituality, success, strength, and protection.

The Lunar Phase

The lunar phase is important in determining the best times for magic.

THE WAXING MOON (from the New Moon to the Full) is the ideal time for magic to draw things toward you.

THE FULL MOON is the time of greatest power.

THE WANING MOON (from the Full Moon to the New) is a time for study, meditation, and little magical work (except magic designed to banish harmful energies).

The Moon's Sign

The Moon continuously "moves" through the zodiac, from Aries to Pisces. Each sign possesses its own significance.

ARIES: Good for starting things, but lacks staying power. Things occur rapidly, but quickly pass. People tend to be argumentative and assertive.

TAURUS: Things begun now last the longest, tend to increase in value, and become hard to alter. Brings out appreciation for beauty and sensory experience.

GEMINI: Things begun now are easily changed by outside influence. Time for shortcuts, communication, games, and fun.

CANCER: Stimulates emotional rapport between people. Pinpoints need, supports growth and nurturance. Tends to domestic concerns.

LEO: Draws emphasis to the self, central ideas, or institutions, away from connections with others and other emotional needs. People tend to be melodramatic.

VIRGO: Favors accomplishment of details and commands from higher up. Focuses on health, hygiene, and daily schedules.

LIBRA: Favors cooperation, social activities, beautification of surroundings, balance, and partnership.

SCORPIO: Increases awareness of psychic power. Precipitates psychic crises and ends connections thoroughly. People tend to brood and become secretive.

SAGITTARIUS: Encourages flights of imagination and confidence. This is an adventurous, philosophical, and athletic Moon sign. Favors expansion and growth.

CAPRICORN: Develops strong structure. Focus on traditions, responsibilities, and obligations. A good time to set boundaries and rules.

AQUARIUS: Rebellious energy. Time to break habits and make abrupt changes. Personal freedom and individuality is the focus.

PISCES: The focus is on dreaming, nostalgia, intuition, and psychic impressions. A good time for spiritual or philanthropic activities.

Color and Incense

The color and incense for the day are based on information from *Personal Alchemy* by Amber Wolfe, and relate to the planet that rules each day. This information can be taken into consideration along with other factors when planning works of magic or when blending magic into mundane life. Please note that the incense selections listed are not hard and fast. If you cannot find or do not like the incense listed for the day, choose a similar scent that appeals to you.

Festivals and Holidays

Festivals are listed throughout the year. The exact dates of many of these ancient festivals are difficult to determine; prevailing data has been used.

Time Changes

The times and dates of all astrological phenomena in this almanac are based on **Eastern Standard Time (EST)**. If you live outside of the Eastern time zone, you will need to make the following changes:

PACIFIC STANDARD TIME: Subtract three hours.

MOUNTAIN STANDARD TIME: Subtract two hours.

CENTRAL STANDARD TIME: Subtract one hour.

ALASKA: Subtract four hours.

HAWAII: Subtract five hours.

DAYLIGHT SAVING TIME (ALL ZONES): Add one hour.

Daylight Saving Time begins at 2 am on March 9, 2014, and ends at 2 am on November 2, 2014.

Please refer to a world time zone resource for time adjustments for locations outside the United States.

2014 Sabbats
and Full Moons

January 15	Cancer Full Moon 11:52 pm
February 2	Imbolc
February 14	Leo Full Moon 6:53 pm
March 16	Virgo Full Moon 1:08 pm
March 20	Ostara (Spring Equinox)
April 15	Libra Full Moon 3:42 am
May 1	Beltane
May 14	Scorpio Full Moon 3:16 pm
June 13	Sagittarius Full Moon 12:11 am
June 21	Midsummer (Summer Solstice)
July 12	Capricorn Full Moon 7:25 am
August 1	Lammas
August 10	Aquarius Full Moon 2:09 pm
September 8	Pisces Full Moon 9:38 pm
September 22	Mabon (Fall Equinox)
October 8	Aries Full Moon 6:51 am
October 31	Samhain
November 6	Taurus Full Moon 5:23 pm
December 6	Gemini Full Moon 7:27 am
December 21	Yule (Winter Solstice)

All times are Eastern Standard Time (EST)
or Eastern Daylight Time (EDT)

2014 Sabbats in the Southern Hemisphere

Because Earth's Northern and Southern Hemispheres experience opposite seasons at any given time, the season-based Sabbats listed on the previous page and in this almanac section are not correct for those residing south of the equator. Listed here are the Southern Hemisphere sabbat dates for 2014:

February 2	Lammas
March 20	Mabon (Fall Equinox)
May 1	Samhain
June 21	Yule (Winter Solstice)
August 2	Imbolc
September 22	Ostara (Spring Equinox)
November 1	Beltane
December 21	Midsummer (Summer Solstice)

☽ **Wednesday**
New Year's Day • Kwanzaa ends
Waning Moon
New Moon 6:14 am
Color: Yellow

Moon Sign: Capricorn
Incense: Marjoram

2 **Thursday**
First Writing Day (Japanese)
Waxing Moon
Moon phase: First Quarter
Color: Crimson

Moon Sign: Capricorn
Moon enters Aquarius 12:03 pm
Incense: Nutmeg

3 **Friday**
St. Genevieve's Day
Waxing Moon
Moon phase: First Quarter
Color: Pink

Moon Sign: Aquarius
Incense: Yarrow

4 **Saturday**
Frost Fairs on the Thames
Waxing Moon
Moon phase: First Quarter
Color: Blue

Moon Sign: Aquarius
Moon enters Pisces 11:58 am
Incense: Pine

5 **Sunday**
Epiphany Eve
Waxing Moon
Moon phase: First Quarter
Color: Gold

Moon Sign: Pisces
Incense: Eucalyptus

6 **Monday**
Epiphany
Waxing Moon
Moon phase: First Quarter
Color: Lavender

Moon Sign: Pisces
Moon enters Aries 2:45 pm
Incense: Narcissus

◐ **Tuesday**
Rizdvo (Ukrainian)
Waxing Moon
Second Quarter 10:39 pm
Color: Red

Moon Sign: Aries
Incense: Cinnamon
:

January

8   Wednesday
Midwives' Day
Waxing Moon
Moon phase: Second Quarter
Color: White

Moon Sign: Aries
Moon enters Taurus 9:24 pm
Incense: Lavender

9   Thursday
Feast of the Black Nazarene (Filipino)
Waxing Moon
Moon phase: Second Quarter
Color: Purple

Moon Sign: Taurus
Incense: Balsam

10   Friday
Business God's Day (Japanese)
Waxing Moon
Moon phase: Second Quarter
Color: White

Moon Sign: Taurus
Incense: Orchid

11   Saturday
Carmentalia (Roman)
Waxing Moon
Moon phase: Second Quarter
Color: Brown

Moon Sign: Taurus
Moon enters Gemini 7:26 am
Incense: Patchouli

12   Sunday
Revolution Day (Tanzanian)
Waxing Moon
Moon phase: Second Quarter
Color: Orange

Moon Sign: Gemini
Incense: Almond

13   Monday
Twentieth Day (Norwegian)
Waxing Moon
Moon phase: Second Quarter
Color: Gray

Moon Sign: Gemini
Moon enters Cancer 7:25 pm
Incense: Rosemary

14   Tuesday
Feast of the Ass (French)
Waxing Moon
Moon phase: Second Quarter
Color: Black

Moon Sign: Cancer
Incense: Ylang-ylang

Wednesday

Birthday of Martin Luther King, Jr. (actual)
Waxing Moon
Full Moon 11:52 pm
Color: Brown

Moon Sign: Cancer
Incense: Bay laurel

16 Thursday

Apprentices's Day
Waning Moon
Moon phase: Third Quarter
Color: White

Moon Sign: Cancer
Moon enters Leo 8:00 am
Incense: Myrrh

17 Friday

St. Anthony's Day (Mexican)
Waning Moon
Moon phase: Third Quarter
Color: Coral

Moon Sign: Leo
Incense: Alder

18 Saturday

Assumption Day
Waning Moon
Moon phase: Third Quarter
Color: Black

Moon Sign: Leo
Moon enters Virgo 8:23 pm
Incense: Rue

19 Sunday

Kitchen God Feast (Chinese)
Waning Moon
Moon phase: Third Quarter
Color: Yellow

Moon Sign: Virgo
Sun enters Aquarius 10:51 pm
Incense: Heliotrope

20 Monday

Birthday of Martin Luther King, Jr. (observed)
Waning Moon
Moon phase: Third Quarter
Color: White

Moon Sign: Virgo
Incense: Hyssop

21 Tuesday

St. Agnes's Day
Waning Moon
Moon phase: Third Quarter
Color: Maroon

Moon Sign: Virgo
Moon enters Libra 7:43 am
Incense: Basil

22 Wednesday
St. Vincent's Day (French)
Waning Moon
Moon phase: Third Quarter
Color: Topaz

Moon Sign: Libra
Incense: Honeysuckle

23 Thursday
St. Ildefonso's Day (French)
Waning Moon
Moon phase: Third Quarter
Color: Turquoise

Moon Sign: Libra
Moon enters Scorpio 4:43 pm
Incense: Carnation

◖ Friday
Alasitas Fair (Bolivian)
Waning Moon
Fourth Quarter 12:19 am
Color: Purple

Moon Sign: Scorpio
Incense: Cypress

25 Saturday
Burns' Night (Scottish)
Waning Moon
Moon phase: Fourth Quarter
Color: Gray

Moon Sign: Scorpio
Moon enters Sagittarius 10:13 pm
Incense: Sandalwood

26 Sunday
Republic Day (Indian)
Waning Moon
Moon phase: Fourth Quarter
Color: Amber

Moon Sign: Sagittarius
Incense: Marigold

27 Monday
Vogelgruff (Swiss)
Waning Moon
Moon phase: Fourth Quarter
Color: Silver

Moon Sign: Sagittarius
Incense: Neroli

28 Tuesday
Rizdvo (Ukrainian)
Waning Moon
Moon phase: Fourth Quarter
Color: White

Moon Sign: Sagittarius
Moon enters Capricorn 12:04 am
Incense: Geranium

29 **Wednesday**
Australia Day
Waning Moon
Moon phase: Fourth Quarter
Color: Yellow

Moon Sign: Capricorn
Moon enters Aquarius 11:33 pm
Incense: Lilac

 Thursday
Three Hierarchs Day (Eastern Orthodox)
Waning Moon
New Moon 4:39 pm
Color: Green

Moon Sign: Aquarius
Incense: Mulberry

31 **Friday**
Chinese New Year (horse)
Waxing Moon
Moon phase: First Quarter
Color: Rose

Moon Sign: Aquarius
Moon enters Pisces 10:45 pm
Incense: Vanilla

Magical Vacation

If the longer nights and shorter days of winter are getting you down, you could take a vacation to Tahiti. Or you could try a short magical vacation instead. Find a couple of items that represent your dream get-away and put them on your altar. Light a white or yellow candle. If you want, put on appropriate mood music. Then close your eyes and visualize yourself where you want to be. Call in the elements: hear the sound of the water, or feel the wind in your hair. Invite along the god or goddess who suits the place best. Remember to relax and repeat as needed!

–Deborah Blake

February

1   Saturday
St. Brigid's Day (Irish)
Waxing Moon
Moon phase: First Quarter
Color: Indigo

Moon Sign: Pisces
Incense: Ivy

---

2   Sunday
Imbolc • Groundhog Day
Waxing Moon
Moon phase: First Quarter
Color: Orange

Moon Sign: Pisces
Moon enters Aries 11:55 pm
Incense: Hyacinth

---

3   Monday
St. Blaise's Day
Waxing Moon
Moon phase: First Quarter
Color: Gray

Moon Sign: Aries
Incense: Lily

---

4   Tuesday
Independence Day (Sri Lankan)
Waxing Moon
Moon phase: First Quarter
Color: Red

Moon Sign: Aries
Incense: Bayberry

---

5   Wednesday
Festival de la Alcaldesa (Italian)
Waxing Moon
Moon phase: First Quarter
Color: Topaz

Moon Sign: Aries
Moon enters Taurus 4:47 am
Incense: Honeysuckle

☾   Thursday
Bob Marley's Birthday (Jamaican)
Waxing Moon
Second Quarter 2:22 pm
Color: White

Moon Sign: Taurus
Incense: Clove

---

7   Friday
Full Moon Poya (Sri Lankan)
Waxing Moon
Moon phase: Second Quarter
Color: Purple

Moon Sign: Taurus
Moon enters Gemini 1:44 pm
Incense: Violet

February

8 **Saturday**
Mass for Broken Needles (Japanese)
Waxing Moon
Moon phase: Second Quarter
Color: Black

Moon Sign: Gemini
Incense: Sage

9 **Sunday**
St. Marion's Day (Lebanese)
Waxing Moon
Moon phase: Second Quarter
Color: Yellow

Moon Sign: Gemini
Incense: Frankincense

10 **Monday**
Gasparilla Day (Floridian)
Waxing Moon
Moon phase: Second Quarter
Color: Lavender

Moon Sign: Gemini
Moon enters Cancer 1:33 am
Incense: Clary sage

11 **Tuesday**
Foundation Day (Japanese)
Waxing Moon
Moon phase: Second Quarter
Color: Black

Moon Sign: Cancer
Incense: Ginger

12 **Wednesday**
Lincoln's Birthday (actual)
Waxing Moon
Moon phase: Second Quarter
Color: White

Moon Sign: Cancer
Moon enters Leo 2:15 pm
Incense: Marjoram

13 **Thursday**
Parentalia (Roman)
Waxing Moon
Moon phase: Second Quarter
Color: Crimson

Moon Sign: Leo
Incense: Apricot

☺ Friday
Valentine's Day
Waxing Moon
Full Moon 6:53 pm
Color: White

Moon Sign: Leo
Incense: Thyme

February

15 Saturday
Lupercalia (Roman)
Waning Moon
Moon phase: Third Quarter
Color: Brown

Moon Sign: Leo
Moon enters Virgo 2:26 am
Incense: Magnolia

16 Sunday
Fumi-e (Japanese)
Waning Moon
Moon phase: Third Quarter
Color: Amber

Moon Sign: Virgo
Incense: Juniper

17 Monday
Presidents' Day (observed)
Waning Moon
Moon phase: Third Quarter
Color: White

Moon Sign: Virgo
Moon enters Libra 1:23 pm
Incense: Rosemary

18 Tuesday
Saint Bernadette's Second Vision
Waning Moon
Moon phase: Third Quarter
Color: Scarlet

Moon Sign: Libra
Sun enters Pisces 12:59 pm
Incense: Cedar

19 Wednesday
Pero Palo's Trial (Spanish)
Waning Moon
Moon phase: Third Quarter
Color: Yellow

Moon Sign: Libra
Moon enters Scorpio 10:33 pm
Incense: Lilac

20 Thursday
Installation of the New Lama (Tibetan)
Waning Moon
Moon phase: Third Quarter
Color: Green

Moon Sign: Scorpio
Incense: Jasmine

21 Friday
Feast of Lanterns (Chinese)
Waning Moon
Moon phase: Third Quarter
Color: Rose

Moon Sign: Scorpio
Incense: Rose

February

○ **Saturday**
Caristia (Roman)
Waning Moon
Fourth Quarter 12:15 pm
Color: Gray

Moon Sign: Scorpio
Moon enters Sagittarius 5:12 am
Incense: Patchouli

---

23 Sunday
Terminalia (Roman)
Waning Moon
Moon phase: Fourth Quarter
Color: Gold

Moon Sign: Sagittarius
Incense: Almond

---

24 Monday
Regifugium (Roman)
Waning Moon
Moon phase: Fourth Quarter
Color: Silver

Moon Sign: Sagittarius
Moon enters Capricorn 8:50 am
Incense: Hyssop

---

25 Tuesday
Saint Walburga's Day (German)
Waning Moon
Moon phase: Fourth Quarter
Color: White

Moon Sign: Capricorn
Incense: Basil

---

26 Wednesday
Zamboanga Festival (Filipino)
Waning Moon
Moon phase: Fourth Quarter
Color: Brown

Moon Sign: Capricorn
Moon enters Aquarius 9:55 am
Incense: Bay laurel

---

27 Thursday
Threepenny Day
Waning Moon
Moon phase: Fourth Quarter
Color: Purple

Moon Sign: Aquarius
Incense: Nutmeg

---

28 Friday
Kalevala Day (Finnish)
Waning Moon
Moon phase: Fourth Quarter
Color: Pink

Moon Sign: Aquarius
Moon enters Pisces 9:53 am
Incense: Mint

☽ **Saturday**
Matronalia (Roman)
Waning Moon
New Moon 3:00 am
Color: Blue

Moon Sign: Pisces
Incense: Sage

2 **Sunday**
St. Chad's Day (English)
Waxing Moon
Moon phase: First Quarter
Color: Amber

Moon Sign: Pisces
Moon enters Aries 10:40 am
Incense: Marigold

3 **Monday**
Doll Festival (Japanese)
Waxing Moon
Moon phase: First Quarter
Color: Ivory

Moon Sign: Aries
Incense: Narcissus

4 **Tuesday**
Mardi Gras (Fat Tuesday)
Waxing Moon
Moon phase: First Quarter
Color: Black

Moon Sign: Aries
Moon enters Taurus 2:12 pm
Incense: Ylang-ylang

5 **Wednesday**
Ash Wednesday
Waxing Moon
Moon phase: First Quarter
Color: White

Moon Sign: Taurus
Incense: Lavender

6 **Thursday**
Alamo Day
Waxing Moon
Moon phase: First Quarter
Color: Crimson

Moon Sign: Taurus
Moon enters Gemini 9:37 pm
Incense: Myrrh

7 **Friday**
Bird and Arbor Day
Waxing Moon
Moon phase: First Quarter
Color: Coral

Moon Sign: Gemini
Incense: Orchid

March

○ **Saturday**
International Women's Day
Waxing Moon
Second Quarter 8:27 am
Color: Gray

Moon Sign: Gemini
Incense: Rue

9 Sunday
Daylight Saving Time begins
Waxing
Moon phase: Second Quarter
Color: Gold

Moon Sign: Gemini
Moon enters Cancer 9:33 am
Incense: Eucalyptus

10 Monday
Tibet Day
Waxing Moon
Moon phase: Second Quarter
Color: White

Moon Sign: Cancer
Incense: Lily

11 Tuesday
Feast of the Gauri (Hindu)
Waxing Moon
Moon phase: Second Quarter
Color: Maroon

Moon Sign: Cancer
Moon enters Leo 10:09 pm
Incense: Ginger

12 Wednesday
Receiving the Water (Buddhist)
Waxing Moon
Moon phase: Second Quarter
Color: Yellow

Moon Sign: Leo
Incense: Marjoram

13 Thursday
Purification Feast (Balinese)
Waxing Moon
Moon phase: Second Quarter
Color: Turquoise

Moon Sign: Leo
Incense: Mulberry

14 Friday
Mamuralia (Roman)
Waxing Moon
Moon phase: Second Quarter
Color: Purple

Moon Sign: Leo
Moon enters Virgo 10:17 am
Incense: Cypress

March ♈

15 Saturday
Phallus Festival (Japanese)
Waxing Moon
Moon phase: Second Quarter
Color: Brown

Moon Sign: Virgo
Incense: Magnolia

☺ Sunday
St. Urho's Day (Finnish)
Waxing Moon
Full Moon 1:08 pm
Color: Orange

Moon Sign: Virgo
Moon enters Libra 8:46 pm
Incense: Heliotrope

17 Monday
St. Patrick's Day
Waning Moon
Moon phase: Third Quarter
Color: Silver

Moon Sign: Libra
Incense: Neroli

18 Tuesday
Sheelah's Day (Irish)
Waning Moon
Moon phase: Third Quarter
Color: White

Moon Sign: Libra
Incense: Cinnamon

19 Wednesday
St. Joseph's Day (Sicilian)
Waning Moon
Moon phase: Third Quarter
Color: Brown

Moon Sign: Libra
Moon enters Scorpio 5:13 am
Incense: Honeysuckle

20 Thursday
Ostara • Spring Equinox • International Astrology Day
Waning Moon
Moon phase: Third Quarter
Color: Green

Moon Sign: Scorpio
Sun enters Aries 12:57 pm
Incense: Apricot

21 Friday
Juarez Day (Mexican)
Waning Moon
Moon phase: Third Quarter
Color: Pink

Moon Sign: Scorpio
Moon enters Sagittarius 11:39 am
Incense: Violet

March ♈

22 Saturday
Hilaria (Roman)   Moon Sign: Sagittarius
Waning Moon   Incense: Sandalwood
Moon phase: Third Quarter
Color: Black

☾ Sunday
Pakistan Day   Moon Sign: Sagittarius
Waning Moon   Moon enters Capricorn 4:03 pm
Fourth Quarter 9:46 pm   Incense: Frankincense
Color: Yellow

24 Monday
Day of Blood (Roman)   Moon Sign: Capricorn
Waning Moon   Incense: Clary sage
Moon phase: Fourth Quarter
Color: Gray

25 Tuesday
Tichborne Dole (English)   Moon Sign: Capricorn
Waning Moon   Moon enters Aquarius 6:39 pm
Moon phase: Fourth Quarter   Incense: Bayberry
Color: Red

26 Wednesday
Prince Kuhio Day (Hawaiian)   Moon Sign: Aquarius
Waning Moon   Incense: Lilac
Moon phase: Fourth Quarter
Color: Topaz

27 Thursday
Smell the Breezes Day (Egyptian)   Moon Sign: Aquarius
Waning Moon   Moon enters Pisces 8:10 pm
Moon phase: Fourth Quarter   Incense: Carnation
Color: White

28 Friday
Rizdvo (Ukrainian)   Moon Sign: Pisces
Waning Moon   Incense: Rose
Moon phase: Fourth Quarter
Color: Rose

29 Saturday
Feast of St. Eustace's of Luxeuil
Waning Moon
Moon phase: Fourth Quarter
Color: Indigo

Moon Sign: Pisces
Moon enters Aries 9:54 pm
Incense: Pine

 Sunday
Seward's Day (Alaskan)
Waning Moon
New Moon 2:45 pm
Color: Amber

Moon Sign: Aries
Incense: Hyacinth

31 Monday
The Borrowed Days (Ethiopian)
Waxing Moon
Moon phase: First Quarter
Color: Lavender

Moon Sign: Aries
Incense: Hyssop

Put Out Positive Energy

As Witches, many of us believe that what we put out into the world is what we get back; some call that the Law of Returns. But it is also important to put out "good" even if you aren't going to get anything out of it at all. After all, if our thoughts and words and prayers have the ability to change the world (and they do), why not use them for the good of all? Take a moment each day to say to the gods, "Please help the world to move in a better direction," or send the hope for peace out into the universe. Beam love out into every corner of the world, just because you can.

–Deborah Blake

April ♈

1 Tuesday
April Fools' Day
Waxing Moon
Moon phase: First Quarter
Color: Black

Moon Sign: Aries
Moon enters Taurus 1:20 am
Incense: Geranium

2 Wednesday
The Battle of Flowers (French)
Waxing Moon
Moon phase: First Quarter
Color: Brown

Moon Sign: Taurus
Incense: Lilac

3 Thursday
Thirteenth Day (Iranian)
Waxing Moon
Moon phase: First Quarter
Color: Purple

Moon Sign: Taurus
Moon enters Gemini 7:48 am
Incense: Clove

4 Friday
Megalesia (Roman)
Waxing Moon
Moon phase: First Quarter
Color: White

Moon Sign: Gemini
Incense: Yarrow

5 Saturday
Tomb-Sweeping Day (Chinese)
Waxing Moon
Moon phase: First Quarter
Color: Gray

Moon Sign: Gemini
Moon enters Cancer 5:40 pm
Incense: Sandalwood

6 Sunday
Chakri Day (Thai)
Waxing Moon
Moon phase: First Quarter
Color: Gold

Moon Sign: Cancer
Incense: Juniper

◖ **Monday**
Festival of Pure Brightness (Chinese)
Waxing Moon
Second Quarter 4:31 am
Color: White

Moon Sign: Cancer
Incense: Clary sage

April ♈

8 Tuesday
Buddha's Birthday
Waxing Moon
Moon phase: Second Quarter
Color: Scarlet

Moon Sign: Cancer
Moon enters Leo 5:50 am
Incense: Cedar

9 Wednesday
Valour Day (Filipino)
Waxing Moon
Moon phase: Second Quarter
Color: Yellow

Moon Sign: Leo
Incense: Honeysuckle

10 Thursday
The Tenth of April (English)
Waxing Moon
Moon phase: Second Quarter
Color: Turquoise

Moon Sign: Leo
Moon enters Virgo 6:08 pm
Incense: Jasmine

11 Friday
Heroes Day (Costa Rican)
Waxing Moon
Moon phase: Second Quarter
Color: Purple

Moon Sign: Virgo
Incense: Alder

12 Saturday
Cerealia (Roman)
Waxing Moon
Moon phase: Second Quarter
Color: Blue

Moon Sign: Virgo
Incense: Ivy

13 Sunday
Palm Sunday
Waxing Moon
Moon phase: Second Quarter
Color: Orange

Moon Sign: Virgo
Moon enters Libra 4:33 am
Incense: Marigold

14 Monday
Sanno Festival (Japanese)
Waxing Moon
Moon phase: Second Quarter
Color: Gray

Moon Sign: Libra
Incense: Neroli

April

Tuesday
Passover begins
Waxing Moon
Full Moon 3:42 am
Color: Red

Moon Sign: Libra
Moon enters Scorpio 12:20 pm
Incense: Cinnamon

16 Wednesday
Zurich Spring Festival (Swiss)
Waning Moon
Moon phase: Third Quarter
Color: White

Moon Sign: Scorpio
Incense: Marjoram

17 Thursday
Yayoi Matsuri (Japanese)
Waning Moon
Moon phase: Third Quarter
Color: Crimson

Moon Sign: Scorpio
Moon enters Sagittarius 5:44 pm
Incense: Apricot

18 Friday
Good Friday • Orthodox Good Friday
Waning Moon
Moon phase: Third Quarter
Color: Coral

Moon Sign: Sagittarius
Incense: Vanilla

19 Saturday
Cerealia last day (Roman)
Waning Moon
Moon phase: Third Quarter
Color: Brown

Moon Sign: Sagittarius
Sun enters Taurus 11:56 pm
Moon enters Capricorn 9:28 pm
Incense: Sage

20 Sunday
Easter • Orthodox Easter
Waning Moon
Moon phase: Third Quarter
Color: Amber

Moon Sign: Capricorn
Incense: Almond

21 Monday
Tiradentes Day (Brazilian)
Waning Moon
Moon phase: Third Quarter
Color: Silver

Moon Sign: Capricorn
Incense: Rosemary

◖ **Tuesday**
Earth Day • Passover ends
Waning Moon
Fourth Quarter 3:52 am
Color: White

Moon Sign: Capricorn
Moon enters Aquarius 12:18 am
Incense: Ylang-ylang

23 **Wednesday**
St. George's Day (English)
Waning Moon
Moon phase: Fourth Quarter
Color: Topaz

Moon Sign: Aquarius
Incense: Bay laurel

24 **Thursday**
St. Mark's Eve
Waning Moon
Moon phase: Fourth Quarter
Color: White

Moon Sign: Aquarius
Moon enters Pisces 2:55 am
Incense: Clove

25 **Friday**
Robigalia (Roman)
Waning Moon
Moon phase: Fourth Quarter
Color: Rose

Moon Sign: Pisces
Incense: Thyme

26 **Saturday**
Arbor Day
Waning Moon
Moon phase: Fourth Quarter
Color: Black

Moon Sign: Pisces
Moon enters Aries 6:01 am
Incense: Magnolia

27 **Sunday**
Humabon's Conversion (Filipino)
Waning Moon
Moon phase: Fourth Quarter
Color: Yellow

Moon Sign: Aries
Incense: Eucalyptus

28 **Monday**
Floralia (Roman)
Waning Moon
Moon phase: Fourth Quarter
Color: Ivory

Moon Sign: Aries
Moon enters Taurus 10:23 am
Incense: Narcissus

April

☽ Tuesday
Green Day (Japanese)
Waning Moon
New Moon 2:14 am
Color: Gray

Moon Sign: Taurus
Incense: Basil

30 Wednesday
Walpurgis Night • May Eve
Waxing Moon
Moon phase: First Quarter
Color: White

Moon Sign: Taurus
Moon enters Gemini 4:56 pm
Incense: Lavender

Watch Your Words

Witches say that words have power, but what does that mean to our everyday lives? Since words are a way of putting our intentions out into the universe (which is why we speak our spells aloud), it is important to be sure your words are sending the message you want. Spent a day truly listening to yourself. Are you critical of yourself or others? Is your attitude positive or negative? Are your words kind or hurtful? If you're not happy with what you hear, make an effort to watch what you say in the days that lie ahead. Because words really do have power, but you have power over your words.

–Deborah Blake

May

1   Thursday
Beltane • May Day
Waxing Moon
Moon phase: First Quarter
Color: Green

Moon Sign: Gemini
Incense: Jasmine

2   Friday
Big Kite Flying (Japanese)
Waxing Moon
Moon phase: First Quarter
Color: Pink

Moon Sign: Gemini
Incense: Mint

3   Saturday
Holy Cross Day
Waxing Moon
Moon phase: First Quarter
Color: Brown

Moon Sign: Gemini
Moon enters Cancer 2:13 am
Incense: Pine

4   Sunday
Frost Fairs on the Thames
Waxing Moon
Moon phase: First Quarter
Color: Orange

Moon Sign: Cancer
Incense: Heliotrope

5   Monday
Cinco de Mayo (Mexican)
Waxing Moon
Moon phase: First Quarter
Color: Lavender

Moon Sign: Cancer
Moon enters Leo 1:55 pm
Incense: Rosemary

◑   Tuesday
Martyrs' Day (Lebanese)
Waxing Moon
Second Quarter 11:15 pm
Color: Scarlet

Moon Sign: Leo
Incense: Bayberry

7   Wednesday
Pilgrimage of St. Nicholas (Italian)
Waxing Moon
Moon phase: Second Quarter
Color: Brown

Moon Sign: Leo
Incense: Honeysuckle

May

8 Thursday
Liberation Day (French)
Waxing Moon
Moon phase: Second Quarter
Color: White

Moon Sign: Leo
Moon enters Virgo 2:24 pm
Incense: Balsam

9 Friday
Lemuria (Roman)
Waxing Moon
Moon phase: Second Quarter
Color: Coral

Moon Sign: Virgo
Incense: Rose

10 Saturday
Census Day (Canadian)
Waxing Moon
Moon phase: Second Quarter
Color: Black

Moon Sign: Virgo
Moon enters Libra 1:19 pm
Incense: Patchouli

11 Sunday
Mother's Day
Waxing Moon
Moon phase: Second Quarter
Color: Gold

Moon Sign: Libra
Incense: Frankincense

12 Monday
Florence Nightingale's Birthday
Waxing Moon
Moon phase: Second Quarter
Color: Silver

Moon Sign: Libra
Moon enters Scorpio 9:07 pm
Incense: Hyssop

13 Tuesday
Pilgrimage to Fatima (Portuguese)
Waxing Moon
Moon phase: Second Quarter
Color: White

Moon Sign: Scorpio
Incense: Cedar

☺ Wednesday
Carabao Festival (Spanish)
Waxing Moon
Full Moon 3:16 pm
Color: Yellow

Moon Sign: Scorpio
Incense: Bay laurel

May
♊

15 Thursday
Festival of St. Dympna (Belgian)
Waning Moon
Moon phase: Third Quarter
Color: Turquoise

Moon Sign: Scorpio
Moon enters Sagittarius 1:44 am
Incense: Carnation

16 Friday
St. Honoratus' Day
Waning Moon
Moon phase: Third Quarter
Color: Purple

Moon Sign: Sagittarius
Incense: Cypress

17 Saturday
Norwegian Independence Day
Waning Moon
Moon phase: Third Quarter
Color: Indigo

Moon Sign: Sagittarius
Moon enters Capricorn 4:12 am
Incense: Rue

18 Sunday
Las Piedras Day (Uruguayan)
Waning Moon
Moon phase: Third Quarter
Color: Amber

Moon Sign: Capricorn
Incense: Juniper

19 Monday
Pilgrimage to Treguier (French)
Waning Moon
Moon phase: Third Quarter
Color: White

Moon Sign: Capricorn
Moon enters Aquarius 5:58 am
Incense: Neroli

20 Tuesday
Pardon of the Singers (British)
Waning Moon
Moon phase: Third Quarter
Color: Black

Moon Sign: Aquarius
Sun enters Gemini 10:59 pm
Incense: Geranium

☽ Wednesday
Victoria Day (Canadian)
Waning Moon
Fourth Quarter 8:59 am
Color: Topaz

Moon Sign: Aquarius
Moon enters Pisces 8:18 am
Incense: Lavender

May

22 Thursday
Heroes' Day (Sri Lankan)
Waning Moon
Moon phase: Fourth Quarter
Color: Purple

Moon Sign: Pisces
Incense: Nutmeg

23 Friday
Tubilustrium (Roman)
Waning Moon
Moon phase: Fourth Quarter
Color: Rose

Moon Sign: Pisces
Moon enters Aries 12:01 pm
Incense: Yarrow

24 Saturday
Culture Day (Bulgarian)
Waning Moon
Moon phase: Fourth Quarter
Color: Gray

Moon Sign: Aries
Incense: Ivy

25 Sunday
Urbanas Diena (Latvian)
Waning Moon
Moon phase: Fourth Quarter
Color: Yellow

Moon Sign: Aries
Moon enters Taurus 5:28 pm
Incense: Hyacinth

26 Monday
Memorial Day (observed)
Waning Moon
Moon phase: Fourth Quarter
Color: Gray

Moon Sign: Taurus
Incense: Lily

27 Tuesday
St. Augustine of Canterbury's Day
Waning Moon
Moon phase: Fourth Quarter
Color: Black

Moon Sign: Taurus
Incense: Ginger

☽ Wednesday
St. Germain's Day
Waning Moon
New Moon 2:40 pm
Color: Brown

Moon Sign: Taurus
Moon enters Gemini 12:47 am
Incense: Bay laurel

May

29 Thursday
Royal Oak Day (English)
Waxing Moon
Moon phase: First Quarter
Color: Crimson

Moon Sign: Gemini
Incense: Myrrh

30 Friday
Memorial Day (actual)
Waxing Moon
Moon phase: First Quarter
Color: White

Moon Sign: Gemini
Moon enters Cancer 10:13 am
Incense: Violet

31 Saturday
Flowers of May
Waxing Moon
Moon phase: First Quarter
Color: Blue

Moon Sign: Cancer
Incense: Sage

❖

Explore Religious Diversity

One of the great things about modern Witchcraft is the way we gather what is good and useful from many cultures and experiences and pull them all together into something that works for us as Pagans. But it is easy to get stuck in a rut. If you normally tend towards one particular pantheon or culture (Celtic, for instance, or Greek), why not make the effort to explore something further out of your comfort zone? Find out something about Yemaya, for instance (Africa) or the Norse gods (like Thor). Offer to share some of your Pagan beliefs with others; you'd be surprised how many people have no idea what it is we believe in, and would be interested in learning about it.

–Deborah Blake

June

♊

1   Sunday
National Day (Tunisian)
Waxing Moon
Moon phase: First Quarter
Color: Gold

Moon Sign: Cancer
Moon enters Leo 9:43 pm
Incense: Juniper

2   Monday
Rice Harvest Festival (Malaysian)
Waxing Moon
Moon phase: First Quarter
Color: Ivory

Moon Sign: Leo
Incense: Narcissus

3   Tuesday
Memorial to Broken Dolls (Japanese)
Waxing Moon
Moon phase: First Quarter
Color: Maroon

Moon Sign: Leo
Incense: Cinnamon

4   Wednesday
Shavuot
Waxing Moon
Moon phase: First Quarter
Color: Yellow

Moon Sign: Leo
Moon enters Virgo 10:20 am
Incense: Marjoram

◐   **Thursday**
Constitution Day (Danish)
Waxing Moon
Second Quarter 4:39 pm
Color: White

Moon Sign: Virgo
Incense: Mulberry

6   Friday
Swedish Flag Day
Waxing Moon
Moon phase: Second Quarter
Color: Purple

Moon Sign: Virgo
Moon enters Libra 10:01 pm
Incense: Orchid

7   Saturday
St. Robert of Newminster's Day
Waxing Moon
Moon phase: Second Quarter
Color: Black

Moon Sign: Libra
Incense: Patchouli

June

8 Sunday
St. Medard's Day (Belgian)
Waxing Moon
Moon phase: Second Quarter
Color: Orange

Moon Sign: Libra
Incense: Marigold

9 Monday
Vestalia (Roman)
Waxing Moon
Moon phase: Second Quarter
Color: Silver

Moon Sign: Libra
Moon enters Scorpio 6:38 am
Incense: Lily

10 Tuesday
Time-Observance Day (Chinese)
Waxing Moon
Moon phase: Second Quarter
Color: Red

Moon Sign: Scorpio
Incense: Basil

11 Wednesday
Kamehameha Day (Hawaiian)
Waxing Moon
Moon phase: Second Quarter
Color: White

Moon Sign: Scorpio
Moon enters Sagittarius 11:23 am
Incense: Lilac

12 Thursday
Independence Day (Filipino)
Waxing Moon
Moon phase: Second Quarter
Color: Green

Moon Sign: Sagittarius
Incense: Clove

☺ Friday
St. Anthony of Padua's Day
Waxing Moon
Full Moon 12:11 am
Color: Pink

Moon Sign: Sagittarius
Moon enters Capricorn 1:04 pm
Incense: Thyme

14 Saturday
Flag Day
Waning Moon
Moon phase: Third Quarter
Color: Blue

Moon Sign: Capricorn
Incense: Pine

June ♋

15 Sunday
Father's Day
Waning Moon
Moon phase: Third Quarter
Color: Yellow

Moon Sign: Capricorn
Moon enters Aquarius 1:27 pm
Incense: Almond

16 Monday
Bloomsday (Irish)
Waning Moon
Moon phase: Third Quarter
Color: Lavender

Moon Sign: Aquarius
Incense: Hyssop

17 Tuesday
Bunker Hill Day
Waning Moon
Moon phase: Third Quarter
Color: White

Moon Sign: Aquarius
Moon enters Pisces 2:26 pm
Incense: Ylang-ylang

18 Wednesday
Independence Day (Egyptian)
Waning Moon
Moon phase: Third Quarter
Color: Topaz

Moon Sign: Pisces
Incense: Honeysuckle

◖ Thursday
Juneteenth
Waning Moon
Fourth Quarter 2:39 pm
Color: Purple

Moon Sign: Pisces
Moon enters Aries 5:26 pm
Incense: Apricot

20 Friday
Flag Day (Argentinian)
Waning Moon
Moon phase: Fourth Quarter
Color: White

Moon Sign: Aries
Incense: Alder

21 Saturday
Midsummer • Summer Solstice
Waning Moon
Moon phase: Fourth Quarter
Color: Brown

Moon Sign: Aries
Sun enters Cancer 6:51 am
Moon enters Taurus 11:03 pm
Incense: Sandalwood

June

22 Sunday
Rose Festival (English)
Waning Moon
Moon phase: Fourth Quarter
Color: Amber

Moon Sign: Taurus
Incense: Eucalyptus

23 Monday
St. John's Eve
Waning Moon
Moon phase: Fourth Quarter
Color: White

Moon Sign: Taurus
Incense: Rosemary

24 Tuesday
St. John's Day
Waning Moon
Moon phase: Fourth Quarter
Color: Scarlet

Moon Sign: Taurus
Moon enters Gemini 7:05 am
Incense: Bayberry

25 Wednesday
Fiesta of Santa Orosia (Spanish)
Waning Moon
Moon phase: Fourth Quarter
Color: White

Moon Sign: Gemini
Incense: Marjoram

26 Thursday
Pied Piper Day (German)
Waning Moon
Moon phase: Fourth Quarter
Color: Turquoise

Moon Sign: Gemini
Moon enters Cancer 5:05 pm
Incense: Jasmine

☽ Friday
Day of the Seven Sleepers (Islamic)
Waning Moon
New Moon 4:08 am
Color: Rose

Moon Sign: Cancer
Incense: Mint

28 Saturday
Ramadan begins
Waxing Moon
Moon phase: First Quarter
Color: Indigo

Moon Sign: Cancer
Incense: Magnolia

June

29 **Sunday**
Feast of Saints Peter and Paul
Waxing Moon
Moon phase: First Quarter
Color: Gold

Moon Sign: Cancer
Moon enters Leo 4:43 am
Incense: Frankincense

30 **Monday**
The Burning of the Three Firs (French)
Waxing Moon
Moon phase: First Quarter
Color: Gray

Moon Sign: Leo
Incense: Neroli

Celebrate the Dark Moon

Most of us focus our practice on the Full Moon, when the goddess smiles down on us in all Her light and glory. But other times of the moon cycle have power, too. The dark moon, when Her face is hidden, is a good time for banishing rituals or protective work. It is well suited for looking inward, as well as divination work of all kinds. Folklore tells us to plant certain things during the dark moon, like root vegetables that grow underground. And if you want to try shamanic journeying, the dark moon is the perfect time to crawl down into the earth and visit the lower worlds. Just be sure to come back up in time to celebrate the rest of the lunar cycle!

–Deborah Blake

July

1   **Tuesday**
Climbing Mount Fuji (Japanese)
Waxing Moon
Moon phase: First Quarter
Color: Black

Moon Sign: Leo
Moon enters Virgo 5:24 pm
Incense: Ginger

2   **Wednesday**
Heroes' Day (Zambian)
Waxing Moon
Moon phase: First Quarter
Color: Topaz

Moon Sign: Virgo
Incense: Lilac

3   **Thursday**
Indian Sun Dance (Native American)
Waxing Moon
Moon phase: First Quarter
Color: Crimson

Moon Sign: Virgo
Incense: Carnation

4   **Friday**
Independence Day
Waxing Moon
Moon phase: First Quarter
Color: White

Moon Sign: Libra
Moon enters Libra 5:43 am
Incense: Alder

☾   **Saturday**
Tynwald (Nordic)
Waxing Moon
Second Quarter 7:59 am
Color: Gray

Moon Sign: Libra
Incense: Rue

6   **Sunday**
Khao Phansa Day (Thai)
Waxing Moon
Moon phase: Second Quarter
Color: Amber

Moon Sign: Libra
Moon enters Scorpio 3:33 pm
Incense: Hyacinth

7   **Monday**
Weaver's Festival (Japanese)
Waxing Moon
Moon phase: Second Quarter
Color: Silver

Moon Sign: Scorpio
Incense: Clary sage

July

8 **Tuesday**
St. Elizabeth's Day (Portuguese)
Waxing Moon
Moon phase: Second Quarter
Color: Red

Moon Sign: Scorpio
Moon enters Sagittarius 9:24 pm
Incense: Cedar

9 **Wednesday**
Battle of Sempach Day (Swiss)
Waxing Moon
Moon phase: Second Quarter
Color: Yellow

Moon Sign: Sagittarius
Incense: Bay laurel

10 **Thursday**
Lady Godiva Day (English)
Waxing Moon
Moon phase: Second Quarter
Color: Purple

Moon Sign: Sagittarius
Moon enters Capricorn 11:24 pm
Incense: Nutmeg

11 **Friday**
Revolution Day (Mongolian)
Waxing Moon
Moon phase: Second Quarter
Color: Coral

Moon Sign: Capricorn
Incense: Violet

☺ Saturday
Lobster Carnival (Nova Scotian)
Waxing Moon
Full Moon 7:25 am
Color: Brown

Moon Sign: Capricorn
Moon enters Aquarius 11:07 pm
Incense: Sage

13 **Sunday**
Festival of the Three Cows (Spanish)
Waning Moon
Moon phase: Third Quarter
Color: Orange

Moon Sign: Aquarius
Incense: Heliotrope

14 **Monday**
Bastille Day (French)
Waning Moon
Moon phase: Third Quarter
Color: White

Moon Sign: Aquarius
Moon enters Pisces 10:40 pm
Incense: Rosemary

July

15 Tuesday
St. Swithin's Day
Waning Moon
Moon phase: Third Quarter
Color: Gray

Moon Sign: Pisces
Incense: Basil

16 Wednesday
Our Lady of Carmel
Waning Moon
Moon phase: Third Quarter
Color: Brown

Moon Sign: Pisces
Incense: Lavender

17 Thursday
Rivera Day (Puerto Rican)
Waning Moon
Moon phase: Third Quarter
Color: Turquoise

Moon Sign: Pisces
Moon enters Aries 12:07 am
Incense: Balsam

◑ Friday
Gion Matsuri Festival (Japanese)
Waning Moon
Fourth Quarter 10:08 pm
Color: Purple

Moon Sign: Aries
Incense: Rose

19 Saturday
Flitch Day (English)
Waning Moon
Moon phase: Fourth Quarter
Color: Blue

Moon Sign: Aries
Moon enters Taurus 4:43 am
Incense: Pine

20 Sunday
Binding of Wreaths (Lithuanian)
Waning Moon
Moon phase: Fourth Quarter
Color: Gold

Moon Sign: Taurus
Incense: Marigold

21 Monday
National Day (Belgian)
Waning Moon
Moon phase: Fourth Quarter
Color: Ivory

Moon Sign: Taurus
Moon enters Gemini 12:36 pm
Incense: Narcissus

22 Tuesday
St. Mary Magdalene's Day
Waning Moon
Moon phase: Fourth Quarter
Color: Maroon

Moon Sign: Gemini
Sun enters Leo 5:41 pm
Incense: Geranium

23 Wednesday
Mysteries of Santa Cristina (Italian)
Waning Moon
Moon phase: Fourth Quarter
Color: White

Moon Sign: Gemini
Moon enters Cancer 10:59 pm
Incense: Marjoram

24 Thursday
Pioneer Day (Mormon)
Waning Moon
Moon phase: Fourth Quarter
Color: Green

Moon Sign: Cancer
Incense: Myrrh

25 Friday
St. James' Day
Waning Moon
Moon phase: Fourth Quarter
Color: Pink

Moon Sign: Cancer
Incense: Thyme

☽ Saturday
St. Anne's Day
Waning Moon
New Moon 6:42 pm
Color: Black

Moon Sign: Cancer
Moon enters Leo 6:42 pm
Incense: Ivy

27 Sunday
Ramadan ends
Waxing Moon
Moon phase: First Quarter
Color: Yellow

Moon Sign: Leo
Incense: Almond

28 Monday
Independence Day (Peruvian)
Waxing Moon
Moon phase: First Quarter
Color: Lavender

Moon Sign: Leo
Moon enters Virgo 11:37 pm
Incense: Lily

29 **Tuesday**
Pardon of the Birds (French)
Waxing Moon
Moon phase: First Quarter
Color: Gray

Moon Sign: Virgo
Incense: Ylang-ylang

30 **Wednesday**
Micman Festival of St. Ann
Waxing Moon
Moon phase: First Quarter
Color: Brown

Moon Sign: Virgo
Incense: Honeysuckle

31 **Thursday**
Weighing of the Aga Kahn
Waxing Moon
Moon phase: First Quarter
Color: White

Moon Sign: Taurus
Moon enters Libra 12:09 pm
Incense: Carnation

Creativity and Spirit

Witches believe that there are five elements: earth, air, fire, water, and spirit. But we tend to concentrate on the first four, and sometime forget to celebrate the fifth. Feeding the fires of creativity helps spirit to blossom and grow, so try and find a way to integrate some form of art or craft with your magical practice. You don't have to be an artist, or even particularly good at whatever you do; finger-painting is just as worthwhile as creating a fine masterpiece in oils. What's important is expressing your spirituality with a creative flair, whether you are sewing an altar cloth, making your own Book of Shadows, or writing a poem. If you need help, call on Brigid, goddess of creativity.

–Deborah Blake

1   Friday
Lammas
Waxing Moon
Moon phase: First Quarter
Color: Rose

Moon Sign: Libra
Incense: Cypress

---

2   Saturday
Porcingula (Native American)
Waxing Moon
Moon phase: First Quarter
Color: Indigo

Moon Sign: Libra
Moon enters Scorpio 10:57 pm
Incense: Magnolia

☽   **Sunday**
Drimes (Greek)
Waxing Moon
Second Quarter 8:50 pm
Color: Yellow

Moon Sign: Scorpio
Incense: Juniper

---

4   Monday
Cook Islands Constitution Celebration
Waxing Moon
Moon phase: Second Quarter
Color: Gray

Moon Sign: Scorpio
Incense: Lily

---

5   Tuesday
Benediction of the Sea (French)
Waxing Moon
Moon phase: Second Quarter
Color: White

Moon Sign: Scorpio
Moon enters Sagittarius 6:19 am
Incense: Basil

---

6   Wednesday
Hiroshima Peace Ceremony
Waxing Moon
Moon phase: Second Quarter
Color: Topaz

Moon Sign: Sagittarius
Incense: Lavender

---

7   Thursday
Republic Day (Ivory Coast)
Waxing Moon
Moon phase: Second Quarter
Color: Purple

Moon Sign: Sagittarius
Moon enters Capricorn 9:38 am
Incense: Clove

August

---

8   Friday
Dog Days (Japanese)   Moon Sign: Capricorn
Waxing Moon   Incense: Vanilla
Moon phase: Second Quarter
Color: Coral

---

9   Saturday
Nagasaki Peace Ceremony   Moon Sign: Capricorn
Waxing Moon   Moon enters Aquarius 9:52 am
Moon phase: Second Quarter   Incense: Sandalwood
Color: Black

☺   Sunday
St. Lawrence's Day   Moon Sign: Aquarius
Waxing Moon   Incense: Eucalyptus
Full Moon 2:09 pm
Color: Gold

---

11   Monday
Puck Fair (Irish)   Moon Sign: Aquarius
Waning Moon   Moon enters Pisces 8:55 am
Moon phase: Third Quarter   Incense: Hyssop
Color: Silver

---

12   Tuesday
Fiesta of Santa Clara   Moon Sign: Pisces
Waning Moon   Incense: Ginger
Moon phase: Third Quarter
Color: Maroon

---

13   Wednesday
Women's Day (Tunisian)   Moon Sign: Pisces
Waning Moon   Moon enters Aries 9:00 am
Moon phase: Third Quarter   Incense: Honeysuckle
Color: Yellow

---

14   Thursday
Festival at Sassari   Moon Sign: Aries
Waning Moon   Incense: Jasmine
Moon phase: Third Quarter
Color: Green

August

15 Friday
Assumption Day
Waning Moon
Moon phase: Third Quarter
Color: Pink

Moon Sign: Aries
Moon enters Taurus 11:58 am
Incense: Violet

---

16 Saturday
Festival of Minstrels (European)
Waning Moon
Moon phase: Third Quarter
Color: Brown

Moon Sign: Taurus
Incense: Sage

 Sunday
Feast of the Hungry Ghosts (Chinese)
Waning Moon
Fourth Quarter 8:26 am
Color: Amber

Moon Sign: Taurus
Moon enters Gemini 6:41 pm
Incense: Heliotrope

---

18 Monday
St. Helen's Day
Waning Moon
Moon phase: Fourth Quarter
Color: Ivory

Moon Sign: Gemini
Incense: Rosemary

---

19 Tuesday
Rustic Vinalia (Roman)
Waning Moon
Moon phase: Fourth Quarter
Color: Black

Moon Sign: Gemini
Incense: Bayberry

---

20 Wednesday
Constitution Day (Hungarian)
Waning Moon
Moon phase: Fourth Quarter
Color: Brown

Moon Sign: Gemini
Moon enters Cancer 4:45 am
Incense: Lilac

---

21 Thursday
Consualia (Roman)
Waning Moon
Moon phase: Fourth Quarter
Color: White

Moon Sign: Cancer
Incense: Apricot

August

22 Friday

Feast of the Queenship of Mary (English)
Waning Moon
Moon phase: Fourth Quarter
Color: Purple

Moon Sign: Cancer
Moon enters Leo 4:49 pm
Incense: Orchid

23 Saturday

National Day (Romanian)
Waning Moon
Moon phase: Fourth Quarter
Color: Blue

Moon Sign: Leo
Sun enters Virgo 12:46 am
Incense: Patchouli

24 Sunday

St. Bartholomew's Day
Waning Moon
Moon phase: Fourth Quarter
Color: Orange

Moon Sign: Leo
Incense: Frankincense

☽ Monday

Feast of the Green Corn (Native American)
Waning Moon
New Moon 10:13 am
Color: Lavender

Moon Sign: Leo
Moon enters Virgo 5:33 am
Incense: Clary sage

26 Tuesday

Pardon of the Sea (French)
Waxing Moon
Moon phase: First Quarter
Color: Gray

Moon Sign: Virgo
Incense: Cedar

27 Wednesday

Summer Break (English)
Waxing Moon
Moon phase: First Quarter
Color: White

Moon Sign: Virgo
Moon enters Libra 5:54 pm
Incense: Bay laurel

28 Thursday

St. Augustine's Day
Waxing Moon
Moon phase: First Quarter
Color: Crimson

Moon Sign: Libra
Incense: Mulberry

29 Friday

St. John's Beheading
Waxing Moon
Moon phase: First Quarter
Color: White

Moon Sign: Libra
Incense: Yarrow

---

30 Saturday

St. Rose of Lima Day (Peruvian)
Waxing Moon
Moon phase: First Quarter
Color: Black

Moon Sign: Libra
Moon enters Scorpio 4:53 am
Incense: Rue

---

31 Sunday

Unto These Hills Pageant (Cherokee)
Waxing Moon
Moon phase: First Quarter
Color: Gold

Moon Sign: Scorpio
Incense: Hyacinth

Connect with Nature

Pagans follow a nature-based religion, and that connection with the natural world and the planet we live on is at the core of a Witchcraft practice. But it can be hard to make that connection in the midst of our busy lives, usually filled with technology and the noise of civilization. Make a commitment to take ten minutes a day to try and reconnect with nature. Take a walk and leave the earbuds out; listen to the birds instead. Open a window. Grow a plant. Smell a flower. Visit a body of water and rejoice at all the life it supports. Plant a tree. Look at the moon and the stars. Put your feet in the dirt. Dance in the rain.

–Deborah Blake

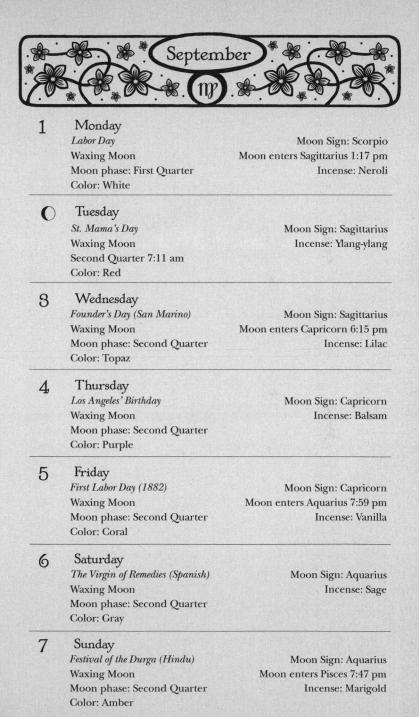

September ♍

1 Monday
Labor Day
Waxing Moon
Moon phase: First Quarter
Color: White

Moon Sign: Scorpio
Moon enters Sagittarius 1:17 pm
Incense: Neroli

Tuesday
St. Mama's Day
Waxing Moon
Second Quarter 7:11 am
Color: Red

Moon Sign: Sagittarius
Incense: Ylang-ylang

3 Wednesday
Founder's Day (San Marino)
Waxing Moon
Moon phase: Second Quarter
Color: Topaz

Moon Sign: Sagittarius
Moon enters Capricorn 6:15 pm
Incense: Lilac

4 Thursday
Los Angeles' Birthday
Waxing Moon
Moon phase: Second Quarter
Color: Purple

Moon Sign: Capricorn
Incense: Balsam

5 Friday
First Labor Day (1882)
Waxing Moon
Moon phase: Second Quarter
Color: Coral

Moon Sign: Capricorn
Moon enters Aquarius 7:59 pm
Incense: Vanilla

6 Saturday
The Virgin of Remedies (Spanish)
Waxing Moon
Moon phase: Second Quarter
Color: Gray

Moon Sign: Aquarius
Incense: Sage

7 Sunday
Festival of the Durga (Hindu)
Waxing Moon
Moon phase: Second Quarter
Color: Amber

Moon Sign: Aquarius
Moon enters Pisces 7:47 pm
Incense: Marigold

September ♍

Monday
Birthday of the Virgin Mary
Waxing Moon
Full Moon 9:38 pm
Color: Silver

Moon Sign: Pisces
Incense: Narcissus

---

9 Tuesday
Chrysanthemum Festival (Japanese)
Waning Moon
Moon phase: Third Quarter
Color: Black

Moon Sign: Pisces
Moon enters Aries 7:33 pm
Incense: Cinnamon

---

10 Wednesday
Festival of the Poets (Japanese)
Waning Moon
Moon phase: Third Quarter
Color: Yellow

Moon Sign: Aries
Incense: Marjoram

---

11 Thursday
Coptic New Year
Waning Moon
Moon phase: Third Quarter
Color: Turquoise

Moon Sign: Aries
Moon enters Taurus 9:17 pm
Incense: Carnation

---

12 Friday
National Day (Ethiopian)
Waning Moon
Moon phase: Third Quarter
Color: White

Moon Sign: Taurus
Incense: Cypress

---

13 Saturday
The Gods' Banquet (Roman)
Waning Moon
Moon phase: Third Quarter
Color: Blue

Moon Sign: Taurus
Incense: Patchouli

---

14 Sunday
Holy Cross Day
Waning Moon
Moon phase: Third Quarter
Color: Orange

Moon Sign: Taurus
Moon enters Gemini 2:26 am
Incense: Frankincense

September ♍

○ Monday
Birthday of the Moon (Chinese)
Waning Moon
Fourth Quarter 10:05 pm
Color: Ivory

Moon Sign: Gemini
Incense: Lily

16 Tuesday
Mexican Independence Day
Waning Moon
Moon phase: Fourth Quarter
Color: Maroon

Moon Sign: Gemini
Moon enters Cancer 11:24 am
Incense: Geranium

17 Wednesday
Von Steuben's Day
Waning Moon
Moon phase: Fourth Quarter
Color: White

Moon Sign: Cancer
Incense: Lavender

18 Thursday
Dr. Johnson's Birthday
Waning Moon
Moon phase: Fourth Quarter
Color: Green

Moon Sign: Cancer
Moon enters Leo 11:10 pm
Incense: Nutmeg

19 Friday
St. Januarius' Day (Italian)
Waning Moon
Moon phase: Fourth Quarter
Color: Rose

Moon Sign: Leo
Incense: Thyme

20 Saturday
St. Eustace's Day
Waning Moon
Moon phase: Fourth Quarter
Color: Brown

Moon Sign: Leo
Incense: Rue

21 Sunday
UN International Day of Peace
Waning Moon
Moon phase: Fourth Quarter
Color: Gold

Moon Sign: Leo
Moon enters Virgo 11:54 am
Incense: Eucalyptus

September

22 Monday
Mabon • Fall Equinox
Waning Moon
Moon phase: Fourth Quarter
Color: Lavender

Moon Sign: Virgo
Sun enters Libra 10:29 pm
Incense: Rosemary

23 Tuesday
Shubun no Hi (Chinese)
Waning Moon
Moon phase: Fourth Quarter
Color: Gray

Moon Sign: Virgo
Moon enters Libra 11:59 pm
Incense: Ginger

☽ Wednesday
Schwenkenfelder Thanksgiving (German-American)
Waning Moon
New Moon 2:14 am
Color: Yellow

Moon Sign: Libra
Incense: Honeysuckle

25 Thursday
Rosh Hashanah
Waxing Moon
Moon phase: First Quarter
Color: White

Moon Sign: Libra
Incense: Clove

26 Friday
Feast of Santa Justina (Mexican)
Waxing Moon
Moon phase: First Quarter
Color: Pink

Moon Sign: Libra
Moon enters Scorpio 10:29 am
Incense: Cypress

27 Saturday
Saints Cosmas and Damian's Day
Waxing Moon
Moon phase: First Quarter
Color: Indigo

Moon Sign: Scorpio
Incense: Pine

28 Sunday
Confucius's Birthday
Waxing Moon
Moon phase: First Quarter
Color: Amber

Moon Sign: Scorpio
Moon enters Sagittarius 6:50 pm
Incense: Almond

29 **Monday**
Michaelmas
Waxing Moon
Moon phase: First Quarter
Color: Gray

Moon Sign: Sagittarius
Incense: Hyssop

30 **Tuesday**
St. Jerome's Day
Waxing Moon
Moon phase: First Quarter
Color: White

Moon Sign: Sagittarius
Incense: Basil

⌘

Nurturing Animals and Children

The goddess comes to us as Maiden, Mother, and Crone—but for many of us, it is her nurturing aspect that is the most comforting. As Witches, we try to manifest god and goddess in our daily lives, channeling them through our actions in a positive way. And there is no better way to channel the goddess (and the god, as healer and provider) than to care for an animal or a child. By nurturing those who are vulnerable, we bring light to the world and to our own spirits. Whether you are caring for your own child/pet or volunteering with those that belong to others—or to no one—your actions are divine, in every meaning of the word.

–Deborah Blake

October

○ **Wednesday**
Armed Forces Day (South Korean)
Waxing Moon
Second Quarter 3:33 pm
Color: Topaz

Moon Sign: Sagittarius
Moon enters Capricorn 12:41 am
Incense: Bay laurel

2 **Thursday**
Old Man's Day (Virgin Islands)
Waxing Moon
Moon phase: Second Quarter
Color: Crimson

Moon Sign: Capricorn
Incense: Apricot

3 **Friday**
Moroccan New Year's Day
Waxing Moon
Moon phase: Second Quarter
Color: Purple

Moon Sign: Capricorn
Moon enters Aquarius 4:00 am
Incense: Violet

4 **Saturday**
Yom Kippur
Waxing Moon
Moon phase: Second Quarter
Color: Black

Moon Sign: Aquarius
Incense: Ivy

5 **Sunday**
Republic Day (Portuguese)
Waxing Moon
Moon phase: Second Quarter
Color: Orange

Moon Sign: Aquarius
Moon enters Pisces 5:24 am
Incense: Hyacinth

6 **Monday**
Dedication of the Virgin's Crowns (English)
Waxing Moon
Moon phase: Second Quarter
Color: White

Moon Sign: Pisces
Incense: Clary sage

7 **Tuesday**
Kermesse (German)
Waxing Moon
Moon phase: Second Quarter
Color: Scarlet

Moon Sign: Pisces
Moon enters Aries 6:07 am
Incense: Bayberry

October

♈ **Wednesday**
Okunchi (Japanese)
Waxing Moon
Full Moon 6:51 am
Color: Brown

Moon Sign: Aries
Incense: Honeysuckle

9 Thursday
Sukkot begins
Waning Moon
Moon phase: Third Quarter
Color: Turquoise

Moon Sign: Aries
Moon enters Taurus 7:44 am
Incense: Balsam

10 Friday
Health Day (Japanese)
Waning Moon
Moon phase: Third Quarter
Color: Pink

Moon Sign: Taurus
Incense: Alder

11 Saturday
Medetrinalia (Roman)
Waning Moon
Moon phase: Third Quarter
Color: Blue

Moon Sign: Taurus
Moon enters Gemini 11:51 am
Incense: Magnolia

12 Sunday
National Day (Spanish)
Waning Moon
Moon phase: Third Quarter
Color: Gold

Moon Sign: Gemini
Incense: Juniper

13 Monday
Columbus Day (observed)
Waning Moon
Moon phase: Third Quarter
Color: Silver

Moon Sign: Gemini
Moon enters Cancer 7:30 pm
Incense: Narcissus

14 Tuesday
Battle Festival (Japanese)
Waning Moon
Moon phase: Third Quarter
Color: Gray

Moon Sign: Cancer
Incense: Cedar

○ **Wednesday**
Sukkot ends
Waning Moon
Fourth Quarter 3:12 pm
Color: Yellow

Moon Sign: Cancer
Incense: Lilac

16 **Thursday**
The Lion Sermon (British)
Waning Moon
Moon phase: Fourth Quarter
Color: White

Moon Sign: Cancer
Moon enters Leo 6:29 am
Incense: Jasmine

17 **Friday**
Pilgrimage to Paray-le-Monial
Waning Moon
Moon phase: Fourth Quarter
Color: Rose

Moon Sign: Leo
Incense: Orchid

18 **Saturday**
Brooklyn Barbecue
Waning Moon
Moon phase: Fourth Quarter
Color: Brown

Moon Sign: Leo
Moon enters Virgo 7:08 pm
Incense: Patchouli

19 **Sunday**
Our Lord of Miracles Procession (Peruvian)
Waning Moon
Moon phase: Fourth Quarter
Color: Amber

Moon Sign: Virgo
Incense: Almond

20 **Monday**
Colchester Oyster Feast
Waning Moon
Moon phase: Fourth Quarter
Color: Lavender

Moon Sign: Virgo
Incense: Lily

21 **Tuesday**
Feast of the Black Christ
Waning Moon
Moon phase: Fourth Quarter
Color: Black

Moon Sign: Virgo
Moon enters Libra 7:12 am
Incense: Ylang-ylang

22 Wednesday
Goddess of Mercy Day (Chinese)
Waning Moon
Moon phase: Fourth Quarter
Color: Topaz

Moon Sign: Libra
Incense: Lavender

☽ Thursday
Revolution Day (Hungarian)
Waning Moon
New Moon 5:57 pm
Color: Purple

Moon Sign: Libra
Sun enters Scorpio 7:57 am
Moon enters Scorpio 5:10 pm
Incense: Mulberry

24 Friday
United Nations Day
Waxing Moon
Moon phase: First Quarter
Color: Coral

Moon Sign: Scorpio
Incense: Rose

25 Saturday
Islamic New Year
Waxing Moon
Moon phase: First Quarter
Color: Gray

Moon Sign: Scorpio
Incense: Sage

26 Sunday
Quit Rent Ceremony (English)
Waxing Moon
Moon phase: First Quarter
Color: Yellow

Moon Sign: Scorpio
Moon enters Sagittarius 12:40 am
Incense: Marigold

27 Monday
Feast of the Holy Souls
Waxing Moon
Moon phase: First Quarter
Color: Ivory

Moon Sign: Sagittarius
Incense: Neroli

28 Tuesday
Ochi Day (Greek)
Waxing Moon
Moon phase: First Quarter
Color: Red

Moon Sign: Sagittarius
Moon enters Capricorn 6:03 am
Incense: Cinnamon

29 **Wednesday**
Iroquois Feast of the Dead
Waxing Moon
Moon phase: First Quarter
Color: Brown

Moon Sign: Capricorn
Incense: Marjoram

◐ **Thursday**
Meiji Festival (Japanese)
Waxing Moon
Second Quarter 10:48 pm
Color: Green

Moon Sign: Capricorn
Moon enters Aquarius 9:52 am
Incense: Carnation

31 **Friday**
Halloween • Samhain
Waxing Moon
Moon phase: Second Quarter
Color: White

Moon Sign: Aquarius
Incense: Vanilla

❧

Talk to the Gods

Many of us invoke the god and goddess during ritual and call on them during times of crisis. This is good. But taking that communication one step further is even better. After all, the gods are always there, ready to listen (and sometime comment back, if you are paying attention). Try greeting them at the start of each new day, and saying "thank you" for all the blessings in your life as the day draws to an end. Spend a couple of minutes at your altar, just checking in. Or bring them your worries, your problems, your fears—opening yourself to the comfort they offer, and maybe even an answer or two, if you are listening.

–Deborah Blake

November

1 Saturday
All Saints' Day
Waxing Moon
Moon phase: Second Quarter
Color: Blue

Moon Sign: Aquarius
Moon enters Pisces 12:37 pm
Incense: Sandalwood

2 Sunday
All Souls' Day • Daylight Saving Time ends
Waxing Moon
Moon phase: Second Quarter
Color: Orange

Moon Sign: Pisces
Incense: Heliotrope

3 Monday
St. Hubert's Day (Belgian)
Waxing Moon
Moon phase: Second Quarter
Color: Ivory

Moon Sign: Pisces
Moon enters Aries 1:53 pm
Incense: Rosemary

4 Tuesday
Election Day (general)
Waxing Moon
Moon phase: Second Quarter
Color: Maroon

Moon Sign: Aries
Incense: Geranium

5 Wednesday
Guy Fawkes Night (British)
Waxing Moon
Moon phase: Second Quarter
Color: Topaz

Moon Sign: Aries
Moon enters Taurus 4:33 pm
Incense: Lilac

☺ Thursday
Leonard's Ride (German)
Waxing Moon
Full Moon 5:23 pm
Color: White

Moon Sign: Taurus
Incense: Nutmeg

7 Friday
Mayan Day of the Dead
Waning Moon
Moon phase: Third Quarter
Color: Purple

Moon Sign: Taurus
Moon enters Gemini 8:45 am
Incense: Orchid

November

8 Saturday
The Lord Mayor's Show (English)
Waning Moon
Moon phase: Third Quarter
Color: Black

Moon Sign: Gemini
Incense: Rue

---

9 Sunday
Lord Mayor's Day (British)
Waning Moon
Moon phase: Third Quarter
Color: Yellow

Moon Sign: Gemini
Incense: Eucalyptus

---

10 Monday
Martin Luther's Birthday
Waning Moon
Moon phase: Third Quarter
Color: Silver

Moon Sign: Gemini
Moon enters Cancer 3:38 am
Incense: Lily

---

11 Tuesday
Veterans Day
Waning Moon
Moon phase: Third Quarter
Color: Scarlet

Moon Sign: Cancer
Incense: Cinnamon

---

12 Wednesday
Tesuque Feast Day (Native American)
Waning Moon
Moon phase: Third Quarter
Color: White

Moon Sign: Cancer
Moon enters Leo 1:44 pm
Incense: Bay laurel

---

13 Thursday
Festival of Jupiter (Roman)
Waning Moon
Moon phase: Third Quarter
Color: Turquoise

Moon Sign: Leo
Incense: Clove

◑ Friday
The Little Carnival (Greek)
Waning Moon
Fourth Quarter 10:16 am
Color: Rose

Moon Sign: Leo
Incense: Alder

15 Saturday
St. Leopold's Day
Waning Moon
Moon phase: Fourth Quarter
Color: Indigo

Moon Sign: Leo
Moon enters Virgo 2:08 am
Incense: Ivy

16 Sunday
St. Margaret of Scotland's Day
Waning Moon
Moon phase: Fourth Quarter
Color: Gold

Moon Sign: Virgo
Incense: Frankincense

17 Monday
Queen Elizabeth's Day
Waning Moon
Moon phase: Fourth Quarter
Color: Lavender

Moon Sign: Virgo
Moon enters Libra 2:30 pm
Incense: Clary sage

18 Tuesday
St. Plato's Day
Waning Moon
Moon phase: Fourth Quarter
Color: Black

Moon Sign: Libra
Incense: Bayberry

19 Wednesday
Garifuna Day (Belizean)
Waning Moon
Moon phase: Fourth Quarter
Color: Yellow

Moon Sign: Libra
Incense: Lavender

20 Thursday
Revolution Day (Mexican)
Waning Moon
Moon phase: Fourth Quarter
Color: Purple

Moon Sign: Libra
Moon enters Scorpio 12:31 am
Incense: Jasmine

21 Friday
Repentance Day (German)
Waning Moon
Moon phase: Fourth Quarter
Color: White

Moon Sign: Scorpio
Incense: Mint

November

 Saturday
St. Cecilia's Day
Waning Moon
New Moon 7:32 am
Color: Gray

Moon Sign: Scorpio
Sun enters Sagittarius 4:38 am
Moon enters Sagittarius 7:19 am
Incense: Magnolia

---

23 Sunday
St. Clement's Day
Waxing Moon
Moon phase: First Quarter
Color: Orange

Moon Sign: Sagittarius
Incense: Juniper

---

24 Monday
Feast of the Burning Lamps (Egyptian)
Waxing Moon
Moon phase: First Quarter
Color: White

Moon Sign: Sagittarius
Moon enters Capricorn 11:31 am
Incense: Hyssop

---

25 Tuesday
St. Catherine of Alexandria's Day
Waxing Moon
Moon phase: First Quarter
Color: Gray

Moon Sign: Capricorn
Incense: Ginger

---

26 Wednesday
Festival of Lights (Tibetan)
Waxing Moon
Moon phase: First Quarter
Color: Brown

Moon Sign: Capricorn
Moon enters Aquarius 10:30 am
Incense: Marjoram

---

27 Thursday
Thanksgiving Day
Waxing Moon
Moon phase: First Quarter
Color: Crimson

Moon Sign: Aquarius
Incense: Balsam

---

28 Friday
Day of the New Dance (Tibetan)
Waxing Moon
Moon phase: First Quarter
Color: Pink

Moon Sign: Aquarius
Moon enters Pisces 5:03 pm
Incense: Violet

November

1

○ **Saturday**
Tubman's Birthday (Liberian)
Waxing Moon
Second Quarter 5:06 am
Color: Blue

Moon Sign: Pisces
Incense: Pine

30 **Sunday**
St. Andrew's Day
Waxing Moon
Moon phase: Second Quarter
Color: Amber

Moon Sign: Pisces
Moon enters Aries 8:14 pm
Incense: Hyacinth

❖

Be Kind to the Earth

As Witches, we are more closely connected to the Earth than most. That is both a joy and a responsibility. Because we view Gaia (the Earth) as our mother, we know how important it is to treat her well. Look at the way you are living, and see if there is anything in your daily life you can do better to help our planet thrive. Can you recycle, reuse, or repurpose more? Use less energy or be more efficient with what you do use? This can be as simple as turning off a light you're not using. You don't have to do anything drastic; just be mindful of how what you do affects the Earth, and strive every day to do a little bit better.

–Deborah Blake

December

1 Monday
Big Tea Party (Japanese)
Waxing Moon
Moon phase: Second Quarter
Color: Gray

Moon Sign: Aries
Incense: Narcissus

2 Tuesday
Republic Day (Laotian)
Waxing Moon
Moon phase: Second Quarter
Color: Maroon

Moon Sign: Aries
Incense: Basil

3 Wednesday
St. Francis Xavier's Day
Waxing Moon
Moon phase: Second Quarter
Color: Brown

Moon Sign: Aries
Moon enters Taurus 12:15 am
Incense: Honeysuckle

4 Thursday
St. Barbara's Day
Waxing Moon
Moon phase: Second Quarter
Color: White

Moon Sign: Taurus
Incense: Myrrh

5 Friday
Eve of St. Nicholas' Day
Waxing Moon
Moon phase: Second Quarter
Color: Coral

Moon Sign: Taurus
Moon enters Gemini 5:28 am
Incense: Thyme

☺ Saturday
St. Nicholas' Day
Waxing Moon
Full Moon 7:27 am
Color: Black

Moon Sign: Gemini
Incense: Rue

7 Sunday
Burning the Devil (Guatemalan)
Waning Moon
Moon phase: Third Quarter
Color: Gold

Moon Sign: Gemini
Moon enters Cancer 12:34 pm
Incense: Marigold

8 Monday
Feast of the Immaculate Conception
Waning Moon
Moon phase: Third Quarter
Color: Silver

Moon Sign: Cancer
Incense: Lily

9 Tuesday
St. Leocadia's Day
Waning Moon
Moon phase: Third Quarter
Color: White

Moon Sign: Cancer
Moon enters Leo 10:14 pm
Incense: Ylang-ylang

10 Wednesday
Nobel Day
Waning Moon
Moon phase: Third Quarter
Color: Yellow

Moon Sign: Leo
Incense: Lavender

11 Thursday
Pilgrimage at Tortugas
Waning Moon
Moon phase: Third Quarter
Color: Green

Moon Sign: Leo
Incense: Apricot

12 Friday
Fiesta of Our Lady of Guadalupe (Mexican)
Waning Moon
Moon phase: Third Quarter
Color: Purple

Moon Sign: Leo
Moon enters Virgo 10:19 am
Incense: Yarrow

13 Saturday
St. Lucy's Day (Swedish)
Waning Moon
Moon phase: Third Quarter
Color: Gray

Moon Sign: Virgo
Incense: Ivy

◑ Sunday
Warriors' Memorial (Japanese)
Waning Moon
Fourth Quarter 7:51 am
Color: Amber

Moon Sign: Virgo
Moon enters Libra 11:05 pm
Incense: Almond

December

15 Monday
Consualia (Roman)
Waning Moon
Moon phase: Fourth Quarter
Color: Lavender

Moon Sign: Libra
Incense: Neroli

16 Tuesday
Posadas (Mexican)
Waning Moon
Moon phase: Fourth Quarter
Color: Red

Moon Sign: Libra
Incense: Cedar

17 Wednesday
Hanukkah begins
Waning Moon
Moon phase: Fourth Quarter
Color: White

Moon Sign: Libra
Moon enters Scorpio 9:52 am
Incense: Marjoram

18 Thursday
Feast of the Virgin of Solitude
Waning Moon
Moon phase: Fourth Quarter
Color: Turquoise

Moon Sign: Scorpio
Incense: Nutmeg

19 Friday
Opalia (Roman)
Waning Moon
Moon phase: Fourth Quarter
Color: Pink

Moon Sign: Scorpio
Moon enters Sagittarius 4:55 pm
Incense: Vanilla

20 Saturday
Commerce God Festival (Japanese)
Waning Moon
Moon phase: Fourth Quarter
Color: Indigo

Moon Sign: Sagittarius
Incense: Magnolia

☽ Sunday
Yule • Winter Solstice
Waning Moon
New Moon 8:36 pm
Color: Yellow

Moon Sign: Sagittarius
Sun enters Capricorn 6:03 pm
Moon enters Capricorn 8:25 pm
Incense: Frankincense

December

22 Monday
Saints Chaeremon and Ischyrion's Day
Waxing Moon
Moon phase: First Quarter
Color: Ivory

Moon Sign: Capricorn
Incense: Rosemary

23 Tuesday
Larentalia (Roman)
Waxing Moon
Moon phase: First Quarter
Color: Black

Moon Sign: Capricorn
Moon enters Aquarius 9:52 pm
Incense: Cinnamon

24 Wednesday
Christmas Eve • Hanukkah ends
Waxing Moon
Moon phase: First Quarter
Color: Topaz

Moon Sign: Aquarius
Incense: Lilac

25 Thursday
Christmas Day
Waxing Moon
Moon phase: First Quarter
Color: Crimson

Moon Sign: Aquarius
Moon enters Pisces 11:07 pm
Incense: Mulberry

26 Friday
Kwanzaa begins
Waxing Moon
Moon phase: First Quarter
Color: White

Moon Sign: Pisces
Incense: Mint

27 Saturday
Boar's Head Supper (English)
Waxing Moon
Moon phase: First Quarter
Color: Brown

Moon Sign: Pisces
Incense: Sandalwood

☽ Sunday
Holy Innocents' Day
Waxing Moon
Second Quarter 1:31 pm
Color: Orange

Moon Sign: Pisces
Moon enters Aries 1:31 pm
Incense: Juniper

December

29 Monday
Feast of St. Thomas à Becket
Waxing Moon
Moon phase: Second Quarter
Color: White

Moon Sign: Aries
Incense: Lily

30 Tuesday
Republic Day (Madagascan)
Waxing Moon
Moon phase: Second Quarter
Color: Scarlet

Moon Sign: Aries
Moon enters Taurus 5:56 am
Incense: Geranium

31 Wednesday
New Year's Eve
Waxing Moon
Moon phase: Second Quarter
Color: Yellow

Moon Sign: Taurus
Incense: Bay laurel

Beat the Drum

Almost every Pagan culture, no matter where in the world it was located or when it existed, used drums during rituals. Sometimes the drums were made from the skins of sacred animals. Sometimes they were created from hollow logs. But no matter what materials they were formed from, drums served the same purpose for those folks as they do for us. The rhythmic beat of the drum mimics the beat of the human heart and can bring on trance states if beaten slowly, or an ecstasy of spirit if beaten rapidly. You can dance or sing or chant to drums; you can also pray. When many people beat drums in unison, it brings their energies together and amplifies them. So get yourself a drum and join in!

–Deborah Blake

Fire Magic

Winter Fire Magic
by James Kambos

If we had never learned how to tame fire, civilization as we know it would not exist. Around fire, humankind created the first permanent home—the cave. Then the cave floor became the first hearth, and when the first fires burned upon that hearth, it brought a sense of security. Fire allowed our ancient ancestors to defend themselves against the fang of the wild beast and the bite of the winter cold. Around those early fires, the ancients gathered for safety and comfort. They communicated. Friendships were formed, and from those friendships clans came into being. The clans turned into villages, then cities, and from cities great nations grew and ultimately mighty civilizations flourished. None of these would have been possible if we were still shivering in the dark.

The element of fire is the most "alive" of all the elements. Because of this, it was utilized early on in spiritual and religious ceremonies. It was used for divination, purification, and spellcasting. Although fire is associated with summer and the Sun, its magical properties seem to be most appreciated during the dark days of winter.

In our computerized age, many of us have lost touch with the magical significance of fire. We have furnaces, thermostats, and battery-operated "candles." These are great conveniences, but fail to convey the primal energy of fire itself.

I've always had an intimate relationship with fire. As a child in rural Ohio, we'd keep the fireplace burning for days during severe cold snaps. Today I heat my home with wood and have come to respect the magical power and beauty of fire. What follows is a collection of magical information, spells, and rituals incorporating fire that I've gathered over the years and have used during the winter. Naturally, many of you don't have fireplaces or wood stoves, but these rituals may still be performed using only candles and a cauldron, or other heatproof container. If you do use a fireplace or wood stove, be sure to have it cleaned and inspected by a chimney sweep. Safety is of the utmost importance when working any form of fire magic.

Winter Purification Rituals

During the winter, stagnant energy and negativity can build up in our homes. Fire is a natural purifier and is excellent to use during the winter to cleanse our living space. Here are three rituals for you to try.

This ritual uses winter spices to help clear the home of negativity. Combine a pinch each of allspice, ginger, and clove. Sprinkle these spices onto the fire. Using a small pine branch, trace the shape of the pentagram in the air over the hearth. At first, hold the pine branch above the flames and visualize any negativity being sucked up the chimney. Then lay the pine branch directly into the flames, if it pops and cracks a lot, then you did have some negative energy hanging around. If you perform this ritual in your cauldron or other dish, when the ashes cool, sprinkle them away from your home.

To create a calm atmosphere in the home and to purify yourself of any negative thoughts, this spell combines snow (or ice), rose water, and fire. First, in a bowl combine some fresh snow, or a few ice cubes, and a teaspoon of rose water. Place the bowl in front of the fire and let the snow or ice melt. When melted, stir the mixture with your hand and anoint your forehead and each wrist. The scent of the rose water should calm you—let go of any bad thoughts. Take this mixture around your home and sprinkle it in front of doors and windows. Return to your hearth and bless the fireplace and chimney. Pour any extra mixture outside.

As a good general cleansing technique, after you have built a fire or when the wood is glowing brightly, sprinkle a handful of regular table salt onto the fire. This serves to bless and purify any space, as a bonus the salt also helps to slow any creosote build-up in the chimney. I use this once a day in my wood stove.

Winter Fire Magic for Love

The winter fire is a symbol for passion and heat. Love spells performed before a winter fire are especially powerful. Here are two quick and easy spells.

For this spell you'll need two pine cones, a length of red yarn, and, of course, a fire. With the yarn, tie the two pine cones together as you think of romance coming into your life. As you tie them together, say:

Fire, fire, child of the Sun,
Fire, fire, bring me that special one.

Toss the pine cones into the fire. Watch them burn and gaze into the flames, look for any pictures or signs the fire may give you as to who the spell could bring into your life.

For this next love spell, we'll use three "warm" love attracting scents—clove, cinnamon, and orange—plus a candle of your choice. In an envelope, mix a pinch each of clove, cinnamon, and grated orange peel, but don't seal the envelope closed. Select a votive candle with a wintry scent such as apple/cinnamon, or pumpkin spice for example. Sit before a fire or just light your candle and look deeply into the flame. Hold the envelope in front of you and say this charm:

> *Fire, hear what I say,*
> *Fire, clear the way,*
> *Fire, bring love my way.*

Now seal the envelope and think of the qualities you'd like in a romantic partner. Let the candle burn out. Put the sealed envelope in a secret place. In one lunar month, cast the envelope into a ritual fire as an offering to keep the spell working.

Divining with the Winter Fire

People have divined, scryed, and sought to see omens of the future by gazing into the flames of a winter fire since before recorded history. For many, "seeing" the future by observing the flames of a winter fire was a pleasant form of entertainment and a fun way to spend a winter evening. In many ways, it became a parlor game and helped families pass time during the long, dark winter nights.

Witches and other occultists realized, however, that the winter fire was an important scrying tool. They also knew the winter fire was an effective way to cast spells. We can only imagine the times a village witch has sat by a glowing hearth on a cold winter night, scrying into the dancing flames and casting a spell.

To see the future by using the winter fire and smoke is both exciting and powerful. It lets you tap into the primal energy of fire. These are two methods for you to try. If you can, do this on a cold winter eve when the wind roars through the trees and howls down the chimney.

A Scrying Spell For a Winter's Eve

This spell allows you to scry and at the same time bring a wish into your life. Have on hand three twigs—one of oak (for strength), one of hawthorn (for wishes), and one of ash (for energy). On a night or two before a Full Moon, start a fire—but don't burn your three twigs yet. Gaze at the flames as you think of your wish. Toss the twigs into the fire and say:

> *Seasons turn, fire burn,*
> *Twigs of oak, hawthorn, and ash,*
> *Burn, so what I want shall come to pass.*

Watch the flames for any signs or visions. If you notice a lot of blue flame, there is a good chance your wish will come true quickly. The fire and smoke will release your wish into the unseen realm.

To Conjure A Vision With Fire

To work this spell, gather some apple peel, dried leaves of chrysanthemum, and rosemary. You'll also need one white feather. Cast the peel, chrysanthemum leaves, and rosemary into the flames and say:

> *Life and death,*
> *Fire's breath,*
> *Flames crackle and flare.*
> *Let me see*
> *A face, a name, or sign upon the air.*
> *Smoke gray, smoke white,*
> *Let me see my future this night.*

With the feather, fan the smoke gently, letting it curl about you. Gaze at the fire and smoke for as long as you wish, looking for signs. Leave the fire to burn for the rest of the evening. As a sign of gratitude, leave the feather before the hearth or on the fireplace mantel.

≈

To the Ancients, the winter fire was an echo of the Sun—of life itself. During the winter, our ancestors gave thanks to the slowly increasing power of the Sun as the year made its steady climb toward spring and summer. To do this, they'd raise a glass of beer or ale before the winter fire as a sign of respect. Using your favorite beverage you can continue this custom.

become part of the very problem they otherwise see so clearly.

The Space in General

I also mean clearing your environment literally. Clean it up. Get rid of dust bunnies, wipe down as much of it as possible with a solution of one part vinegar, two parts water, and make it shiny clean. If you've got a rug, sprinkle it with baking soda and let it stand overnight, then vacuum it up. (Check with maintenance to see if it's okay to have them do it at your office). If you can get the privacy, try doing a space-clearing ritual at your office, and definitely do one at home. For ongoing space clearing, I put together a spray bottle with 25 drops of eucalyptus oil, 15 drops of cinnamon oil, and 10 drops of lemon oil in a cup of vodka mixed with a cup of distilled water. Whenever I am alone in the office, I give the air a good spritzing, and always on Monday morning.

Take a look at your environment(s), both work and home. While you are looking, ask yourself:

- Is the space clean and uncluttered?
- Does it excite and inspire me?
- Does it provide me access to the tools I need to work and live effectively?
- Does it make me feel happy and productive?
- What can I do to make this space a more enjoyable and productive place to spend my time?

Make your space as clutter-free as possible—get rid of everything that just takes up space and distracts you. Ask yourself: Do I love this? Do I use this? and, Do I need this? If the answer is no, get rid of it and make room for what you do love and use and need.

Then, Clear Your Mind

Ideally, we'd all walk around clearheaded and right-thinking, each at our best. In reality, some days it's about all we can do to just to walk around, never mind with a clear head or thinking right. This section is guidance for working toward the ideal, not an admonishment that we haven't achieved it.

Two things that make a huge difference in being able to have a positive outlook are getting enough quality sleep and getting some exercise. Apparently most of us are sleep deprived—not getting the 7.5 to 8 hours of sleep we need every night. And exercise seems to be the cure for all ills. Getting 30 minutes of exercise that makes you sweat and slightly out of breath on a daily basis seems to clear the mind and refresh your outlook on life, as well as improving your overall health.

The real work of clearing the mind comes about by paying close attention to our thoughts. Every time we recognize negative thoughts and words, we need to immediately stop and reframe the thought into an alternative reference, one that is positive and optimistic. If you can't "hear" your thoughts, start with your emotions.

The word emotion comes from the Latin *emovere*, meaning to "move through or out." So emotions in their pure state do not cling to us or leave a residue—they are simply another form of information about our physical state. But most of us feed our emotions with negative thoughts. In short order, the guests take over the house, leaving us feeling out of control. To turn around this unhelpful pattern, we must sharpen our awareness so that we become sensitive to smaller versions of these emotions, early on, before they've grown out of control.

Microemotions come up all the time in our everyday experiences. For example, someone makes a snide remark to me at a party. It isn't a direct attack, but it puts me out of sorts, and I find myself a bit upset. The party isn't as fun anymore, and I'm not feeling like I want to be social anymore. Perhaps I'll leave earlier than planned—all because of one small comment. But if, instead I can recognize that I am feeling out of sorts, and that the cause is external, I can then also see how the emotion is influencing me and choose whether or not I really want to stay or go.

This is hard work. There is no time off, no way to make it easier—it's just a repetitious creation of a pattern of thinking. The good news is that it gets easier as it becomes more habitual. There is great value in understanding all the connections between the many layers and aspects of our reality. We learn to recognize how our interpretation of events affects how we feel, and that in turn affects what we think, say, and do. This becomes the basis for a powerful feedback loop and shows us where we have choices that previously went unrecognized.

Now You're Ready for Magickal Aikido

Initially, recognizing our choices won't shift things completely. But as we start to actually make more micro-decisions, the momentum turns, and those everyday moments help break our unconscious patterns. Perhaps before, that snide remark might've led to spending the next ten minutes on coming up with a smart rejoinder. Now I might say, "Hey, that was pretty snarky. Is something bothering you?" In doing so, I give myself the opportunity to connect on a deeper level with another person. I may be giving them a chance to realize their negativity and reframe it. I may be given a chance to help another person heal.

Over my desk—both at home where I am writing this article and at work—I have a picture of a set of Chinese *kanji*. One depicts crisis and opportunity and reminds me that "opportunity is always present in the midst of crisis." The other depicts chaos, "where brilliant dreams are born." These images are constant and active reminders of the value of disorder, or the unplanned, the unforeseen. They remind me to take advantage of the crisis and allow it to show me new opportunities, thereby taking a negative state (bawk! bawk! arms flailing) and turning it into a positive one (Hey, look, we can improve this if we …).

As we become more self-aware, it can seem like the amount of negativity in and around us increases—it's a side effect of the process, and it will pass. While it's happening, you may want to use some specific responses.

1. Be aware and contemplative about the negative situation. Whenever possible, take time before responding and try to get perspective. Don't look for blame, but acknowledge that conflict requires two participants and look for how you contributed. Look for the place where the misunderstanding occurred and be aware of it for the future.

2. Choose not to accept the negativity when it's spewed your way. My manager recently lost his temper in a meeting and ended up shouting at us. He left the meeting twice, and returned both times to yell some more. It was seriously unpleasant, but I reminded myself throughout that it was not MY fault that he was upset. I tried to note specific items he was upset about so I could look into them further. I made a conscious effort to keep my body and breathing relaxed. I acknowledged that there was nothing I could do about his anger in the moment, but I didn't need to take it on.

3. Pay attention to how you respond to negativity. In the above example, I mentioned how I consciously kept my breathing and body relaxed. I've learned that when I'm freaked out, I start to hunch my shoulders, and my breathing gets shallow. One way to keep me from freaking out is to not let my body dictate my response, so I've trained myself to notice when I'm showing physical signs of stress.

4. Let people own their own negativity. Sometimes it feels good to just "dump" for a while. Wallowing in it isn't healthy, but if you can be there for a friend or colleague and help them work through the negative situation, you can end up doing a lot of good. Talk to your

friends and loved ones. It may seem obvious, but raising the topic allows you to get more information and may allow your friend to open up about their concerns. Helping another person feel better about a scary situation is a wonderful way to feel better about it yourself.

5. When talking, it is better to stick to the facts and information you know than to speculate. For example, if you are talking about body scanners at the airport, it's okay to mention your concerns that TSA agents aren't allowed to wear radiation tags and that the incidence of cancer among TSA employees has been increasing. You would probably want to avoid trying to figure out how a bomber would get around the security measures.

⁓

One of the worst aspects of external negativity is the sense of helplessness it engenders. The best way to combat that is look for ways to engage our normal resiliency and make positive changes. Looking into a topic more deeply is a good place to start, as learning about an issue can make it more familiar, which can often defuse our stress. You may then choose to raise awareness in others about a terrible situation to try and change it. If you show empathy and courage to others, you will encourage them to do the same, creating an ever-expanding pool of strength in the face of a terrible situation. Every story of hope and triumph over a serious problem began with someone who refused to give up. That story could be yours.

Solar Power and Your Physical Space

by Kelly Surtees

The Sun's power has been revered throughout history. Ancient cultures created stone monuments like Stonehenge, Newgrange, and the pyramids, to honor the Sun's light at solstice and equinox points.

In Vastu Shastra, or Indian feng shui, beliefs around the Sun go one step further. Vastu practitioners honor the duality of the Sun's light. They believe the Sun's eastern light (morning sun) provides positive ultraviolet rays and that the north, or overhead, Sun provides access to magnetic energy, also positive. Conversely, Vastu holds that the Sun's connection to gamma rays from the west (where the Sun sets) and infrared rays from the south (dark Sun at night) are depleting.

Vastu is ancient and comprehensive, yet it offers simple suggestions about layout and design to help you benefit from the Sun's power. Vastu "helps us enjoy the Sun's healthy properties and avoid its harmful properties." Indian sages, writing in the Rig Veda, between 8 BC and 4 BC, state "Only when illuminating light shines/everything else shines."

Whatever your personal beliefs, the Sun is our primary source of energy. If you've watched a sunrise, you'll understand the intention behind the phrase "something dawned on me." Dawn is a time of insight and awakening, when recognition of something new, or fresh clarity, is possible. Sunset represents the end, that this day is done. There is no more to be gained from this time. Aligning your space and life to the Sun's arc can help you live in line with this prime energy.

In *The Way of Vastu*, Michael and Robin Mastro describe your home as "the body of your body," highlighting how your external space influences your inner experience. By arranging your space and furniture according to the Sun, you tap into powerful forces.

Declutter

While solar-inspired design is ancient, a very modern clearing or decluttering is needed before you begin. Old, unused, or pushed-aside stuff creates stagnant energy and acts as a barrier to success and happiness. Holding onto stuff from the past is akin to holding onto the past itself. Allocating a few hours or even a weekend for recycling, throwing out, or repurposing accumulated clutter—including larger items like broken appliances or worn-out furniture—is an essential first step to creating a space that is ready for a solar recharge.

Time of Day

The Sun's energy is potent and most favorable when it shines from the east and north. The areas or rooms of your house that receive morning or midday sun are naturally infused with this positive, enlivening light. The Sun's light from the east and north is active, so placing a home office, playroom, or living room in these directions can help you maximize the natural influence of the Sun.

The Sun's energy in the evening and at night, linked to west and south, is depleting. Thus, heavier furniture, storage and shelving, darker colors and quieter rooms are best in these directions. These are spaces for reflection, rest, and recuperation. They benefit from décor and layout changes that add warmth, heat, and solidness, either literally or symbolically.

Layout and Design

Ideally, your property has a lower, or sloped, angle in the north and east. This creates a dynamic where the natural lay of the land helps provide protection from the more difficult energies in the south and west. If your property slopes down to the north and east, it's naturally higher or raised in the south and west. You can bring this high-low approach inside, adding raised platforms in the south or west areas of different rooms.

Entryway

The entry to your home is like a transition space into your sacred world. Whether you have a path, porch, stoop, or just a door, it's important to keep this space open and clear. The direction your entryway faces will guide you to the kinds of objects and colors to use here. (See below.)

Morning Sun

Capture the promise of the morning Sun by hanging sun-catcher crystals in your east windows. These transform a single sunbeam into a rainbow of color, which then energizes or "lights up" otherwise dark corners of rooms, hallways, and staircases. You might consider strategic placement of flat-bottom, pyramid-style sun catchers on railings, bookcases, or coffee tables to act as conduits to transfer the morning sunlight into neglected or dull parts of your space.

In the Garden

You can add protective barriers like fencing, stone or rock features, and solid hedging or landscaping in the south or west. Consider raising the garden beds in this direction. Keeping the north and east open, clear, and as bright as possible enhances the positive solar energy from these directions. Mirrors, water

features (like a pond, birdbath, or pool), or a birdfeeder help amplify the positive energy in the north and east.

Furniture

In *The Power of Vastu Living*, Kathleen Cox suggests following the vastu guideline "of lightweight or delicate furnishings in the north and east quadrants and heavy or tall furnishings in the south and west quadrants." This provides maximum openness and receptivity in the north and east while improving the ability of your space to hold on to the good flowing in from these directions by building up and strengthening the west and south.

The Bed

The southwest is generally good for the bed, with the east as second choice. These directions refer to the wall on which the headboard is placed. Avoid placing your bedhead on the north wall. Cox states, "When you sleep in the same direction as the earth's magnetic pole, the two poles behave like magnets. They repel each other and interfere with your sleep." Her suggestion if the only option is for your bedhead to be on the north wall? When you go to sleep, sleep upside down in the bed, i.e. with your head at the south end.

Conventional Candle Wisdom:
True or False?

by Denise Dumars

Most of us know and follow conventional candle wisdom, if not to the letter, then as much as possible. However, some candle customs are merely superstitions, not necessary magical practices, and once their origins are understood, can safely be ignored. Let's look at a few of them in the context of "true or false" and with good critical thinking.

Don't use matches to light a candle used in rituals or for spells. FALSE.

The origin of this myth has nothing to do with pagan or magical practice as we know it today. It actually originated in the nineteenth century when matches became common and were often called "lucifers" because they contained phosphorus and had a sulfurous odor. They—and indeed both sulfur

and phosphorus—were thought to be "evil" and unsuitable for spiritual work because of associations with the devil. None of this folklore has anything whatsoever to do with current Pagan or magical traditions, so one can safely use matches to light sacred candles. My Iseum does it all the time, but since we are an open circle and sometimes newcomers attend, we keep the matches in a big matchbook from Lithuania that has the likeness of the fire god Perkunas on the cover, which lends Pagan credibility to their use to fend off any complaints!

Don't blow out a candle; pinch it out or use a candle snuffer. FALSE.

While using a candle snuffer looks elegant and there's no reason not to use one, there is no need to be superstitious or to burn your fingers rather than blow out candles. The origin of this myth came about because it was thought that one's breath would "blow away" the magic and invalidate the spell. Wow, if one's breath is that powerful, then a spell probably isn't even needed, right? In addition, some religious traditions feel it is unclean or irreligious to risk getting one's saliva on sacred candles, so if you are in a church, follow their traditions. Otherwise, this, too, can be safely ignored among modern Pagans.

Always let a candle used in a spell burn continuously until it is burned out. FALSE in some traditions; TRUE in others.

This is simply not safe and safety trumps anything else. Even though many advise putting the candle in the bathtub until it burns out, I live in earthquake country, and even in the tub a bathroom curtain or other object could fall in and start a fire during a tremor or quake. I always snuff a spell candle before I leave the house and simply burn it again when I am home; I do this each time I am home until it burns down, and this is what I recommend to everyone. Candle use with small children and pets around is iffy at best; a friend who has several pets doesn't even light real candles.

She lights "astral candles" that she can visualize in her mind without risking accidents, and if you believe that magic is in the intent, not in its trappings, then I would suggest trying her method if you have animals or small children at home.

However, in some traditions, such as hoodoo and some gypsy spellwork, a candle must burn down all the way without being relit, so it is recommended that a tea candle, votive, or small taper candle be used that will safely burn out quickly rather than a larger candle, such as the nine-day glass candles that are commonly used.

Don't use broken or dirty candles in spellwork. TRUE, but with qualification.

A candle that has its "back" broken, as in a broken taper, is simply unfit for spellwork if only because of its psychological effect on the spellcaster. A candle that is enclosed in glass that is cracked is unsafe to use, and if a votive or other glass candleholder cracks, it should be thrown out for safety's sake as well.

A dirty candle, on the other hand, needs to be considered before using. Is it just a little dusty? If so, then olive oil or appropriate ritual oil can be rubbed on the candle prior to lighting it in order to cleanse it. Some people also pass the candle through a purifying incense such as sage or dragon's blood before use. However, if the candle—especially a glass candle—has been in a shop for so long that its color is fading and there is a lot of dust or dirt on the top, then do you really want to use it anyway? Better to buy a newer, cleaner candle someplace where ritual supplies are treated with more respect.

Burn Patterns and Meanings

There are many traditional ideas about the symbolism of *how* a candle burns especially when considering candles in glass containers, so let's look at some of them.

First, when buying a candle, look to see if the wick is off-center. If it is, then the candle will not burn correctly. If

the wick can be moved to the center easily, then it should be all right. Now, with a candle that is poured evenly and has a straight wick and is enclosed in glass or can be put in a glass or other container—such as a votive candle—let's look at those traditional beliefs about how the candle burns.

If a candle burns unevenly and leaves black soot on one side of the glass, someone is working against you. FALSE, most likely.

Of course, it's possible that this is happening, but before you buy into this idea, check the following: First, make sure there aren't any air currents affecting the candle flame, such as a fan blowing it to one side. Then, check to see if your candle wick is off-center. If it is, use something fireproof to gently center it. If you can find no logical explanation for the candle's behavior and if it continues to happen while you are doing a ritual, performing a spell, or saying prayers, then there may well be someone or something attempting to affect you.

If a candle goes out and refuses to relight, someone is trying to repel the magic, or spiritual forces are telling you not to perform this ritual. FALSE.

A candle that goes out and does not relight may have gotten wet and enough water remained in the wick and/or wax so that it will never relight. In this case, you'll have to throw it away and start over. Or, as in some inexpensive candles, the wick is poorly made and the candle itself may not even be truly flammable! Nothing supernatural here, just a poorly made candle. Get a better quality candle and start over.

A candle that hisses and sizzles and suddenly burns higher or brighter is trying to tell you something. POSSIBLY TRUE.

Either that, or it's gotten wet. (See above.) If you have anointed the candle with oils and/or herbs, then those substances may well affect the candle's burning pattern, too. However, I've found that sometimes a candle flame will do something odd if a certain phrase is spoken or question asked. I cannot prove that the candle is trying to tell me something, but it doesn't hurt to note when and under what circumstances this occurred if there is no other logical explanation.

A candle that tips over or lights something on fire indicates the presence of an evil force or someone working magic against you. Probably FALSE.

I'm not sure how you'd prove this 100 percent false, but I do know that most candles that tip over do so because they are not firmly placed to begin with. This is actually fairly common with tapers, which is why I rarely use them in ritual or spells. People in the circle can get clumsy, and someone knocking over a candle might be too embarrassed to admit it. And because candle flames do vary in size and height naturally throughout the burning process, anything placed too close to the candle can catch on fire if the candle flares, so be careful!

Use of Colored Candles

There are a few superstitions regarding candle colors as well. Many of the disagreements about the meaning of candle colors and how they should be used can be chalked up to cultural differences between practitioners, but some lore is simply personal perception. Mostly, where the lore disagrees is in the use of the following candle colors.

Red: When I think of **red**, I think of passion, love, Valentine's Day. It's my favorite color, so I loved going to Chinatown as a child because they used so much **red** in their decor because in their culture it is a lucky color. However, there are those who do not recommend **red** candles for love spells. Some see **red** as emblematic of lust, not love, and say that if you are seeking a long-term, loving relationship instead of a one-night stand, use a **pink** candle instead of a **red** one. Some cultures also identify **red** with blood, anger, and violence, and so do not advise using it except in very negative spells, which I wouldn't recommend doing at all. Examine your own feelings about the color **red** and then go with a spell that fits your own beliefs.

Green: Hoodoo and modern American magic seems to always equate **green** with prosperity, but this idea has only been around since the United States started printing "greenback dollars." In the past, **gold**, **yellow**, and **silver** candles were used for money and prosperity, as they symbolized precious metals. In Asian traditions, large, round "golden" fruits like oranges and grapefruit are put on prosperity altars, and so **yellow** and **orange** candles stand for money. **Green** candles originally stood for abundance, which is not exactly the same thing as prosperity; **green** was the color of healthy vegetation, which symbolized lush crops and therefore healthy gardens, animals, and human beings. It is associated with the Green Man archetype, of course, who is the patron of **green** growing things and animal and human fertility. So, unless you are in a country such as the United States, which prints **green** currency, you may wish to use a **golden yellow** candle if your wish is simply for money.

Black: Probably no candle color is so controversial. This is because of Western culture's negative associations with the color, which modern society tries hard to dispel in other areas, yet the negative association attributed to **black** candles still remains. Many people see a **black** candle and immediately associate it with "**black**" magic and placing curses. This is simplistic and superstitious thinking, but it is widespread. However, not all cultures see it this way; for example, in New Orleans, you can buy **black** patchouli-scented candles to burn for St. Expedite, whose statue stands in the Virgin of Guadalupe chapel! Many Pagans who celebrate Samhain and those of us in the Southwest who also celebrate the Mexican Day of the Dead use **black** candles, sometimes also patchouli-scented, as symbolic of the fact that the wheel of the year is turning from the light to the dark and the veil between the worlds is thin. It was once common to leave such a candle in the window to welcome the spirit of a departed loved one. **Black** candles are also used to "uncross" persons who feel they have been crossed by others, by circumstances, or even by themselves. A double-action candle—one that is **black** halfway and another color the other half—is used to first dispel the negativity, then to bring what the person wants—usually **red** to bring love, **green** to bring money, etc. Remember that in some cultures, **white**, not **black**, is the color associated with death and mourning. **Black** is beautiful; embrace it!

Now, I have a curious candle story. On my Egyptian altar I have two identical tealight holders. One is on the right side of the altar and the other on the left. It seemed to me that the candle on the left side always burned longer than the one on the right, regardless of what type or brand of candle I used. It wasn't the air currents in my home, either. Had that been the case, the left candle would have been the one affected and would most likely have been the one to burn out sooner. So I decided it must be something to do with the candleholder itself, for even two mass-produced items are not exactly alike.

I switched the positions of the candleholders. I put in fresh tealights.

Yes, you guessed it; the one on the left side of the altar still burned longer even though it was now in the candleholder that had been on the right side. This one I can't explain. Any ideas?

∾

In conclusion, use good common sense and safety precautions when burning candles. Respect others' candle-burning traditions, but do not allow superstition to frighten you or keep you from utilizing candles in the way that you think best. Remember, it's your energy that you're putting into the candle work, so go with what works best for you!

Enchanted Entryways

by Blake Octavian Blair

We pass through entryways every day, in and out of our homes, within our homes, at businesses, at our jobs. Many people do not give them a second thought. However, entryways are an integral part of our daily lives and are of great energetic importance. Magickal folks have realized this throughout history and have developed magickal treatments and customs for these portals. Once we view them through the lens that they are magickal portals into our sacred places and spaces that allow for people and energy to flow into and through our environments (or not!), the desire to address them in a conscious and magickal way becomes clear.

Whether you wish to enchant your home's front door, bedroom door, business entrance, or the entryway to your office cubicle—many of the goals, principles, and techniques remain the same. Although there is some overlap, many techniques can be used in more than one area. For ease of organization, I'll break the options down into the three basic areas of an entryway: inside the entryway, the door and threshold itself, and outside the entryway.

Inside the Entryway

Let's begin inside the entryway and work our way outward. When adding magickal enchantments to an entryway, many people tend to focus heavily on the door itself and tend to forget that the areas immediately in and outside of it are equally important. In the Eastern practice of feng shui, the front door of one's home or office is considered the "mouth" of the dwelling, where *chi* or life-force energy enters to flow throughout the rest of the space. You will want to keep the inside of your entryway as clear of clutter and unnecessary objects as possible to promote the energetic flow. Try to organize essential items like shoes, winter coats, or umbrellas on a rack. A good rule of thumb—if you can't move freely, neither can the energy.

Now that you've given your entry a little tidying, let's look at a few magickal touches you can add. Crystals and stones are an easy way to add desired energy to your entry. Choose your stones based on the qualities you wish to attract and promote within your home. For example, try placing a couple pieces of black obsidian on each side of the door inside your entryway. Black obsidian is said to have properties of protection on physical and emotional levels and lends an energy of stability to its environment.

Placing a small, living green plant in your entryway also adds a touch of vibrant life force and earth energy, giving those who enter a welcome and uplifting boost. Another way I have utilized plant magick in the entryway to my own home is by creating a swag out of dried grapevine and dried herbs. I purchased the swag ready-made at my local craft store and also picked up some of the dried herbs. You can, of course, grow and dry your own herbs as well. The grapevine has protective properties, and I used eucalyptus for good health and healing, as well as yarrow for its

qualities of nurturing love. I hung the swag above the inside of our front door and all those who enter must pass under it.

Hanging things above, to the side, or behind the door serves double duty. Not only does it accomplish your magical goal while adding to your décor, it helps keep the floor space clear—and the energy flowing. Many homes do not have a formal entryway, and the entry area in many apartments is small to nonexistent. Consider hanging a plaque of a rune, sigil, or a symbol of your faith in your entryway. While this may not be appropriate for a workspace outside the home, it is perfectly fitting within your home. Popular symbols such as pentacles, awens, and the triple moon are popular standards for Pagans; however, many eclectics who still honor their ancestry or blend paths may also consider other faith symbols such as the Star of David, the Celtic cross, the Om, or a mezuzah (generally placed on the outside door frame).

You may decide to create a mojo bag or witch bottle for your desired enchanting goals to place in your entryway. Whether it be for prosperity, good health, calmness, protection, or a combination of goals, a mojo bag can be a nice inconspicuous option. Simply hang it high toward the ceiling, or even in plain sight from the key rack. You'll be surprised how little attention it attracts! The witch bottle can be used in multiple areas. It can be placed inside the entryway or buried in the ground (or in a plant pot) outside the entryway and can be tailored to many goals. Options for ingredients to include in bags and bottles are endless and consulting your magical reference library will help you make just the right choices.

Another of my favorite techniques is to create a home guardian. Choose a statue—it can be a dragon, gargoyle, fu dog, angel, lion, or any other creature you feel would serve as a good guardian protector. Consecrate the statue according to your own methods and traditions, and touch the third eye of the creature (I like to anoint it with an oil as well) while stating your intent for it to serve and protect all those who live in the dwelling. Now, place it in your entryway facing toward your door. If you wish, you can also do this with a statue outside your front door, in which case you'd place it by your door, but facing outward. The guardian works well for office spaces and dealing with toxic coworkers, too! The bonus is that if you choose your guardian wisely, it can simply pass as décor to dress up your workspace.

Many find comfort and effectiveness in placing a small shrine or image of a personal patron or threshold deity in the entryway of their home. This can be as simple as a small statue, and an offering bowl on a small table or even just a framed picture on the wall. Some deities who have associations with thresholds and crossroads (they share much in common energetically!) are the Hindu god Ganesha, Legba from the African diasporic traditions, and the ever-popular Hecate, among others.

The Door Itself

For many, an image of their front door is the first thing that comes to mind when they hear the term entryway. Enchantments for the door itself range from the visibly witchy to the virtually invisible. One of the more inconspicuous treatments for the door is its color. The energetic effect of color on our emotions and perceptions is something even real estate agents are aware of— even if they don't refer to it as magick! Red has long been a traditional color for the front door of homes for its associations with vibrancy, protection, blessings, and prosperity. Blue is considered by many to be a good color choice for magickal practitioners and is said to protect from evil in addition to being associated with the element of water. Blue also evokes serene and calming energies. Brown gives off earthy and grounding vibes, while green can symbolize growth, prosperity, and healing. If you are able to paint your door, give your color choice some thoughtful consideration.

Another stealthy enchantment for doors is to use a wash. Washes (often termed "floor washes") are used often in hoodoo magick. A wash is a liquid infused with various ingredients such as oils, essences, and herbs that align with a magical goal. If you choose to use a wash, be sure to literally clean the door before applying the magical wash! For a nice uplifting and cleansing wash, I like a citrus and sage combination. There are varying opinions on the proper method to create a wash, so the instructions I give here are for my adaptation. Into a large empty bucket, squeeze the juice of a large citrus fruit (two if the fruits are smaller) and then add its peel. Add two to three teaspoons of crushed white sage to the bucket, fill with hot water, and allow to steep for fifteen minutes. Once the wash is made, it is applied to the door, as if washing it, with a rag or sponge. (I also periodically use holy waters/washes to anoint the door by dipping a finger and drawing sacred symbols upon it.) When application to door is finished, leftover wash can be applied to the floor inside the entryway or to the doorstep/porch. When finished, pour any unused wash (herbs, peels, and all) upon the earth.

The system of feng shui takes into consideration shars in relation to the entryway of the home. Author Richard Webster tells us, in *101 Feng Shui Tips for Your Home,* that shars can be thought of as (energetic) poison arrows formed by straight lines or sharp angles that point toward your entryway. Examples are angles and corners of other buildings as well roads that head directly toward your door. The enchantment to fix this is to hang a feng shui remedy known as the *pa-kua* mirror, an octagonal plaque with I Ching trigrams inscribed upon it with a mirror in the center, on the outside of the door. It effectively diverts and sends the shar away from your dwelling.

In addition, an option that can be witchy or covert is hang a magickally designed wreath on your door. That's right, wreaths aren't just for the holidays anymore! The design process for choosing components for a wreath is very similar to that of the swag I mentioned making earlier in this article and grapevine wreaths are readily available in craft shops. With a wreath, you can go over the top and add visibly witchy items such as crystals, pentacles, and faux cobwebs (very protective!) or you might take a more low-key approach by adding foliage and herbs aligning with your goals. And remember, if your home consists of perhaps a rented room inside a larger house, a dorm room, or any situation where you cannot or do not want to put a wreath on the outside of your door, they are equally effective hung inside the door, which has the perk of adding a festive element to your environment.

Outside the Entryway

We've now worked our way through the threshold and to the exterior of the entryway. This is an important area—it welcomes you every time you approach, it welcomes your guests, and energy will pass through here before going through your door and into your space. One of the easiest ways to make this space more hospitable is to choose an appropriate doormat. It goes a long way to making the entry feel welcoming and also affords opportunity for some magickal enchantment. During my university years, I even had a few professors who put doormats in the hallway in front of their office doors. It said a lot about their personality and made them seem more approachable and welcoming to students and visitors. For our own home, my husband and I chose a doormat that

features Celtic knotwork. Not only attractive in appearance, the knotwork also provides a nice protective element.

Another benefit to doormats is that you can put things under them. The aforementioned floor washes work great for front stoops. I also regularly draw protective runes, such as Eolh, in chalk under the doormat. Eolh also conveniently has the added benefit of being associated with beneficial new influences entering one's life—a fitting symbol for the entryway! Be creative with your choices and choose something that resonates with you. Don't forget to employ color magick when choosing your chalk!

Hanging a horseshoe above your door is another magickal enchantment with a long folk history. The use of them as an amulet for entryways is so far ingrained in Western culture that you'll see them above doors far from any sight of equestrian activity. It is said that when hung points up as a "U," that it collects prosperous blessings and luck. Additionally, they are often made of iron, a metal with protective properties. While they are traditionally hung above the door, I have one friend who has placed hers to the side of the door, low to the ground, in the points-up position. It has been put to the test and its magick is working equally as well! This piece of low-key magick didn't even catch my eye until I had already made several visits. A new horseshoe works just as well as an old one, and they can be easily purchased at equestrian tack shops, tractor supply stores, and flea markets.

~

For centuries and across cultures, magickally minded folk have been enchanting their entryways. The methods may be numerous and differ widely but the goals remain universal. Our personal spaces, whether they be at work or at home, should serve as a sanctuary—a place we want to feel safe and hopefully at peace. Hopefully the ideas presented here will be a springboard for you to develop your own ways of enchanting your entryways.

For Further Study:

Cunningham, Scott. *Cunningham's Encyclopedia of Magical Herbs.* St. Paul, MN: Llewellyn Publications, 1985.

Cunningham, Scott, and David Harrington. *The Magical Household: Spells & Rituals for the Home.* St. Paul, MN: Llewellyn Publications, 1983.

Whitehurst, Tess. *Magical Housekeeping: Simple Charms & Practical Tips for Creating a Harmonious Home.* Woodbury, MN: Llewellyn Publications, 2010.

Webster, Richard. *Color Magic for Beginners: Simple Techniques to Brighten & Empower Your Life.* Woodbury, MN: Llewellyn Publications, 2006.

Webster, Richard. *101 Feng Shui Tips for Your Home.* Woodbury, MN: Llewellyn Publications, 1998.

Alvarado, Denise. *The Voodoo Hoodoo Spellbook.* Scotts Valley, CA: CreateSpace, 2009.

Peschel, Lisa. *A Practical Guide to the Runes: Their Uses in Divination and Magick.* St. Paul, MN: Llewellyn Publications, 1989.

Carnival Magic

by Sybil Fogg

Under the light of the full moon, a caravan of recreational vehicles, vardos, and trucks pull off a dirt road and fill a field in what seems like a haphazard pattern, but has an eerie sense of order to it. The reds, blues, and yellows of nature mixed with mechanical fumes are muted in the night shadows. Exhaust coils upward into the autumn sky as engines erupt once more and then fall silent. The evening air holds still for just a moment in anticipation. And then men, women, and children pour forth from the various modes of transportation and stretch their legs into the earth and their arms to the sky. They turn to each other, and voices begin to spin through the field and up into the surrounding forest. As if summoned forth, lightning bugs dance in the tall grass and a magic whirls from them, weaving up and around, through the workers who have begun pulling equipment and parts from the trucks and setting them on the ground. A make-shift kitchen is set up. Before too long, the carousel is up, the Ferris wheel is spinning, drumming can be heard from the dancer's tent, and the fortune-teller is polishing her crystal ball. Jugglers practice near the stilt walkers. Fire breathers and sword swallowers show off on the midway as they all gear up for tomorrow's show. The carnival has come to town.

Since the nineteenth century, the United States has been home to the traveling carnival. Often these shows included amusement park–type rides, a burlesque show, games of chance, and the sideshow entertainment, often referred to as "the midway." It was here that magic could be found in the realm of those who claimed to see the future in a spectator's hand or through cards, mirrors, or other reading devices.

It is commonly believed that the 1893 Chicago World's Fair was the event that brought us the traveling carnival. The event's full name was the World's Fair: Columbian Exposition, an event created to celebrate the 400th anniversary of Christopher Columbus's arrival in the New World in 1492. New York City, Washington D.C., and St. Louis all vied with Chicago for the honor of hosting the event but each lost out to the Windy City. The exposition spread across more than 600 acres and featured nearly 200 temporary buildings of mainly neoclassical design, canals, lagoons, and people representing various cultures from around the world. Dedication of the fairgrounds was made on October 21, 1892, but the exposition was not open to the public until May 1, 1893.

One of the most popular attractions at the fair was the Ferris wheel, named for its creator. George Washington Gale Ferris, Jr. was a civil engineer specializing in steel frameworks built specifically for bridges and tunnels, but when he heard about the World's Fair, Ferris hoped to build a structure that would surpass the Eiffel Tower, which had been part of the Paris Exposition four years earlier. It was then that Ferris drafted an enormous revolving observation wheel. His plan was to create a structure of steel that would allow people to view the world in a completely new way. His wheel would be 264-feet high, spinning 36 elegantly dressed passenger cars that could hold 40 to 60 people each. This wheel would be spun by steam engines and brought to a standstill by a colossal air brake. The design was similar to the smaller wooden "pleasure wheels" that had been in operation since the 1600s. It took some convincing to plan, but eventually Ferris's metal ride modeled on a bicycle wheel passed. (http://web.mit.edu/invent/iow/ferris.html.)

At its opening on June 21, 1893, the Ferris wheel was the showpiece of the Exposition. As one reviewer put it, "You cannot advertise the wheel, anyway, any more than you can advertise the fair, or the Atlantic Ocean. They are all too big." (http://thepittsburghhistoryjournal.com/post/460792449/george-washington-gale-ferris-jr-wiki-on-this.) After a six-month run, the fair closed, and over time most of the buildings were moved or destroyed. The beloved wheel remained until April of 1894 when it was dismantled and stored. A year later, it was rebuilt near an affluent neighborhood on Chicago's North Side. It operated there until 1903, when it was taken down and brought to St. Louis for the 1904 World's Fair. Eventually, the original Ferris wheel was demolished on May 11, 1906. (http://www.hydeparkhistory.org/newsletter.html.)

But the dream continued. On the edge of the grounds was an avenue called the Midway Plaisance that held a variety of thrill rides, food vendors, game booths, and sideshow acts. When the World's Fair ended, an independent showman formed the Chicago Midway Plaisance Amusement Company and took thirteen acts on a tour of the Northeast. The show folded in less than a year due to poor money management, but a few members started their own companies—and thus, the traveling carnival was born. The Midway remains within

the carnival and that is where we find the sideshow acts of today.

There is another side to the carnival or perhaps it would be better to describe it as a different type of event. According to the Encylopedia Britannica website (www.brittanica.com /EBchecked/topic/96363/Carnival), the word "carnival" stems from the Latin *carnem levare* or *carnelevarium* meaning to "put away or remove the meat." A long time ago in Italy, followers of Catholicism began the tradition of throwing a wild party right before Lent. As they were not to eat meat during this time, they named their celebration accordingly. Over time, the celebration became so popular it spread to other areas where groups of Catholics resided.

Columbus brought the carnival through the Caribbean and into the Americas. Later the slave trade added a new dimension and element to the carnival through use of masks, stilt walkers, giant puppets, drumming and stick fighting (www.allahwe.org/History.html). These additions had roots in spirituality and magic. Carnival found a strong foothold in areas heavy in Catholic settlements and the slave trade including New Orleans, areas throughout the Caribbean, and South America (think of Brazil). Many a Pagan will argue that carnival holds its true roots in the ancient Winter Solstice celebration of Saturnalia. This holiday began with rituals and sacrifices to the Sun God and culminated with a feast and wild celebration.

What do we get when we add all of this together? We definitely find ourselves with an entire entity ripe with magical opportunity. In Ferris's contribution to the traveling carnival, we find the sun wheel, or the wheel of the year. The masks of Carnival hold spiritual power as representatives of deity, ancestors, or animal totems. Stilt walking represents growth and good luck in addition to having been used in farming and harvest rituals. Juggling lends itself to spells cast for peace within multitasking and, of course, the fortune-tellers found in the carnival naturally lend themselves to magical workings.

When you first arrive, try meeting up with the different fortune-tellers often found at traveling carnivals to guide you in your visit. A good reading will present ideas to work on throughout the day. This information can help you form a spell to work with the help of various fair attractions.

For instance, when riding the Ferris wheel, do a meditation on the sun and how we travel around it. While waiting in line, ticket clutched in hand, think about what you'd like to manifest with this simple spell. Now would be a perfect time to think of what you'd like to draw toward you. Maybe you have been working on a creative project that is stuck. Analyze the way the Ferris wheel moves. It stops, lets people off and takes on new passengers, and then it moves anew. Someone is sitting at the very top, waiting for the wheel to advance. Do you ever feel similar? You're progressing on a project and suddenly come to a halt? You have to wait for the wheel to begin rotating again. Use this moment to gather thoughts on what you would like to unglue. The queue becomes the spoke of a spiral as you wait. Each step forward moves you toward an inward journey. Once you take your seat, don't forget to thank the attendant and then close your eyes for a moment. Bring an image forward of the project you are working on. Keep it in your mind's eye as the wheel begins moving. Imagine a light spreading into you as you go higher, closer to the sun. Roll over all the different avenues you could take. When you reach the peak, turn your face towards the sun (but don't look directly at it) and let yourself and your creativity be bathed in enlightenment. As the Ferris wheel brings you through a full circle, thank the Sun god for his assistance. Don't forget to throw a happy thought to George Washington Gale Ferris, Jr. for making the spell possible.

Now would be a good time to seek out the stilt walkers, preferably ones that also juggle. While entertained, take a moment to reflect on how stilt walkers have been used in various cultures to evoke harvest luck. The taller a stilt, the taller and more verdant the plants will be. Imagine that your artistic endeavor will grow fertile, nurtured by the stilt walker's dance. This, combined with the juggling, will help you to keep all of your pins in the air metaphorically. So often, we find ourselves multitasking, trying to keep all aspects of our life on the move from the holy to the mundane. Use the juggler's skill to infuse the many aspects of your life so that you may keep them well managed.

Now it's time to find a dancer to weave your spell into existence. Different carnivals rely on different forms of dance ranging from burlesque to belly dancing, but all styles can be used in your meditation. If you're viewing a burlesque show, imagine that each piece of clothing removed is a layer of anxiety, worries, and stresses that are keeping you from working to your potential being stripped away. If your dancer is a snake dancer, let the serpent's spirit coil around your difficulties or pains and soothe them away. Dancers' feet are in tune with Mother Earth. As they tap the ground, they awaken the mother and she will hear your wishes, so ask with an open heart and soul.

If you want, try your hand at the various games. There is not much magic to be had in this activity, as often carnival games are near impossible to win. This would be a good exercise for steeping your life in whimsy and playfulness. That is an integral part of magic that is often overlooked and will allow you time to add a splash of joy to your workings.

To complete your spell, find the sword swallowers and fire performers. A good sword-swallowing performance is not only compelling, it will give your spell that push inward so that it will begin to manifest. Finally, deliberate on the fire performance as a way to use the Sun's element to send your spell into completion. You might want to whisper throughout some words that fit your intention, but don't forget to end it with "So mote it be" when the fire goes out.

Now is a good time to stop for a snack to replenish energies depleted by magical workings. Fair food is tasty, but not particularly good for you, so it is wise to use moderation here. Don't forget to keep a little left over for an offering to the God and Goddess for their part in your spell.

After you've returned home from your outing, clean your altar and decorate it with reminders from the day. Perhaps small bits of wood like toothpicks to represent the stilt walkers, a small pin or ball for the juggler, a pocket knife for the sword swallower, coins for the games, tickets for the rides, etc. Whatever you can think of will work. A symbol of what you worked on should be placed in the center alongside the food offering. When you lay your carnival gifts on the altar, light a candle and contemplate the day's events and ponder what other uses you might find for carnival magic.

Phoenix Fuels:
Woods and Resins for Spellcraft

by Elizabeth Barrette

Fire was among the earliest of humanity's great discoveries, following tool use in shaping our future. Today, fire is one of the elements in the Western system commonly used in Pagan traditions. We use candles, bonfires, and other such things to raise power and direct our magic. We also use fire as natural lighting for our rituals because it creates a more mystical mood than artificial light. The more we understand about how it works, and especially how to feed it, the better results we get.

Remember that fire magic requires extra care for safety's sake. Make sure all flames are in secure containers where nobody can bump into them. Avoid touching hot things with bare skin. Wear snug clothes. Keep a fire extinguisher handy.

The Magic of Fire

Fire is the most lifelike of the elements. It's born, it grows, it dies. It eats and breathes and moves. It responds to its environment. All of these factors encourage us to treat it almost like a living thing. We can sense its energy.

As an element, fire is hot and dry. It corresponds to summer, south, and masculine energy. It matches the astrological signs Aries, Leo, and Sagittarius. Its personality traits include leadership, passion, bravery, arrogance, and aggression. In tarot, fire represents passion and transformation. Fire makes a good servant but a poor master; as useful as it is, it can wreak great harm. It requires care and control to use safely.

Fire magic can be used for many things. It raises energy. It can grant courage and forge will. It deals with lust—although for love, water is also needed. (Remember that fire and water make steam!) It purifies, protects, banishes, and transforms.

With so many powers, how does fire know what we want from it? We can use incantations, complex spells, or many other methods. However, the most straightforward way involves fuel. All fire requires something to burn. What we choose to use as fuel, or what we add to the fire as it burns, can focus the nature of the magic. This is why so many traditions speak of sacred woods or incenses to be burned in magical fires. Dressing oils are applied to candles for similar purpose. It's even possible to change the color of flames with the right ingredients.

Resins and Other Incenses

Incense comes in many forms. Stick or cone incense may be burned for fire/air magic. For tuning fire magic to a particular purpose, however, the most useful types are resin or loose powder incenses. These are placed atop lit charcoal within a censer, or thrown into a larger fire. Some of them, particularly the resins, have very strong and persistent smoke, which makes them distinguishable even outdoors or in a sizable fire. Use them sparingly indoors.

Amber protects, shields, and mellows. It supports mental focus and emotional stability. It transmutes negative energy to positive energy.

Ambergris strengthens dreams and psychic abilities. It blends fire and water magic. In love spells, it attracts men and enhances male virility.

Balm of Gilead brings love and protection. It soothes stress and aids healing. It can summon spirits and support manifestation.

Balsam grants strength and stability. It breaks up negative energy and blocks.

Bayberry attracts good luck and money. It heals and relieves stress.

Benzoin is good for prosperity and purification. It soothes tension while reducing irritability, anxiety, and depression. It enhances concentration, focus, and generosity. Add it to incense for divination or for attracting customers.

Camphor is among the strongest purification ingredients. It also boosts personal influence, dreams, psychic awareness, and divinatory ability. Add it to any incense for extra strength, or to incense for purifying and blessing a new home.

Copal is a good ingredient for love or purification incenses.

Dragon's blood provides energy, purification, and protection. It banishes negative influences and breaks bad habits. Add it to increase the strength of incense blends.

Frankincense cleanses, purifies, protects, and consecrates. It brings successful ventures and manifestation. Use it in works for self-discipline or will. Add it to offertory or blessing incenses. A blend of frankincense and myrrh is a traditional sacred incense

across several traditions, making it a good choice for interfaith work; and its strong, carrying smoke suits it to outdoor rituals.

Gum Arabic conveys protection, prosperity, and friendship. It enhances psychic and spiritual development. Burn it in a censer to consecrate chests, boxes, cabinets, or other containers for ritual equipment. Add it to meditative incense blends.

Musk boosts self-esteem and strengthens the root chakra. It enhances desirability and attracts women. It helps extend a sexual or romantic connection into the spiritual realm.

Myrrh promotes meditation, healing, and peace. It opens spiritual channels. Use it in blends for consecration; add to any blend for extra strength. It is traditionally combined with frankincense.

Xanthan gum is used as a blending base for incense. It also works for binding, setting limits, and cooperation.

Magical Woods

Each woody plant has its own magical signature and mystical properties. Most magical wood comes from trees, but some comes from bushes or woody vines instead. Fuel woods are available in large quantities, often burned as whole logs—maple, oak, etc. Less common woods may be added as twigs or wood shavings. It's easy to find chips of mesquite, hickory, apple, and others intended for flavoring in smokers or barbecue grills. Pine, cedar, and a few other options appear as shavings in the pet aisle. They make good firestarters for sacred fires, and may also be tossed in as offerings.

Poor firewood types include cottonwood, elm, spruce, and willow. They are not recommended for fire magic.

Apple is an excellent fuel overall. It produces a low amount of intensely sweet smoke when burned. It gives few sparks and good coals. It conjures feminine energy and is the sacred tree of the *bandraoi* or woman-druids. Use it in rituals for enchantment, divination, love, or female fertility. To find large quantities of apple wood, try asking at an orchard if they have pruned branches (spring) or have cut down any damaged trees (autumn to winter).

Ash is an excellent fuel overall. It yields low smoke, sparks, and fragrance but produces good coals. This is the world-tree Yggdrasil in Norse tradition; ash is also sacred to Poseidon. Therefore it's ideal for use in Asatru or Hellenic ritual fires. It links the inner and outer worlds, magical and mundane. It grants strength and clarity of purpose. It grants influence over the sea and protection from drowning. Burn it in spells for healing, karma, or magical enhancement.

Black walnut is an excellent fuel overall. It puts out low smoke, few sparks, and good fragrance. It also produces good coals. Use it for banishing or binding spells.

Cedar is not ideal as a fuel, but makes a good additive. It produces a bright, sharp fragrance and many sparks. Cedar is sacred to Artemis and Persephone. It cleanses negativity and consecrates sacred space. Use it in rituals for healing, protection, or ancestor work.

Hickory is an excellent fuel overall. It puts out low smoke and sparks. It burns hot and long, giving a rich smoky flavor to anything cooked over it. Hickory is sacred to sun gods such as Lugh and Apollo. It conveys command and discipline. It aids in finding direction and promotes generosity. Use it in rituals for abundance, wholeness, and presence.

Lilac produces very bright, tall, hot flames with moderate sparks. Add a few branches of it to boost the performance of bonfires. Magically, lilac drives away evil and grants protection. This makes it ideal for the balefires of Beltane and Samhain.

Maple is an excellent fuel overall. It gives off low smoke, few sparks, and good fragrance. It burns down to an excellent bed of coals. Magically, it brings success and abundance. For the latter in particular, a bonfire made entirely of maple is ideal.

Mesquite is a good fuel overall. It burns slowly and very hot. For this reason, a few mesquite logs in a bonfire help keep it going long-term. Its smoke gives a distinctive musky, bittersharp flavor to anything cooked over it. Mesquite has feminine energy; it is ruled by the Moon and the element of Water. Use it in rituals for healing, abundance, or purification. It's an ideal wood for housewarming fires because it strengthens a homestead.

Oak is an excellent fuel overall. It gives off low smoke, few sparks, and good fragrance. It produces an excellent bed of coals. If at all possible, use oak for a fire intended for heat or cooking. It's popular as a Yule log for its duration and thermal qualities. This is the sacred tree of the Druids, considered a wood of

sacrifice and offering. It is a guardian and liberator. Use it in rituals for endurance, prosperity, or power. It also conveys masculine stamina and fertility, and lust. These latter aspects make it popular in Beltane fires.

Pine is a fair fuel overall. It sends up many bright sparks and a medium amount of fragrant smoke, burning down to fair coals. Use it after dark when you want a vivid light show, particularly if you plan to throw in things to change the color of the flames or sparks. Similarly, if you don't have pine logs but you want sparks, add pine shavings or pine cones. Pine is not ideal for use in fireplaces or woodstoves because it leaves a lot of buildup inside the chimney. Magically, pine conveys strength, longevity, and rejuvenation. Its fragrance helps relieve feelings of guilt.

Vine grows in a spiral, making it potent for all magical purposes and especially those relating to the Wheel of the Year. Add it to sabbat fires. It can inspire exhilaration, joy, or wrath. Use it for rebirth or working with Faerie.

Dressing Oils

Candles may be enchanted for a specific purpose by dressing them with oil. Use genuine essential oil, not fragrance oil. For summoning a quality, point the base of the candle toward you, then stroke from the wick to the base. For banishing a quality, stroke from the base to the wick.

Basil banishes negativity and brings good luck. Use on lovers candles to promote fidelity or mend a damaged relationship.

Cassia promotes clarity, power, and concentration. Use it to enhance meditation or divination. On a male or female candle it promotes romance (pink candle) or lust (red candle).

Gardenia evokes peace, spirituality, and psychic awareness on a white candle. Use it for healing on a green candle. It can also be used for spiritual or nonromantic love on a bride-and-groom candle.

Honeysuckle inspires creativity, prophetic dreams, and psychic awareness. Use on a black-and-white candle for balance. Put it on a green candle to attract money.

Jasmine is good for meditation, astral projection, and psychic enhancement. Use it in spells for justice or honor. It brings restful sleep (on a deep blue candle) or prophetic dreams (on a light blue candle). For peace and harmony, put it on a white candle.

Lavender promotes chastity, peace, and longevity. It focuses the mind and aids creativity on a blue candle.

Patchouli deals in the Earth and the underworld. Use it on a male or female candle for fertility and lust. Use it on a black skull for meditation on death or communing with the ancestors.

Rose attracts love, peace, and pleasant dreams. It relieves stress and promotes household harmony. It attracts fairies. Put it on a lady candle for beauty spells.

Sandalwood is good for protection, exorcism, and warding. It is a popular offering in general. Use with a skull candle for reincarnation work, or a black cat for wish magic.

Coloring Agents

Certain materials make flames change color. This makes it possible to combine fire magic and color magic. Some companies sell sprinkles or firestarters made with these materials, but you can also make your own. Ideally, use one color per fire to get a vivid effect. Some of the commercial products try for multiple colors, but it's very difficult to do well and the result is often an ordinary yellow flame. Several coloring agents are available in grocery stores, and are recommended for beginners. If you're experienced at working with fire, you can look for fancier supplies from a company specializing in fireworks or model rocketry. Don't use coloring in a fire intended for cooking.

There are several ways to employ coloring agents. 1. Put dry coloring directly into a fire. This works great with "found" materials such as green cardboard, which often contains enough copper to make a green flame. 2. Soak wood in a solution of coloring, then allow it to dry before burning. Choose an absorbent wood such as maple or cork. 3. Make firestarters with the coloring. This works especially well if you dip pinecones in melted wax, sprinkle on the coloring, and then add more wax as sealant.

Borax gives a yellowish-green flame. Look for powdered borax among laundry supplies.

Copper sulfate produces green flame. It typically comes as a liquid, sold for swimming pool maintenance.

Potassium chloride yields a purple flame. It's used as a substitute for table salt, found in the spice section.

Magnesium sulfate produces a bright white flame. It's commonly known as Epsom salts, available in cleaning supplies or the pharmacy.

~

As with all magic, the use of fire in ritual requires clarity of purpose. You must know your goal and then choose the spell components best suited to that. Remember that all fuels are flammable (obviously) and some of them extremely so; handle them with care. Likewise, fire energy is highly volatile and requires thoughtful control. Success and safety depend on maintaining your focus even with an exciting bonfire or leaping magic present. You may wish to moderate it with other elements for easier control.

Water Magic

The Joy and Magic of Water

by Penny Billington

Water: cascading, trickling, streaming. The source of life, health, and well-being—and the symbol of the nurturing power of the divine feminine. We float in the womb, and, as the waters break, we enter incarnation; and to water we can always return for regeneration.

So let's first look at what is actually there in the real world. Where is your nearest well, stream, river? Where did local people originally get their water?

Ancient watercourses are with us, but they are often withdrawn from our attention. We can learn to notice them afresh—rivers, ancient fords, bridges, and landing posts that remind us of past industry. It's often possible to hear water roaring below pavements or to glimpse a stream trickling along the edges of backyards. Our job is to know our own area intimately—a lifetime's study. We might discover a water source that will take on special significance, and we'll think about how to use that later on.

Water symbolically represents flow, love, nurturing, emotion, and cleansing. If you feel "water deficient," in your temperament or in the way you are living your life, then resolve to work with water in all its forms.

Making the Relationship

So, you have found a local source of water. You believe in a living, enspirited world, and folklore that tells us many lakes, pools, and springs have a guardian spirit. But how do you begin to make a relationship?

Well, how do you do it with a new friend? Not by telling them what a great person you are or overwhelming them. Take time. Say hello. Introduce yourself, then listen to the voice of the water and see what it evokes in you. Peace? Sadness? Release? Joy? There are no correct answers; this is purely subjective. Allow the emotions this meditative approach brings up to flow through you. Don't feel the need to explain and understand them…just release them by breathing them out gently. And then say thank you.

If you wish to take water for a ritual, always ask first, and then wait for permission, perhaps coming as a bird call, a gurgling wave, a caressing breeze, or just a feeling. Once again, say thank you for the gift.

Relationship starts with noticing and appreciation, so be consciously thankful for the gift of clean water—a rarity in some places in the world—as you fill the kettle, clean your teeth, or as you flush. Gratitude is a potent transformative magic.

Ritual Preparation and Practice

So, water sprites, mermen, and nymphs—how will you celebrate this year? Preparation for ritual is a common Pagan practice. So even before you begin, resolve now to really relish this, using water…

Cleansing, Rejuvenating, and Healing

Sing in your ritual bath or shower, symbolically washing away your everyday concerns, revealing your authentic self for ceremony.

Imagine an undine—a water sprite—emerging from a deep pool, arms outstretched, fluid, graceful, joyous, and loving: face and hair are formed of drops and ribbons streaming from a cascading waterfall, sparking rainbows in the sun. Water is deep and loving: now evoke that feeling in yourself every time you shower to invigorate and rejuvenate yourself.

Take a ritual bath when life is hard. When you need the nurturing qualities of water to support you, as they did in the womb. Prepare your room with candles, and relaxing scents, and slip into the waters.

Allow a beautiful image to form in the place of your third eye; a chalice of crystal tilting, pouring out the magical essence of love, forgiveness and healing through your body as your stresses dissolve. Float, weightless and supported by the higher powers. Evoke the love, peace, and forgiveness of the eternal Mother of the Waters within you, and ask for the help of the higher powers with your problems. Relax, and feel stirring within you the sense of support and strength. Set your intention to work with love and trust… say thank you for the gift, for the time of respite, then pull the plug, and, as the waters gurgle, just let go.

And have fun! Be creative! Scent your bath or shower water with herbs or soften it with a scrubbing bag, made by tying oatmeal securely into a piece of cheesecloth to soften the water with its "milk." Research herbs and oils to find out what is safe, appropriate, and seasonal, and then make your choices. Enjoy! Scent your hair rinse to give you the allure of Morgan le Fey! *Morgan* means "from the sea," and, as a holder of deep wisdom, she was one of the queens who took Arthur across the water to the mystical Isle of Avalon. Your own practice will supply the right names for other nymphs or guardians you can conjure up in this way. And when you are clean, you can make your other watery preparations for ritual.

Infusing and Imbuing

Using the purest water possible, you can infuse water with the essence of the season—snowdrop, trefoil, hawthorn, rose, grain, apple, or nut. Pick vegetation early, but after the dew evaporates. Choose respectfully, asking the plant for its gifts and leaving a token in exchange—maybe a kiss, a hair, or a line of a poem. "Infusing" usually means extracting with hot water, but you can also steep your herbs using cosmic influences as befits your ritual—leave some in a bowl of pure water under the high hot sun for the summer festivals, in a crystal goblet under the full moon for lunar rituals, or out in the garden during a thunderstorm—you are limited only by your imagination.

Doing this ensures that you are out in the real world, and connecting to the elements and the cosmic bodies, taking your right place in the natural order.

Blessing and Consecrating

Science tells us that water molecules have a memory, so it makes sense to bless water frequently. The magic is in your intent, reinforced by gesture, so you might harness your imaginative power best when pointing, holding your hand flat over the water, or through a sinuous, gathering motion of the hands, which then focuses on the surface of the water. Remember, the rule is, do what feels right for you.

In your mind's eye, see blessings pouring into the water; see colored streams of energy permeating it. See it sparkle. For your tea, your baby's food, or the water you'll use in ceremony, using water intentionally and treating it—and all the elements—with respect reminds us of its sacred nature.

And then use the water to lustrate in ceremony. Sprinkle fragranced water and feel its energy consecrating your circle for magic. Use and do what is right for you—but never drink water "with additions" unless you are totally sure of your herbs! Make and dedicate water to each purpose just before you use it, and then bless the thirsty earth by pouring out the residue. Magic doesn't work with stock solutions growing cobwebs—it is of *this* time, *this* place, and *these* people. Respect your work by making it fresh whenever possible.

Water and the Seasons

And then there are the festivals—our opportunities to celebrate life, the seasons, and the elements. At each turn of the wheel we can celebrate water.

See now the frozen stasis of the ice of midwinter that mirrors the heart-stopping pause before the Sun's return; running streams of melt water at Imbolc; the Vernal Equinox rain that fuels the growth of new plants, and the thankful showers on the hot farmlands of Midsummer. And, as the wheel turns full circle, the rains of the Autumnal Equinox swell the fruit, and the lashing Samhain storms saturate the soil ready for the dropping seeds and clear the trees of dead leaves.

On your land the continuing dance of sun and rain fuels the turning of the seasons, magically different every year. Witnessing and celebrating that difference is what makes us active Pagans, partners in the dance of life. So if you get wet in your rituals, laugh with the element of water, and give thanks!

Connection to Otherworlds and Respect

Water also has a respected role as a passage down to the Otherworld, which we remember in the custom of throwing coins into wishing wells.

The ancient tradition of votive offerings—ceremonially casting valuable jewelry and weaponry into water—connects people across cultures. We can only speculate on why. To propitiate the gods? To give thanks? As gifts for loved ones far away in time and space? To mark significant occasions? Copying our forebears is an ideal way to forge a relationship. Give gifts to water, just as you would to a friend.

Tell your local stream your news, hopes, and wishes as it flows toward the sea of connection. Trust that you are magnetizing yourself to receive your needs on the return tide. Throw in an acorn as a symbol of your growing projects, a heart-shaped stone for a new relationship, a silver coin for your wishes or a

pentacle for your magical life. Send thanks downstream as you notice every good thing in your life.

And when you come to the time of partings, water will gently receive those things that burden you: your tears can join the nurturing water to give you gentle release, and messages can be carried back to source. At Samhain, give thanks for all that you've loved that has now gone from your life. Make a boat out of half a walnut shell; set in it a small candle and send it on its way to the places of mystery, to the enchanted Isles of the Blessed, with your love.

Respect for Water

Water, like all the elements, can bless, or kill. A real understanding of the immense force of all the elements is essential to understanding our true place in the world. The very noise of the ocean, so soothing when you meditate from the right distance, can buffet your sensibilities, too. Similarly, waves of emotion can cleanse us or, bursting out inappropriately, can be profoundly damaging. Water can glamour us; stay aware, to learn life lessons about balance, allowing grace and beauty to enter. We are small, but we have a right to our place in the world; we can also be mighty in our effect, so we should deal compassionately with each other. And, like the tides, our fortunes will wax and wane. This is being human, being alive. Be joyful!

Water takes the line of least resistance, yet remains completely itself. Waves may fret around large obstructions, but the river's impetus carries it inexorably onward. Water constantly moves in a cycle, evaporating, becoming clouds and dispersing as rain, hail, or sleet to rejoin the earth or sea. Amphibians and many insects live dual lives between water and the land. These are seed-thoughts for visualizations, which will keep us on course in the changing, moving flow of life.

～

Whether presently in the shallows or combating the rapids, feel the joy of life! And remember water's role in transporting us.

In your mind's eye, take a magical barge and then, by the power of magical imagination, allow the boat to travel with you to the place you wish to be—the safe harbour of the future you wish for yourself, where you are loved, secure, and content. A place where you can express your true self absolutely. Where the life you live is magical; where how you think reflects back into the world, connecting you to its subtle changes…

Our brains are 70 percent water, the feeling element. Take the lessons of water deep into your being. Embrace love and life in all its fullness; drink pure water; gaze deep into the well…You are not only nymph, water sprite, or merman, but ruler of your life. Celebrate!

Beach Magick

by Cassius Sparrow

The shoreline is often regarded as a crossroads, where earth meets water. It is a union of two feminine energies: the fertile, strong, enduring energies of the earth, and the healing, cleansing and purifying energies of water. For some, the call of the ocean and its mysteries is strong, inspiring them to follow a path of Sea Witchery. They prefer a long stretch of shoreline, with its crashing waves and rushing waters, using the many gifts of the sea in their spells, and honoring the spirits and gods of the waters. They follow the tides rather than the cycles of the moon and plan their magickal workings accordingly. While the path of the Sea Witch is not for everyone, beach magick can be incorporated into everyday spells and rituals to draw upon the powers of earth, water, and the crossroads where they meet.

Using the Gifts of the Sea

The sea provides many gifts that can be used in magickal workings. Seawater can be used in asperging to cleanse and bless sacred areas. A set of shells similar in shape and size can be inscribed with runes and used in divination. Larger oyster and clamshells can be used as smudging bowls and for burning loose incense. Sand dollars, which are marked with holes spaced like the five points of a star, make an excellent representation of a pentacle for altar decorations. Carve and decorate driftwood for a wand. Coral found naturally along the shoreline can be used to promote harmony and happiness within the home, and assist creativity, communication, and the imagination.

Remember to leave an offering to the sea spirits in thanks when taking a gift from the shoreline. Offerings must not harm the environment, or be seen as litter. Coins, fresh breads or small cakes, sprigs of herbs such as thyme, lavender, and rosemary, or a small bunch of flowers are a few examples of great offerings.

A Wish by the Sea

Wishes are often written on slips of paper, tucked into bottles, and tossed in the sea. This spell re-creates the concept without the litter. Find a flat shell large enough to write on it. Using a water-soluble ink or paint, write your desires on the shell, including symbols and runes corresponding to your wish. Include your name or identifying information. Holding the shell in your hands, charge it with your intentions. Visualize your wish coming true: If you're looking for a promotion at work, visualize your new office and yourself shaking hands with your boss. If your wish is more monetary, imagine your wallet full of cash or that long-expected check arriving in the mail. When you feel the shell has been charged, whisper your wish aloud over it and toss it into the sea. Be sure to thank the sea spirits and leave offerings for them when your wish has been fulfilled.

Happy Home Cleansing Spell

Go to the beach on a day that is calm and bright—early morning hours are great for this. Take a deep breath, releasing stress and anxiety on the exhale, and gather a jar or bottle of seawater. At home, pour the water into a clean, clear bowl and dip a fresh white cloth in it. Use the seawater to wash the doorframes, windowsills and other thresholds of your home with it. Hum, sing, play peaceful music, or do all three, all the while focusing your energy into banishing negativity and unpleasant energies from your home. Invite positivity, love, and happiness. Wash the cloth in the seawater when you are finished, making sure to wring all of the water out of the cloth and into the bowl. Return to the sea, and pour the water back into the ocean, allowing it to carry away all stress, anxiety, and negativity.

Sea Amulet for Protection

This amulet can be either worn or carried in a pocket or bag. Use a shell with a naturally formed hole because drilling or punching a hole runs the risk of cracking or breaking the shell. Any type of shell can be used, although scallop, oyster, and clamshells offer a larger canvas. Choose a shell that resonates for you, and carefully carve or paint runes and symbols of protection. Place the shell into a pouch or charm bag with a pinch of sea salt, a silver coin, a sprig of sage and rosemary, and a tiny sand dollar. Anoint the bag with a drop or two of High John the Conqueror oil, and attach the bag to a cord and wear it as a necklace, attach it to your keychain, or simply carry it in your pocket or bag.

Sea Scrying

The full moon is a perfect time to scry by the waterside. Travel to the shoreline and gather a dish of seawater, using a dark, flat-bottomed dish for best results. Sit comfortably on the sand close to the water and let the soothing sounds of the ocean wash over you, relaxing your body and mind. Use your left (or nondominant) hand to reveal the image, and your right to strengthen it. Move your hands over the water, palms down, nondominant hand first, and wait for the image to appear. Remember to blink! By not blinking, you are straining your eyes and could distort images that appear. When you are finished, return the water to the sea and thank the sea spirits for their help. Feel free to stay and meditate on the images that came to you while scrying.

A Spell for Prosperity

This spell works best when performed during a waxing or full moon, but if you're in a pinch, it can be cast any time. For this spell, carry a piece of aquamarine in your pocket, and bring basil incense and your wand or athame to the shore.

This is a good time to use your shell incense burner and your driftwood wand. While facing the sea, cast your circle or draw a pentacle in front of you with your wand. Light the incense and call upon the spirits of the sea to bring you prosperity. If you have a specific sea deity that you honor, address them with your desires. Otherwise, speak your affirmations to the water:

As there are grains of sand in the sea
So shall be my health and prosperity

If you need a specific sum of money, use your wand or athame to write it in the sand close to the water so the waves will carry your wish out to sea. Take time to meditate; the waters may provide an answer to your money problems immediately. When the incense has burned out, extinguish the charcoal or flames with sand, then be sure to clean up after yourself before you leave. Thank the sea spirits and deities. Sleep with the piece of aquamarine tucked inside your pillow each night. The aquamarine serves as an avenue of communication between you and the sea. While you dream, the spirits of the

sea may come to you with the answers to your money problems. When your situation has been improved or resolved, return to the same spot where the spell was cast, and offer the aquamarine to the sea, thanking it once again for its help.

Banishing a Bad Habit

On a particularly windy day, such as right before a storm—but not in the middle of a storm or anytime lightning is present—travel to the sea. As you walk down to the water, look for a stone or broken shell and pick it up, charging it with your intent as you approach the sea. Stand facing the water, and hold the stone or shell in your dominant hand, careful not to cut yourself. Visualize yourself free of the bad habit that you have replaced it with a good habit, one that is healthier. Feel the stone warm in your hand and you watch the turbulent waters roar as the waves crash in front of you. When you are ready to let go, throw the stone as hard and as far as you can into the water while shouting:

Away from me, I am free of you!

Visualize your bad habit rushing away from you into the waves, swallowed by the sea, never to trouble you again. Turn around and walk away without looking back, leaving the habit far behind.

～

Some spells that require a crossroads can be performed at the water's edge, and many spells that you already use can be altered slightly to incorporate the gifts and energies of the sea. The only limit to beach magick is your own imagination, whether you choose to follow the path of the Sea Witch, or simply decide to incorporate the sea into your magickal workings more often. The sea is a wealth of power, energy, and magickal resources, as long as we approach it mindfully and with respect.

Witches to the Rescue: Emergency Healing Requests

by Mickie Mueller

As magical workers, we often find ourselves in situations where someone needs some emergency healing energy sent for anything from colds or headaches to a stay in the hospital. In the age of social media, these requests have multiplied. We also often learn about current events like natural disasters or situations where many people are hurt and we would love to send some healing energy to help. But if you were to answer every one of the healing requests with a full ritual, you would spend your entire day casting circles and lighting candles and have no time for anything else, wouldn't you?

Not necessarily. The world needs more healing, but there are many ways to accomplish this with large amounts of energy sent through surprisingly simple methods.

I've been a Reiki master/teacher since 2001; I've learned a lot about healing. In fact, the study of Reiki teaches methods for sending healing energy to more than one person at a time. (If you ever have the opportunity to learn this modality, it's a great addition to your magical toolbox.) I will mention Reiki from time to time here as a reference, but even if you aren't a practitioner, there are many ways to apply the principles of distance healing using your own magic so that you can streamline your healing requests for the greatest good of all.

Avoiding an Energy Drain

I have heard some magic workers complain that doing healing work—especially for many people—can leave them feeling drained. That's because they are sending their own personal energy toward healing someone else and keeping less for themselves. Personal energy means that you are sending energy from your own personal energy field, your aura. This is a twofold problem: First of all, if you deplete your own personal energy by doing healing for others, you won't be able to help yourself or anyone else. The second problem is that when you send personal energy, you can leave an open channel for the receiver's energy to flow back to you, which is also unacceptable because they are sick. Besides depleting them, you end up receiving the bad energy their body is releasing due to illness, thus putting your energy field at risk. However, this is never a problem for Reiki practitioners because energy naturally flows only one way and is channeled from universal energy, not your personal energy. Witches who are not Reiki trained can still learn to use the spiritual concepts of energy channeling and energy flow to assist them in their magical healing work. Here are a couple of simple tricks you can use to successfully send energy for multiple emergency healing requests without worrying about depleting your own energy.

First, you need to access another power source other than yourself. Tapping into earth energy is a great option. Earth energy is naturally healing and the earth is constantly absorbing all kinds of energy, cleansing it, and making it neutral, which makes earth energy perfect to program for healing work. You can channel it by imagining roots coming from your feet and growing down into the earth. Allow energy to rise up through those roots, flowing from the earth, through you, and out through your hands. Use this earth energy to charge your candle, crystal, or whatever you're using to send the energy. You can also do this with the intention for the earth energy to continue to flow to each person in need of healing for a set period of time.

Now the source of energy is solved, so how to prevent that back flow? When you send healing energy to another person, you should create a buffer. Instead of sending the earth energy charged with healing intention directly from you to the people you're doing work for, a magical buffer will regulate the flow of energy keeping it going in the right direction. Send it through something like a crystal or a candle—you can even use a slip of paper with the receiver's name on it as a magical buffer. Draw an fletched arrow pointing from left to right under the receiver's name, this is a symbol that will program the magic to flow only in one direction, toward the

person who needs healing and preventing any back flow. If using a candle, simply etch an arrow pointing up toward the flame. If you're using a crystal, program the crystal with the intent that it will only send energy and not receive. Hold the crystal and visualize the direction of energy flow while telling the crystal this is how you want it to act; crystals are not hard to program with your intention. When you create a magical buffer in this way, you are merely making the connection between the earth's healing energy and the receiver. Visualize it like a watering hose: you are turning on the hose and pointing the healing power in the hose toward the receiver, facilitating the healing through your intention. Now you have the basic magical tools in place to send emergency healing for anyone who needs it.

Maintaining Effectiveness

Now let's address the idea that you have to send healing for each individual person. If you do it right, you can actually send healing energy to multiple people all at one time and you won't be dividing the energy between them, but sending a full "dose" to each individual. How, you ask? Simple, it's all about intention. When we set the proper intention with our magic, we can truly work wonders!

For instance, say that you have three people on Facebook and an aunt who have all asked you to send healing energy their way for different problems. You can group these requests and send them all general healing energy at the same time. The trick to doing this is that you set the intention by saying something during your healing work like, "May all the people I'm sending healing to receive all the healing they need for the next twenty-four hours." You can group them in many ways, but be sure to add your magical "buffer arrow" symbol to these groupings and then get creative. Many energy workers use a box and put each name on a piece of paper in the box, then send healing energy to everyone in the box daily. Similarly, I made a small pillow with a pocket on it that I have stuffed with healing herbs. Then I place the names of everyone I'm sending healing to in the pillow's pocket and I send healing to them all at once every night when I go to bed. You can also create a crystal grid: a circle of crystals pointing toward a container in the center holding all the names of your healing receivers. We have a local shop in my town with a healing book—they just add names to the book and send healing to the entire book. Some magic workers name individual ribbons for people and then tie them onto a hoop and send healing energy to the whole hoop.

If you get a lot of requests on the Internet, keep a pen and paper handy and jot the names down to send energy when you're ready to do your group send. You could also open up a document on your computer and copy and paste the names into the document, then you can just hit the print button when you're ready. Another way to use a computer document is to drop it in a folder on your computer dedicated solely for healing. Fill the folder with images of healing symbols, deities, and positive intentions. You can add names to the document and take them off when they no longer are in need of healing. Send healing energy to the folder on your computer by opening the folder once a day and looking at the list while you charge a candle with healing energy, then you can close the document and light the candle and you're done.

One of my favorite methods is to have an actual healing altar. This can be as simple as a shelf on the wall. You can include a small box with a lid for names, candleholder, healing crystals, and a healing deity representation. This can be a great way to send emergency healing because everything you need is at your

fingertips. The space will always be used for your emergency healing work, so it will be easy to tap into healing energy there. You can get creative and come up with ideas of your own to combine and send energy; these ideas can get you started and jump-start more ideas of how you can tailor your healing spells. Healing work doesn't have to be difficult to be effective. In fact, the more we simplify our healing work, the more often we can make it part of our lives and the more easily energy can flow.

To Heal or Not to Heal?

I would be remiss in writing this article without discussing the ethics of healing. You may say, "But healing is good isn't it? How can I possibly go wrong doing healing?" If you think really hard, you can probably remember a time in your life when someone did something against your will "for your own good" that was not helpful. The number one rule: only send healing energy if it is requested or if you have permission from the receiver.

This is not a guideline. It's a rule.

Pushing your spell on someone even if it's for healing is not acceptable because you're interfering with the will of another. Never assume that you know what's best for someone else—if you don't have permission, don't do it. You may ask, "Can I light a candle for you and include you in my prayers?" If anyone is reaching out publicly for healing help, you may always send energy their way, but never against someone's will.

If there is someone you really think needs help and either won't ask or isn't able to ask, there is another option. You simply do your usual healing work, but you send the energy into the universe with the intention that it has been placed there on "reserve" for that person. If they at some point through their own spirit ask for help, healing, or assistance from their higher power, that energy is there for them. Using this method, it's up to them and you're not forcing anything on them. This is also the best method that I've found for sending healing energy to a large emergency like a natural disaster. You send healing energy into the universe tagged for people affected by the specific situation, and anyone who needs it may access it through their higher power. This means if an emergency worker says a quick prayer before entering a burning building or a woman trapped in her car with her children asks for help from a guardian angel or goddess, the energy is there for them and it can help the situation as a whole.

It may seem strange, but those who work with healing energy regularly have almost all seen the phenomenon that occasionally people have to work through a spiritual issue in a physical manifestation. In other words, their spirit is learning from an illness and won't be able to heal until they are ready. By leaving energy on reserve for them in the universe, you are honoring their higher power and allowing them control of their personal spiritual path. Oftentimes, these people come to a conclusion on their own and eventually tap into that energy on their own terms. If they don't, the energy will dissipate and become part of the universal energy and flow toward the greater good.

Remember, It's Not Just about You

Another healing pitfall to avoid is allowing ego to get in the way. Several problems can occur from doing this. When doing healing work, it's very important to always combine our magical efforts with common sense. Magical healing should only augment practical medical healing but can never replace it. If you've got a broken arm or high blood pressure on your hands, by all means light that candle, but do it in *addition* to having a doctor address the issue! Another reason to check your ego is that if we're not careful, we can take the results personally as a reflection of our magical skills. Any time you are doing magical work for someone else, the other person is a large part of the equation. We have to remember that while they may be asking for healing, if they are unable or unwilling to accept the healing—even on a subconscious level that is part of their path—it won't work. And only the receiver can change that part of the equation. We should also remember that offering healing should never be done as a way to manipulate another person. If you send healing energy for someone, do so without ego attached.

That said, when you do provide help, you should try to be as effective as possible. Whether you decide to create a healing altar, box, pillow, or other method for grouping and sending healing, it can be very helpful to add some healing correspondences in order to boost magical energy and intention. Here is a list of correspondences that you may want to consider adding to your practice when working your emergency healing magic. This is not a complete list, but it will get you started.

Deities: Brighid, Airmed, Quan Yin, Apollo, Asclepius, Panacea, Eir, Cardea, Isis, Artemis, Heka

Stones: Quartz, rose quartz, calcite, peacock ore, and amethyst are especially good for distance-healing work

Herbs: Rowan, yarrow, lavender, mint, dandelion, ginger, and sage are among herbs that are good healing communicators

Candle colors: White, green, purple, blue; for healing animals you may also use brown

Scents for oils and incense: Frankincense, olive, rose, rosemary, sandalwood, violet, nag champa

~

Doing healing work is a very rewarding practice. It allows us to do something good for the world and makes us feel good in the process. When people reach out to us, it's good to know that we have the ability to whip up some quick emergency healing magic to send their way and that we don't have to perform a huge elaborate ritual to get the job done. As witches, we know that magic can be a force for positive change in the world, and that has never been truer than when magic is applied for the power of healing.

Releasing Emotional Baggage: A Journey to the Edge of the Universe

by Barbara Ardinger, PhD

I first created and used this visualization back in the early 1980s when the momentous love affair of my life was sputtering to an end. I thought he walked on water; he turned out to be a cad. Distressed and depressed, I wanted revenge.

At the time, I was reading *The Cosmic Doctrine*, a book of vast abstraction and esoteric wisdom channeled by occultist Dion Fortune in 1923 to 1924. Fortune describes the Ring-Pass-Not, which is the outer limit of the universe, as a purely abstract ring of energy that protects our universe from demons in other universes.

I have long believed in recycling. So I put the book down and asked myself: Why couldn't I recycle my overwhelming emotional burden? I could carry it to the Ring-Pass-Not and dump it there. Let it disintegrate into the primal atoms that exist in the Ring. Both the energy and I could come back free and clean.

We all have miseries in our lives, not just broken love affairs but job loss and long-term unemployment, sickness and injury, the deaths of family and friends, bullying, crime... the list goes on. Stop and think a minute: what has happened in your life that has you distressed and depressed? It doesn't matter if it happened many years ago or yesterday. If you're carrying that emotional baggage, and it's ruining your life and got you down, then it's time to get up, release it, and recycle the energy.

When we use creative visualization, we work at a level of reality where anything is possible. That's the magic. Let us therefore move into a solar system like the "real one" we live in but also filled with mystical energy.

Visualize the Cosmos

Close your eyes, take several deep, easy breaths, and enter your alpha state. Know that you are safe in the mystical universe where you're going to be recycling old energy.

Visualize the emotional baggage you're carrying. See it as a giant, dark gray, lumpy sack you're carrying on your back like an old-fashioned peddler's pack. It's so big and heavy that you're bent over and prematurely aged from carrying it. How tired are you? How heavy is your burden of miserable energy? Can you feel sharp edges cutting into your body? Does your back ache from the weight? Is it so awful and heavy that you can hardly move under it? It's time to get rid of your emotional baggage!

Now build yourself a nice, handy-dandy spaceship. It can be as big and shiny-clean as the Enterprise, or it can be a sort of used-car Millennium Falcon. Or maybe you're seeing a little Jetsons' flying car. (Make sure there's room for your huge emotional burden under that dome.) Board your spaceship. As you try to stow your emotional baggage, however, you discover that it won't let go of you. Even if you set it down, it remains attached to you by straps and sticky tentacles.

Take another deep, easy breath. In your imagination, see your spaceship flying away from your home, away from your city, away from your state and continent, away from the earth. Fly past the moon and turn left. Your first stop is the planet Venus.

Land on the planet and exit your spaceship. The baggage comes with you. It won't let go. Venus is an emerald-green planet, and you feel her energy rising around you, touching you, flowing into you. This is the energy of love, pleasure, harmony, and nature. Feel the energy of Venus beginning to infiltrate the emotional burden you're carrying. It's wrapping itself around that heavy sack, it's pushing into it. Spend a few minutes on Venus and let the emerald-green energy do its work. Don't try to force it to do anything. Let it move as it will.

Take another deep, easy breath. Get back in your spaceship and take off. Is this liftoff easy or difficult? Is your emotional baggage lighter or heavier? If it's heavier, it's probably the green energy still working.

Now you are landing on Mars, the red planet. The energy of Mars is strong. It's assertive and powerful. Recall that Mars was not originally a war god, but Juno's son, a Latin god of agriculture who always protected his people and his land. Feel the red energy of Mars rising to meet the emerald-green energy of Venus. Together, Venus and Mars, green and red energy, go to work on that huge emotional burden that's still on your back. Feel the red energy of Mars beginning to tear at the straps and sticky tentacles. Feel it beginning to lift the sack away from you. Let the energy of Mars work to protect you from the negative energy of your burden. Don't try to force it to do anything. Let it move as it will.

When you're ready, take another deep, easy breath and board your spaceship again. Your next stop is the planet Jupiter, whose energy promotes justice, enthusiasm, optimism, and expansion. The energy of Jupiter is deep, rich purple. It's the energy of growth. Feel this energy joining the red and green stream of Mars and Venus. Jupiter's energy is as big as your emotional baggage. It pummels the sack and begins to pry the burden off your back. It makes you feel strong. Feel that energy. You're getting stronger. You're beginning to realize that you can indeed dump that old emotional baggage. You don't have to keep carrying it around with you. You don't have to let it ruin your life. You can move on. Let the energy of Jupiter work to strengthen you. Don't try to force it to do anything. Let it move as it will.

Take another deep, easy breath and board your spaceship. Now in your imagination you are landing on another giant planet, Saturn. The energy of Saturn is as deep and dark and quiet as the night. It's Saturn's energy that gives you your sense of duty and responsibility—it gives you justice and discipline. It's a necessary balance to the energies of the other planets. The deep, dark energy of Saturn begins to work into the huge burden. It also begins to work its way into you. It inspires you to think in ways you may not have considered before. Are any parts of that burden yours alone? Did any thoughts or actions of yours help to build that burden? Is it possible that you enabled the construction of that emotional burden? It's time to take some responsibility for the burden you're carrying. Watch Saturn's energy at work, and now you can see parts of the burden beginning to disengage. They lift away. Some of them dissolve. The whole burden isn't gone yet, but perhaps it's measurably lighter because you understand the roots and causes and outcomes better. Let the energy of Saturn work to bring you greater understanding. Let the energy bring justice and discipline into your life. Don't try to force it to do anything. Let it move as it will.

Take another deep, easy breath, and almost before you're back in your spaceship you're suddenly landing on an indigo planet. This is Uranus, whose energy pushes you to evolve and awaken to your intrinsic freedom. Uranian energy brings unexpected happenings into your life. This is the energy of the visionary, the one who sees ahead. Feel this wonderful energy joining the energies of the other planets, but more than that, feel it penetrating your mind and heart. Where does your freedom lie? How can you handle unexpected events? Your burden, while still huge, is becoming measurably lighter as this indigo energy digs into it and chips more pieces of it off. Let the energy of Uranus bring new awareness into your life. Let it help you see more clearly. Don't try to force it to do anything. Let it move as it will.

Take another deep, easy breath, get in your spaceship again and take off. This liftoff is easier than any previous one. Now you're landing on Neptune. This planet's energy is electric blue. It gives you the ability to dissolve old energies and thoughts. You're free to imagine new things. And suddenly— suddenly you realize that the energies of Venus, Mars, Jupiter, Saturn, Uranus, and Neptune have all ganged up against your emotional baggage. They've lifted it off your back! You can stand up straight now. Turn around. Take a closer look at your burden. What do you see? Take your time and study what's been building up in this huge gray sack. Don't judge what you find. Just let it know that you recognize it for what it is.

When you're ready, heave that awful old baggage aboard your spaceship and get aboard yourself. You're approaching the edge of the universe, the Ring-Pass-Not. As you travel, continue to study that old burden. Look at its parts—old unhappiness, old guilt, old regrets, old anger. This may be the collection of a lifetime or maybe just the debris from one awful episode. It's dying, but it's still dreadful to see. As you fly through the Milky Way, consider how that burden built itself up, think about all the little hurts and angers you've collected and how sharp they became, and how heavy. Let the planetary energies light and enlighten you as you study that burden.

And here we are at the Ring-Pass-Not. It encircles the whole universe. You can see stars and galaxies and nebulae and comets in it. What does it look like to you? Is it an endless, black, concrete wall? A giant impenetrable wall of dark light? Is it energy that flows like whitewater rapids, but bigger and faster than Niagara Falls? Is the Ring-Pass-Not the mythic ocean that encircles the Earth, the giant serpent lying in wait for explorers who dare to pass the Pillars of Hercules? Is it a huge black hole into which anything that comes too near will vanish, only to be reborn on the other side in some other, unknown universe? What color is the Ring-Pass-Not in your imagination? Does it glitter like diamonds? Can you perhaps glimpse faces, moving mouths, waving hands in it?

You're hovering before the Ring-Pass-Not. Yes, it's very scary, but this is where you leave your emotional baggage to be recycled. Take a strong, deep breath. Take another one. Get ready. Lift your burden in your arms. Is it less sharp than it used to be? Less heavy? Can you see some of its parts, the old angers, hurts, guilt, injustices?

Release that burden. Open the airlock of your spaceship and pitch your burden at the Ring-Pass-Not. The glittering waves of the Ring part slightly. Your burden is captured. Now bid them farewell.

...and so it's time to part,
my dearest loves—
the angers and hurts and guilty feelings
I have cherished for so long:
fed you
borne you
grown comfortable with you.
I nourished you well
and held you in my heart.

But you became too big, too strong, too heavy,
and I could bear you no longer.
You gained too much power over me,
and I can bear you no longer.

Goodbye, burden, so long and farewell,
and when your parts come 'round again,
let them come back as love, justice, and loving kindness.

When you're ready, take another deep, easy breath and come back to earth, to your home and your private space. Open your eyes. Do you feel lighter?

Making a Magical
St. Patrick's Day

by Sandra Kynes

Even though my family roots go back to Ireland, celebrating Saint Patrick's Day was a conundrum for me for quite a long time. After all, it's a Christian celebration and the legend of driving the snakes out of Ireland represents the suppression of the Goddess-worshipping religion. I went back and forth about this for years, wondering how to integrate a celebration of my cultural roots with my Pagan spirituality. I didn't want to be angry about the religious shift in Ireland, so I had to find a way to make this a magical day for me. A little research into the symbolism of Paddy's Day yielded interpretations that I could incorporate into my own way of making it positive and meaningful.

First of all there are the snakes, and the fact that Ireland has never had them because of its geography. The timing just didn't work for the evolution and migration of snakes to coincide with the movement of glaciers and changes in sea level around Ireland. Details aside, we know that the snakes are just a metaphor. Long before Christianity became established and serpents became the embodiment of evil, the snake was a symbol of the Great Mother Goddess. While she was associated with many creatures, her connection with the snake was one of the oldest and most important. It personified her powers of life, energy, and reproduction.

The snake's cycle of shedding its skin seemed to echo the waxing and waning of the moon, which also forged a link with fecundity. Ultimately, this shedding came to represent immortality and the mysterious ability to be reborn. In addition, the snake's ability to go underground brought an association with chthonic deities. As a result, snakes served as a symbol of the ancestors and were sometimes thought of as incarnations of the dead. Furthermore, water snakes added another dimension that connected all of their kind with the Goddess's power over the life-giving forces of water.

While Isis was often portrayed with a cobra, which became the insignia of sovereignty for Lower Egypt, on the island of Crete, depictions of the Minoan snake goddess represented the serpent as a benevolent spirit and guardian. All these connections have been reason enough for me to keep a couple of small plastic snakes in my collection of ritual gear for when I want to symbolically connect with the ancient primal goddess energy. On Saint Patrick's

Day, I bring them out to represent the living and ever-present numinous energy of the Great Mother.

A prominent feature in the lead-up to Saint Paddy's Day is the shamrock. This old Celtic symbol was adopted by Christians to illustrate the trinity, which was not a new concept. It was long believed that three-part things or something repeated three times were magical and carried special energy. In addition, the shamrock harkens back to the very ancient symbol of the triangle and the sacredness of three within one—not just for the Celts, but in numerous cultures. Three triangles linked shamrock-like at their narrow points was a symbol of the Fate goddesses, both the Greek Moirae and the Norse Norns.

In Ireland, the power of three within one is evident with the triple goddesses. The Morrigan triple goddess of fertility, war, and death is represented by Badb, Macha, and Nemain. The Dagda's three daughters named Brigid comprise *the* triple goddess Brigid who presided over poetry, smithcraft, and healing. The eponymous goddess of Ireland comes from the triple Banba, Fodla, and Eriu of the Tuatha de Danann. Each of these goddesses vied to represent the sovereignty of the land. However, while Ireland (Eire) was named for Eriu, Banba remains its poetic name. On a personal level, we can relate to the three within one as maiden, mother, crone or son, father, sage.

To Celtic people, the shamrock, as well as the three-part triskele, represented the sky above, the earth beneath, and the sea around—a trinity by which people would swear an oath. Far from being a static design, the triskele illustrates the threefold interconnected flow and dynamic energy of the world. The triskele and shamrock also represented the three worlds: the human world, the faery realm, and the world of spirit. Not surprisingly, this intertwining flow is often represented as a triple spiral as found in the passage tomb at Newgrange, Ireland. It takes no stretch of the imagination to see the triple spiral as a shamrock. As Saint Patrick's Day approaches with paper shamrocks plastered everywhere, I smile secretly to myself and I think about the unity of three within  one, the goddess and the power of the earth below, the sky above, and the sea around.

On Paddy's Day, my dining table does double duty as an altar. I start with a white tablecloth, which becomes the backdrop for a long green scarf with interweaving Celtic designs. A tall, green candle goes in the center with a vase of pussy willows and another with daffodils off to either side forming a triangle. To the Celts, willow trees represented death and rebirth. Similarly, daffodils symbolize rebirth and new beginnings. The daffodil is an emblem of Wales, another country with Celtic roots and just across the Irish Sea from Ireland.

As I lay out my things on the table, I position the little snakes to peek coyly from around the vases. I also place one or two pieces of triskele jewelry on this temporary altar. Stones and other little things that I brought back from Ireland also come out for the day and I scatter them along the length of the scarf. While I don't have a real harp, I do have a small wooden plaque in the shape of a Celtic harp that I place on the table altar. The harp is the national emblem of Ireland as well as a symbol of harmony and communication. It also represents the immortality of the soul.

Perhaps the most prevalent symbol of the day is the wearing of the green. I wear it as a touchstone of my family's roots and as a Pagan to honor the natural world. Green is the color of Mother Earth's mantle with which she wraps the world in springtime. It is the color of nature's renewal and spiritual regeneration. It is the color of balance at the center of a rainbow as well as the heart chakra, which acts as a fulcrum for the other six. Green is the color of the land that balances the color of the sea, and its varied hues echo the lushness of Ireland.

In the past, green was synonymous with the supernatural, enchantment, and powers beyond human bounds. Wearing it could put one under the protection of tree spirits or in the power of fairies. Green was also worn to encourage the earth to bring forth its bounty. This brings us back to the themes of fertility and the powers of renewal. As we can see, the symbols of this day are as intertwining as a Celtic knot.

Although my family and I like getting out of doors all year round, if our schedules permit on Paddy's Day, we combine a trek to the woods with another mainstream motif, the leprechaun. Well, we actually stretch that a bit to the other wee folk—fairies. There's a wonderful spot in some nearby woods where a number of fairy houses have been built over the years. Nestled under pine trees, they number about twenty or thirty at this point and are constructed with all natural items—no nails, glue, or any other human-made thing. The energy in the place is so magically strong—being located next to the ocean it evokes a connection with the sky above, the earth below, and the sea around. We take along some cake or muffins, which we break into small pieces and place on little seashells. As we do this we sing or call to the fairies with a poem:

> *In the forest on this day,*
> *Bid we fairy, elf, and fey;*
> *Come dance, sing, twirl, and fly,*
> *Next to the sea, under the sky.*

Whether or not time (or weather) permits an excursion to the woods, we leave food offerings in the special fairy place in our backyard. This is tucked under the Tinkerbelle lilac bush, which is still bare at this time of year. Because of this, I like to add extra seashells or long twigs to create a tiny lean-to in which to shelter the food. We also place a bowl of water as an offering to Brigid under the bush or nestled in the nearby snow, which is often still covering the ground.

Although Brigid is a solar deity associated with fire, she was also known for her healing powers and Ireland was dotted with springs called Brigid Wells. For a time during the conversion to Christianity, these were called Lady Wells. Eventually many were reassigned to Christian saints with Patrick getting the lion's share, however, many were also renamed Brigid Wells as the goddess and female saint melded into one. It is common to find places with the combination of a Patrick Well enclosed in a little whitewashed shrine house right next to an older stone-enclosed spring. Not surprisingly, the ones I visited during my travels in Ireland showed signs of activity at both water sources. Ireland was one of the last strongholds of Paganism, and when it adopted Christianity, it did so much on its own terms.

Of course, no celebration is complete without a feast. While here in America the standard fare on Saint Paddy's Day is corned beef and cabbage, in Ireland you're more likely to find bacon and cabbage. Irish stew is popular, too, and of course, soda bread. In Ireland the highly favored potato dish called *colcannon* is often served. The name comes from Irish Gaelic *cál ceannann*, meaning "white-headed cabbage." No matter what else is planned for the meal, I always include colcannon because March is still cold here in New England and this is a wonderfully warming dish—comfort food extraordinaire. There are many ways to make it, but here's my favorite recipe, which can be made with cabbage or kale.

1 large or 2 medium heads of green cabbage (or 2
     bunches of kale), coarsely chopped
2 medium leeks, thinly sliced
6 ounces of light cream

3 pounds of potatoes, peeled and quartered (the amount of potatoes and cabbage should be roughly equal)

8 tablespoons of butter

Instructions: Boil the potatoes until tender and then mash them until smooth. Boil or steam the cabbage separately until tender. Place the leeks in the cream over medium heat for about 10 minutes. Combine potatoes, cabbage, leeks, and cream. Add salt and pepper to taste.

Have the oven preheated to 350 degrees F. Place the mixture in a lightly greased oven dish and form it into a mound. Use a small, rounded bowl or large soup ladle to create a little well in the middle of the mound. Place the colcannon in the oven for about 20 to 25 minutes. Before serving, melt the butter and pour it into the center well. Let each person serve him or herself by taking potatoes from the side and then scooping a dip of butter from the well.

As we sit down to dinner, we listen to Celtic harp music to remind us of the ancient bards and the poetry of Amairgen. As the meal progresses, this soulful music gives way to more lively Irish jigs and impromptu sing-alongs. Before we finish our feast we raise our glasses for a toast to Ireland, that beautiful, mystical land of our ancestors.

~

Each year I feel more gratified to have found a way to observe this as a meaningful and magical day. Rather than feeling glum about the shallow mainstream hoopla and green beer, we have turned it around, back into a celebration that commemorates our cultural roots and enriches our Pagan spirituality.

Healing the Waters of Your Community

by Calantirniel

Many of us magical types who have been doing work toward our prosperity or our health have noticed stagnancy or blockage toward these goals of late, possibly due to the economy. If you live in an area that has experienced deep trauma, even a long time ago, these energies may need some clearing before more beneficial energies can wiggle through and enter your space to provide what you have requested.

Examples of area trauma are far-ranging. Many areas had flourishing industries (logging, mining, etc.) that, unfortunately, were damaging the environment. Laws understandably ended these professions, but no financial recovery ever followed. Other industries were forced politically or economically to relocate overseas, starting with the manufacturing jobs, and now even farming and service jobs. Another factor could be long-ago tribal or territorial wars, places where some residual hostile energies are still present. Many areas of the New World were also settled by our predecessors who endured great hardship when relocating from their homeland. On top of the recent economic conditions, characterized by a lack of good jobs, empty business spaces, and rampant foreclosures, is it any wonder why we often feel powerless and unable to change things?

The area could then understandably experience a long-term depression, wherein families, neighborhoods, and even entire communities experience disempowering thought patterns. When many people surrounding you hold these patterns for a long time, you cannot help but be exposed to and affected by it. This process can be likened to a virus that infects those who do not have a strong immune system—but instead of the virus running its course, it lingers for years, even decades, wearing down our personal power, which then can lead to fear. These fears are often expressed by giving up, e.g., "What's the use?" or "That is the way it has always been."

Even worse, these fears can be expressed by not sharing—even hoarding or stealing. Either way, these viewpoints buy into the idea of limitations. So the idea is to overcome the concept of limitation and realign with the laws of abundance. However, it's up to you to choose what is right for you and appropriate for the real bounds (not the perceived problems) of your area.

Having now lived long-term in more than a few places, I have experienced various places with great feeling and understanding. Thriving city environments with lots of culture and activity (and chaos) have a very different dynamic than slower-moving, even depressed rural areas, which can have more isolated and less diverse viewpoints of the world. While each of us still have a level of individual interpretation and expression of these energies (i.e. planetary energies of our natal astrology charts mapped geographically), connecting with the "spirit of place" to see some of the specifics in your locale is a good idea. Getting out in nature and observing your feeling and heart-space is one way. Learning the geological, seasonal, and historical events will also help pinpoint both the strengths and the issues of your area. If you study astrology or numerology at all, you can find the birthdate of your city (or county or state) and see how this information applies. Once these issues are discovered, think about what can you do.

Healing the Community

I have found the quickest way to start providing deep healing for a community is to work with the element closest to emotion—the water systems available around you. Water seeks its own level, and its quality of utterly absorbing into other water to become one is the exact reason this works so well. The healing work of a small amount of water then energetically infuses all water because of this quality, and goes where it is needed.

This works particularly well if you have a river running through your area, but can still work even if the water is in lakes or the ocean (and an alternative method is also presented here).

You can do the work as a solitary or as a group, but a word of warning—changes begin happening to you first, even in your body, before they work outward into the community. Some people may be overwhelmed if they're not prepared to process so much energy at once.

The methods I present here will include the use of flower essences, since they can be so easily purchased and/or made, and achieve rather amazing results. Additional techniques ranging from Reiki and shamanic healing to homeopathy can also be implemented, so feel free to modify for your spiritual path, talents, and needs.

Gather Your Supplies

You will need a medium to large glass or ceramic bowl (clear or white are the most versatile or use a color you can access and feel is part of the water blessing), one gallon of distilled or spring water, and either prepared flower/gem essences of your choice (or that choose you!), or if this is the right time of year, chosen fresh flowers, leaves, twigs, rocks, shells, crystals, and any other ways to allow healing energies to infuse their essence into the water. It is also ideal for creating this water in sunlight or moon/starlight but some adverse conditions (like high wind, rain, or a lightning storm) may be part of the healing process.

Timing is best just after the full moon, as that energy is washing away or leaving. Having the moon in a water sign (Cancer, Scorpio, and especially Pisces, if possible) will add additional energies.

Alternatively, you may wish to have an empty jar and/or empty spray bottles for the water, and a small amount of vodka or brandy to preserve the blessed waters after their creation.

Prepare the Healing Essence

Fill the bowl about halfway with distilled or spring water. Place in uninterrupted sunlight (or moonlight) to the extent possible. You may pray over the water or place healing symbols, infusing it with intention. Incorporating singing and music is an excellent touch. Place the rocks and crystals in the water first (if none are available, you can use sea salt). Then, you can pick the flowers, leaves, and other nearby plant material and place it into the water. You may also feel called to place herbs or essential oils into this healing water. You can also add prepared flower essences

or remedies—or use these essences in the water bowl on their own, just using a few drops for each essence desired. Allow the bowl to sit in the light for a time, and you can take this time to further sing and intentionally add healing symbols from Reiki or other disciplines. Filter out if needed (particularly if you decide to cleanse and reprogram the crystals). If the water is not going to be administered right away, add one part vodka or brandy to the three parts water to preserve it. Keep in a clean jar (line the lid with wax paper or plastic if needed) or funnel the water into the empty spray bottles.

Administer the Healing Essence

There are a couple of ways to use the blessed water you make. One method is to go a place where the water systems enter into your community. If you have a river running through, try to find a good spot upstream (bonus if there is a waterfall feature!). If a local lake is available, or you live near the ocean, choose a spot that people like to visit. Or, you may know of a well that can distribute the energies in the groundwater systems. Then, perform your ritual in any way you wish that feels natural: singing, toning, meditating, visualization, breathwork, prayers, etc. When the time comes, gently pour the water into the river, stream, lake, or the sea. Visualize this

319

water beginning to infuse all water as it flows into your community, thereby absorbing traumas and pain while bringing the message of love and healing deep into the area, right down to each individual that needs this healing. This process then begins to release toxic emotions and trauma that have been residual for years, even centuries. Notice this process has already started with you, and by the natural laws of energy, will radiate outward and go to exactly where it is needed. Then, the waters will wash it all away by going downstream, transforming the residual energies in the process.

Another way to bring water healing is to fill the spray bottles and randomly spray areas (starting with your own home and working outward) where area residents congregate or visit so that they will encounter and integrate the healing qualities. An example is a nearby grocery store. Spray the outside entrance area, especially the walls and ceiling, as the essence can then radiate healing for a long time. If it is embarrassing, you can do this when the store is closed or at night when fewer people are around. Other creative places are the hospital entrances, employment offices, social service entrances, and places of known trauma—like around the doors of an empty building where many people were once happily employed. One person who does this says he sprays the fans and air ducts of busy places if he has access, for those who need the energy to breathe it in. Again, visualize this water infiltrating the area in all the ways that it will, then organically arriving to every individual that needs healing. See all of the residual energies individually, and collectively, leaving your area to transform and go to Source. Then see the newer energies coming to fill this void that are full of love, light, abundance, and vitality. If this is hard to visualize, see these residual energies as fabric that is woven— unravel these threads, seeing them disappear, right down to the last thread. Then, see the fabric with the new threads of vibrant energy weaving a new fabric that nourishes life on all levels.

At the closing of your ritual, know in the deepest place in your heart that this healing work is very real. See this healing work actually happen in your community and experience the new energies of empowerment that bring gifts of love, wealth, and health!

Spirits and the Spirits:
Libations as Potent Potables

by Denise Dumars

One of my copriestesses was asked to leave a ritual in northern California for having a flask in her pocket. It seems she was unaware that it was a ritual of Pagans in a Twelve-Step program, so there was no alcohol allowed, not even on the altar. While that is certainly understandable, alcohol often plays an important role as an offering in the ceremonies of Pagan and other earth-based religions.

In most Pagan traditions, offering an alcoholic libation to the gods or spirits does not mean one must partake of that spirit. Most modern Pagans warn against becoming intoxicated in sacred space and only drink a sip of an alcoholic beverage during the "cakes and ale" part of the ceremony. Every Pagan group should always have nonalcoholic options for participants. And a good thing to remember is that a beverage on the altar that is intended for the gods should *never* be consumed by a person unless it is explicitly stated as part of the ceremony. The whole purpose of a libation is that it is an offering for the deities. Imagine if it was your drink—you wouldn't want some stranger to take a swig, would you?

A grocery chain makes "Vodka of the Gods," and its label depicts a peasant offering some to a deity. Although this is a cute idea, and there's no reason not to offer it in modern Slavic-pantheon based rituals, unfortunately it is an anachronism. Distilled alcoholic beverages such as vodka, gin, whisky, and rum were not invented until well into the Christian era. The origin of vodka itself is obscure, and Russia and Poland still argue over which country invented it.

It is common knowledge that beer and mead were both invented in ancient Egypt, maybe as early as 6000 BCE, although some scholars say that mead was invented simultaneously in China. Wine was found in the tomb of the famed Scorpion King in Egypt, but it was not locally made—it came from Iran, and the Persians may have been the first to create an alcoholic beverage from grapes.

Based on this timeline, it is clear that ancient cultures would have offered wine, beer, and mead to their gods. Distilled spirits didn't make it out of the alchemists' alembics and into the taverns until twelfth or fourteenth centuries AD.

Why alcohol as an offering? The simplest and most logical reason is that alcoholic beverages, along with fresh meat and fresh flowers, are more expensive than everyday fare—this was especially true in ancient times. An offering, remember, is regarded literally or figuratively as a *sacrifice*, and expensive offerings requires sacrificing the contents of one's wallet. The second reason for using an alcoholic beverage as an offering is that there is something magical about alcohol, as anyone who has experienced the phenomenon of "beer goggles" will tell you!

In the Western Hemisphere, rum is commonly used as an offering. As my friend the Rum Dood would tell you, rum was, in fact, the preferred hard liquor of Americans until those pesky British decided to charge their colonies

And It Harm None Do As Ye Will

huge taxes on sugar and molasses. Then there was a little dust-up and well, that's why this is "the United States" and not "the colonies" anymore. In the meantime, Americans started making whiskey to make up for the lack of rum. In recent decades, rum has rebounded in popularity in American cocktails, and in is the preferred libation Santeria and Vodou traditions. *Cachaca*—another sugarcane-based liquor—is preferred in Brazilian and other South American traditions.

Of course, a few deities and spirits are anti-alcohol, and their stories often include unpleasant experiences with intoxication, meant perhaps as cautionary tales for their followers. And of course, Hindu deities should not be offered alcohol. There is, however, a special drink recipe for the god Shiva that lists marijuana as an ingredient. Some gods prefer alternative intoxicants!

Erzuli Danto, patron *loa* of New Orleans, likes a glass of rum mixed with gunpowder (kids, don't try this at home!). This may reflect the belief that she was one of the main reasons for the success of the Haitian slave revolt. The sex-and-death spirits known as the *Guédés* like rum mixed with cayenne pepper—known colloquially as "Haitian tear gas." Don't expect feisty Brazilian spirit Pomba Gira to even acknowledge you unless you offer her French Champagne, and the female *orishas* sometimes like their drinks sweetened with honey or almond syrup, except for Oya, who likes dry red wine—probably a "big" red like a Cabernet!

Because they originated with the alchemists, it's no surprise that distilled alcoholic beverages are called "spirits." And as long as magic seems to happen when people imbibe, these beverages will be given magical names. Some current brand names include Frozen Ghost Vodka; Thor's Hammer vodka; the various ales made in Wych Wood, Oxfordshire; 7 Tikis Rum, which includes a handout describing the powers of the seven tikis it is named for; Strega liquore; Conjure Cognac; etc. Ask anyone who has met the "Green Fairy" about the properties of absinthe, which is legal again in the United States, Mexico, and most of Europe, after suffering some mostly undeserved bad press in the early twentieth century.

Here are a few recipes for potent potables that are drinkable as well as offerable:

La Santa Muerte

1 oz. Opal Nera (or substitute half cassis and half anisette)
1 oz. amber rum

Chill both liquors and pour into a cordial glass. Offer a glass to La Santa Muerte along with a red rose and a red apple, and write her your petition for healing, love, or success at work or in school. Then mix one for yourself and sip slowly! (Why do I feel like my students are working this spell on me right now?)

Ellegua Eshu

1½ oz. Rhum Barbancourt (or another good Caribbean rum)
1 oz. coconut-pineapple juice
1 oz. coconut water
Maraschino cherries or fresh coconut

Pour rum over ice in an old-fashioned glass. Mix in coconut-pineapple juice and thin with coconut water to taste—this keeps it from being too sweet. Garnish with a cherry or slice of fresh coconut. Offer to Ellegua on Monday and ask him to either "open the door" to new opportunities or to "protect the door" from those who would try to do you harm. I then chant "Eleggua Eshu, Ellegua Elegbara, Legba Esu, Elegba Exu," just to cover all of the permutations of his name. Burn an Ellegua candle, a St. Anthony candle, or a red or black votive. Then mix your own drink and toast him!

Baron Samedi

1¼ oz. Old New Orleans amber rum, or amber Rhum Barbancourt
¼ oz. fresh lime juice
¼ oz. cinnamon-infused simple syrup
¼ oz. Falernum

Recipes for a Baron Samedi cocktail abound. This one is by Beachbum Berry, king of the tiki drinks. He suggests garnishing it with a *gris gris,* lest the "Bawon" come for your soul. I suggest just offering one to the Barons before drinking your own. Or offer this drink to the Baron before visiting your departed loved ones at the cemetery or on a holiday such as Samhain or *El Dia de los Muertos.*

Tears of Persephone

1 oz. ouzo or anisette
1 oz. vodka
3 oz. pomegranate juice

1 pearl onion
1 pearl

Shake first three ingredients with ice, then strain into a chilled martini glass. For the offering, place a pearl in the drink. For your cocktail, garnish with a pearl onion. In the Greek myths, Persephone is suffering from homesickness and longing for her mother after descending to Hades. This drink is an offering to Persephone to ask her to understand if you are missing someone, someplace, or just the good ol' days. As she is Hostess of Hades as well as the Good Daughter, she will sympathize with your tears of nostalgia and help purge your pain.

Slammin' Odin

1 chilled jigger of aquavit or Thor's Hammer vodka

When stress sends adrenaline to your flight-or-fight response with nowhere to go, chill out and tell your troubles to Odin while sipping aquavit with him. Having a little dark rye bread with smoked salmon, crème fraiche, and caviar takes some of the sting out of those slings and arrows as well. Aquavit is a caraway-flavored vodka liqueur and if it seems odd to your non-Viking palate you may substitute Thor's Hammer vodka…just this once!

Hathor's Party

½ tsp. rose water
Lemon juice
Pink or red sanding sugar
1 oz. Pama pomegranate liqueur
1 tsp. almond syrup
2 oz. pomegranate juice
1 pitted date

Dip a chilled martini glass in a mixture of rose water and lemon juice and then in sanding sugar. Shake the pomegranate liqueur, almond syrup, and pomegranate juice over ice and pour. Garnish with a date. Hathor is the party goddess of Egypt; who did you think they were celebrating at the big bash with the golden calf? When you want to invoke the "party" spirits to liven up your life, offer Hathor one of these along with a red rose and her image. Ask her to find it in your friends' and acquaintances' hearts to invite you to their next soirées. Alternatively, give an Egyptian-themed party and offer these decadent drinks to your guests.

Bridge of Ghosts

1 oz. green or red absinthe; I like Mythe or Rustic Absinth brands
1 sugar cube
Peychaud's bitters
2 ounces ice water
Ice cubes

This drink is named after an experience I had in Mexico with absinthe, a bridge, and ghosts (no joke—I have witnesses!) It is meant to be used as a toast, not an offering per se. Chill an absinthe glass or an old-fashioned glass. Pour the absinthe over ice. Set an absinthe spoon or a fork over the glass and place sugar cube atop it. Slowly pour the ice water over the sugar cube until it dissolves and the absinthe louches (gets cloudy). Don't do anything dangerous like setting the sugar cube on fire! Add a dash of bitters to taste. Drink a toast to your favorite departed writer, artist, musician, dancer, or actor, and ask him or her to bless your creative endeavors.

~

Always drink responsibly and abide by all liquor laws of the land, whichever land you happen to land in. If you have a Pagan friend who has a problem with alcohol, a link to a Pagan twelve-step program is listed in the References; one does not have to belong to a traditional religion to utilize the AA program or similar methods for recovery.

For Further Study:

Berry, Jeff. *Beachbum Berry Remixed: A Gallery of Tiki Drinks*. San Jose, CA: Club Tiki Press, 2010.

Khoury. "The Twelve Steps for Pagans." *SybillineOrder. org*. http://www.sibyllineorder.org/psychology/psy_ recovery.htm

O'Hanlon, Harry. "Mystery of Beer Goggles Solved," *Discovery News*, 8-17-10, http://news.discovery.com/ human/alcohol-attraction-symmetry.html.

Rogers, Adam. "Alcohol Alchemist Summons Spirits," *Wired*, July 27, 2011. http://www.wired.com/magazine/2011/09/pl_foodspirits/.

Rum Dood. "Rum 101: Rum in the USA," http:// rumdood.com/2009/06/30/rum-101-rum-in-the-usa-part-1/.

Soap Magic

by Autumn Damiana

Everyone uses soap. Alongside basic staples such as food, water, clothing, and medicine, soap is another universal and fundamental necessity, and can be found in some form or another practically everywhere. There are bars of soap, liquid hand soap, dishwashing soap, laundry soap, soap flakes, and even soap solutions made for foam baths or blowing bubbles. Today, because soap is so common, inexpensive, and readily available, using soap as an ingredient in spells, rituals, or daily magical practices is true cottage witchery. With a little magical ingenuity, however, soap can be elevated from its humble place in the world to become the star component in a variety of workings.

A Brief History of Soap

Legend has it that soap was discovered near Mount Sapo, somewhere near Rome, when salts from ashes mixed with animal fats (presumably from sacrifices) were carried by rain runoff down into nearby rivers, where those who washed clothes and other textiles noticed how easily they came clean. Scholars have ridiculed this explanation as a fanciful and romantic myth, citing that there is no evidence of any "Mount Sapo" (*sapo* is Latin for "soap") and that it is highly unlikely that ashes and fats could accidentally combine to make useable soap. However, the legend persists, possibly because soap is so old that no one actually knows where it came from. Although soap was in use thousands of years ago among the Babylonians, Egyptians, Greeks, and Romans, its origins are probably much older. Most of these early forms of soap were indeed made from animal fats,

but it is interesting to note that there are several species of plants grown around the world that have been known since prehistoric times by folk names like Soap Plant, Soapbark, Soaproot, Soapwort, etc., because they produce "saponins" (soaplike substances) when crushed or pulverized. These were most likely the precursors to the soap produced by the ancients.

Though the connection between health and hygiene has been widely understood for the past few hundred years, the decline of soap use and of sanitation in Europe after the fall of the Roman Empire is essentially what caused the rampant pestilence, disease, and plague in the following centuries. And yet all this time, soap continued to be manufactured in Europe, but the formulas were heavily guarded secrets—soap was expensive because it was considered a luxury item. So while the many benefits of soap were still being enjoyed by Eastern Asian and Islamic cultures, Europeans were largely ignorant of this and would remain so until Medieval times, when using soap became commonplace again. As a routine household chore, the practice of making soap spread as Europeans colonized other parts of the world, but commercially available soap would not come about until the late eighteenth and early nineteenth century. Through industrialization, mass-produced soap was finally cheap and easy to come by. Today, you can still find just about any kind of soap ever invented, including the original recipes made from animal fats, as well as newer concoctions that contain palm, coconut, olive, or other vegetable oils.

Soap Ingredients and Additives

Soap is a deceptively simple compound, primarily made out of some type of fat or oil and the caustic salt known as lye (sodium hydroxide). Together with fragrances, coloring agents, and a plethora of other additives, these raw materials are combined using one of several processes to produce the kinds of soaps that we buy as finished products. However, while soap itself is a familiar commodity, many of the ingredients used in soap are not as well known. Because most of the soap made today is mass-produced, there is often confusion about what exactly is in the soap you are purchasing.

For starters, many of the soap products available on today's market are not "soap" in the traditional sense, but are instead made of petroleum, petroleum distillates, or other synthetic surfactants. These cleaning agents are NOT soap, and are labeled "detergents" because of their artificial, man-made, or nonbiodegradable elements. Some actual bona fide soaps have these agents added to them, supposedly to boost their cleaning power. Unfortunately, "detergents" are not only skin irritants and toxic when absorbed into the body, they can cause potentially long-term health problems. In addition, these types of "soaps" are not considered environmentally friendly. Other additives to look out for are preservatives (the notorious parabens and propylene glycol, for example), alcohols (which dry the skin), "fragrance(s)" that are synthetic (as opposed to essential oils, which are not), and antibacterial agents, which kill the good bacteria on your skin as well as the bad, and might be contributing to the rise in antibiotic-resistant bacteria.

However, even natural, finely crafted soaps can pose problems for the consumer. Obviously allergies and dietary restrictions should be considered, as many soaps contain ingredients like gluten or nuts. Vegetarians and vegans will want to avoid all tallow and lard products (and possibly other animal byproducts like milk or honey) and stick to soap made from plant-derived oils. Folks desiring a greener soap will possibly look for one that is organic, or at least biodegradable and free of any hidden artificial ingredients. And many consumers today are purchasing fair-trade and cruelty-free products. When following an Earth-centered religion or spiritual path, it is important to read labels and do your research in order to make informed decisions and ensure standards are upheld, even for something as simple as buying soap. This goes double for when you are going to use the soap for magical practice, since the quality of your magic will have a lot to do with the quality of your components. Generally speaking, it's good to use vegetable or other plant oil–based soaps with only natural additives. And "natural" doesn't have to mean "no fun," either—there are many kinds of soaps available that use essential oils, herbs, and spices to add scent and color. Some of these come in interesting shapes, too!

Making Magic with Soap

When I hear the word "soap," I automatically think "water." Soap will obviously lend itself well to any water-centered working, especially a bath ritual. But that's not all! Soap is actually incredibly versatile and has a wide variety of magical uses. Bars of soap, especially ones that contain herbs, have a solid, earthy quality. Blowing bubbles is a fun, whimsical way to work air magic. Soap that is applied to the body can be used to attract things such as wealth or love. And naturally, because soap washes things away, it is especially well-suited for use in cleansing, purification, and banishing spells. Here are some ideas for simple soap magic:

Attraction: Find soap with the appropriate magical correspondences. For example, to draw love to you, the soap can be red or pink, shaped like a heart or rose, contain a Venus-ruled herb or essential oil, etc. Consecrate and charge the soap on the first day (or night) after the new moon, and envision it drawing love to you. Wash your whole body with the soap every day for the next two weeks of the waxing moon phase. Use the soap for the last time on the day of the full moon to seal the spell. Repeat every waxing moon phase until the desired results have been achieved or the soap is used up. This spell can be adapted to attract success, health, happiness, or other positive influences by changing the correspondences of the soap.

Banishing: Similar to the spell above, except that the soap must be used during the waning moon phase and you don't need soap with magical correspondences—any bar soap, liquid soap, or even bubble bath will work. Again,

charge and consecrate the soap, this time on the day after the full moon, and use it every day until the moon is new. Every time you use the soap, visualize it washing away whatever you want to banish as it is rinsed off of you and down into the drain. To banish general negativity or purify the aura, use the soap on your whole body. Wash just the face to banish tears or sadness, the hands to rid yourself of bad habits, the feet to avoid stumbling or missteps on your current path. You can also use the soap to target areas on the body that you want to rid of sickness or pain. Repeat every waning moon phase until either the soap or the problem is gone.

Soap prayers: Pick a breezy (but not too windy) day outside. Blow bubbles, concentrating on your hopes, wishes, dreams, prayers, or messages to the gods, and watch as they are carried away into the heavens. Blowing bubbles is also a great alternative to working with smudge sticks or incense to represent air in a ritual.

Cultural connection: After her trip to Australia, my mom brought me back some luscious hand-crafted soap scented with the sweet aroma of the Boronia plant, which is native to Austra-

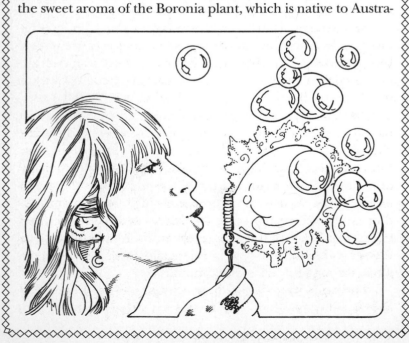

lia. She said that she found the soap in a shop that specialized in local Aboriginal arts and crafts. Whenever I used the soap, I felt connected to these people and their culture, which made me seek to learn more about them. Using soap is such a timeless and everyday part of living that it is the perfect way to tap into another culture, ancient or modern. Try to find soap that would be used by the people you are studying, either made in the customary way or with native recipes or ingredients.

Marking symbols: We've all seen things written on car windows with white soap, usually something like "just married" or "car for sale." People write with soap because it is not permanent, and clean-up is a snap! You can also mark your windows or anything else washable with soap as a component in your spell-casting, using clear glycerin or liquid soap if you prefer that others do not see it. Use a blessed soap to trace pentacles for protection on cars, house windows, mirrors, or even skylights. Write out an incantation on the inside of the tub with soap before taking a magical bath. Or draw an appropriate symbol in soap on the outside of a bottle, glass, or other container that will hold a magical potion or brew.

Snow magic: Soap flakes, which are used as a milder alternative to laundry detergents, can be used in creative ways to represent snow, and therefore help you tap into the energies of the cold winter months. This is especially useful off-season, or when you live in an area like I do where snow is practically nonexistent. Although soap flakes are pretty rare nowadays, you can easily make them yourself just by using a fine cheese grater on a plain, hard bar of Castile or glycerin soap. I put a bowl of soap flakes on my altar when I pray for rain, as our area is prone to drought, and the majority of the much-needed water we use comes from snow high in the mountains that melts and runs down. I also like to add a blessed handful of soap flakes to the laundry when I unpack and wash all the winter blankets and sweaters, visualizing them keeping us warm throughout the coming months.

Carving in soap: While there are tons of soap shapes available to aid in spellcasting, sometimes it's easier to make your own. Anyone who likes to carve or whittle will find it enjoyable to sculpt with bars of soap, but you don't need to be an artist to get results. Strips of soap can be cut with a vegetable peeler for short-term use or instant spells. Words or symbols can be engraved onto the soap. Even cookie cutters can be used to mark the soap or can serve as a guide to chisel out simple shapes. The carved soap can be used in the ideas above, or make up your own uses!

Melt and Pour Your Own

Most methods for making your own soap start from scratch and are not recommended for beginners. However, the melt-and-pour method uses already existing soap and is safe and simple enough that even children can do it (with supervision, of course). By using this method, you can easily cast your own shapes, add your choice of essential oils and/or herbs, and even embed objects in the soap if you wish. In addition, molds for candy, ice, plaster, or candles can also be used when pouring soap, which means that there are literally thousands of shapes available. This takes soap magic to a whole new level, and may be the solution if you can't find the soaps that you need for your workings. Homemade spell soaps also make wonderful Yule gifts! Here are some resources to get you started.

Soapmaking the Natural Way: 45 Melt-and-Pour Recipes Using Herbs, Flowers, and Essential Oils, by Rebecca Ittner (Lark Crafts, 2011). Awesome recipes, with easy to follow directions and gorgeous photos.

Cool Melt & Pour Soap, by Lisa Wagner (Checkerboard Library, 2004). A cute kid's book that explains soap making, also with some clever projects.

Bulk Apothecary: http://www.bulkapothecary.com. Lots of melt-and-pour options, soap molds, and organic supplies.

Bramble Berry: http://www.brambleberry.com. More great soap products, fun kits, and a ton of resources and tutorials.

New Directions Aromatics: http://www.newdirectionsaromatics.com. Large selection of essential oils, plus organic liquid soap base and even soap paints!